Washington County Tennessee

LISTS OF TAXABLES

1778–1801

Transcribed by
Mary Hardin McCown

Heritage Books
2025

HERITAGE BOOKS
AN IMPRINT OF HERITAGE BOOKS, INC.

Books, CDs, and more—Worldwide

For our listing of thousands of titles see our website
at
www.HeritageBooks.com

A Facsimile Reprint
Published 2025 by
HERITAGE BOOKS, INC.
Publishing Division
5810 Ruatan Street
Berwyn Heights, MD 20740

Privately Printed
Johnson City, Tennessee
1964

International Standard Book Number
Paperbound: 978-0-7884-8971-6

WASHINGTON COUNTY, TENNESSEE RECORDS

TRANSCRIBED BY MARY HARDIN McCOWN

VOL. I

WASHINGTON COUNTY LISTS OF TAXABLES

1778 - 1801

⊕§⊕§⊕

ABSTRACT OF WASHINGTON COUNTY MINUTES

COURT OF PLEAS & QUARTER SESSIONS

1778 - 1801

⊕§⊕§⊕

LISTS OF OFFICERS OF WASHINGTON COUNTY

1778 - 1801

⊕§⊕§⊕

MISCELLANEOUS RECORDS IN WASHINGTON COUNTY

Compiled by

MARY HARDIN McCOWN, NANCY E. JONES STICKLEY &

INEZ E. BURNS

Mary Hardin McCown

Privately Printed

Johnson City, Tennessee

1964

TABLE OF CONTENTS

FOREWORD

WASHINGTON COUNTY, North Carolina (later Tennessee), the Mother of all Tennessee Counties, was created in November 1777 by Bill #17 of the General Assembly of North Carolina.

"Endorsed Nov. 28, 1777 - RESOLVED to erect the District of Washington into a county by same name..... Passed the House the 3rd time Dec. 17, 1777"..... The original copy of Bill #17 is in the North Carolina State Archives, Legislative Papers, for Nov-Dec 1777, Box 13, Raleigh, N.C. The published account is in Vol 24, Chapter XXXI, p-141 of North Carolina Colonial Records.

The Courts were to meet the 4th Mondays in February, May, August and November at the house of Charles Robertson. The next Court to meet at the aforesaid place on the 4th Monday in February, next, 1778. Taxes were set and the Court to meet at Charles Robertson's house until a court house could be built. [This house of Charles Robertson's was on the "east (Catbird) branch" of Sinking Creek of the Watauga river, in the area later cut off for Carter County]

Vol 24, Chapter XXVII, p-135, New Bern, Nov. 15, 1777- "Ordered that a road be marked from the house of Charles Robertson, Washington County thru the Mountains to the house of Edward Smith in Burke County. Charles McDowell, John McDowell, Samuel Bright, Ezekiel Smith & Jacob Womack appointed to see about the same..... Chain bearers & markers appointed..... pay to be 8 shillings per day...." (This road is later spoken of as "The North Carolina Road" or "Bright's Trace".)

This Bill enacted by the General Assembly of North Carolina reads as follows:

> "Be it enacted by the General Assembly of the State of North Carolina and by the authority of the same, that the late District of Washington and all that Part of this State comprehended within the following lines shall be enacted into a new and distinct County by the name of WASHINGTON COUNTY, VIZ-
>
> Beginning at the most Northwesterly Part of the County of Wilkes, on the Virginia Line, thence running with the Line of Wilkes County to a point thirty six miles south of the Virginia Line, thence due West to a Ridge of the great Iron Mountain which heretofore divided the hunting Grounds of the Overhill Cherokees from those of the Middle Settlements & Valey, thence running a Southwesterly course along the said Ridge to the Unacoy Mountain where the Trading Path crosses the same on the way from the Valey to the Overhills, thence South with the Line of this State adjoining the State of South Carolina, thence due West to the great River Missipps, thence up the said River the courses thereof to a Point due West from the Beginning, thence due East with the line of this State to the Beginning; and is hereby declared that all that Part of this State comprehended within the Lines aforesaid

shall from henceforth be and remain the County of Washington and shall be and is hereby described to be Part of the District of Salisbury.

An be it further enacted by the Authority aforesaid and it is hereby declared, that all of that Part of this State lying West of Wilkes County & South of the County of Washington shall be and is hereby declared to be a Part of the County of Burke-"

Therefore- On February 23 (4th Monday) 1778, the first Court of Pleas & Quarter Sessions met at the house of Charles Robertson on the Catbird branch of Sinking Creek of Watauga River. Col. Robertson had served as Trustee for the sale of the lands which were purchased on March 19, 1775 from the Cherokees at the Sycamore Shoals of the Watauga. These lands had been leased in 1772 for a ten year period by the Watauga Association, with Col. John Carter, Chairman. The Watauga Purchase took place just two days after the Transylvania Purchase on March 17, between Richard Henderson & Associates from North Carolina and the Cherokees, and at the same site- The Sycamore Shoals.

A Summons to this First Court, on Feb. 23, 1778, was discovered and is given herein. One of the first acts was the appointment of Assessors, who were to assess all the Taxable Property of the Inhabitants, or the heads of families and to make return of this to a Collector. This 1778 List of Taxables appears to have had seven or eight Assessors- not all named. The taxes were one pound, no shillings and six pence (£ 1-0-6) for every one hundred pounds (£ 100) valuation. This was broken down thus:

General Assessment on each £ 100................	0-16-8
For Building the Court House, Prison & Stocks....	2-6
For building the Court House in Salisbury........	-4
(Washington County was in Salisbury District)	
For Contingent charges of the County............	-11
Total	1-0-6

This 1778 List shows the total assessed valuation of the County of Washington without listing the amount of land owned, and the number of White Polls and Slaves. White Polls were taxed from 21 to 50 years, while the Tax paid on Slaves was from ages 12-50 years. Every Male inhabitant was judged to be worth £ 100, regardless of whether he owned any land. Those marked with £ 100 valuation and with Tax to Pay of £ 1-0-6 were most likely single males of 21 years and over, owning no property. This List numbers 433 Males (or heads of families) with a total valuation of £ 148,701-6-0 and with Taxes to Pay of £ 1497-12-10.

In 1779 the number of acres of land and value, usually naming a "manor plantation", horses, cattle, ready money, and Negroes were listed. By then it seems that the County was divided into Districts. Only two Lists were found- one for the First & Fifth Districts, and one for "The Lower District"- and are given herein.

During the 1780s the settlers were greatly disturbed with Indian attacks and wars, so the civil affairs were upset, as evidenced by the Tax Lists. Patterned after the military, the Colonel Commandant of the County appointed the various Militia Company Captains to "Take in the List of Taxables" and make returns to the Clerk. Constables were appointed to "warn the people" to turn in their taxables. This was usually done at the April Muster of the militia company. One list for 1780 & 1781 was not taken until 1781. During these years the value of their currency fluctuated greatly. The Minutes of the early 1780s show that sometime the Constables received $60.00, and once, $100.00 per day as pay for their services. The 1781 List names Horsekind and "Neat Cattle" owned by each. Neat Cattle, as defined by an old Webster Dictionary, was Oxen, an animal most useful for the clearing of the wilderness. The Lists of the mid-1780s, and those during the years of the hectic and turbulent State of Franklin, 1784-1788, are missing, with one exception- that for 1787 of Capt. John Fain's Company, taken by John Hammer (the upper Knob Creek area). This interesting List names "widows", "Feme Soles" and "Feme Coverts", which were legal terms used in old documents. The Minutes show that the Court House was ordered to be built in 1784- John Chisolm was appointed to build the building which was to be a square "24 feet by 24 feet and the roof to be joint shingles hung with pegs". "Alexander Greer was to repair and complete the prison and stocks on the same terms as John Chisolm."

In 1790, after the Territory South of the River Ohio was organized, with Governor William Blount's arrival at the home of William Cobb, ROCKY MOUNT, then located in Washington County, one of the very first acts of the newly appointed governor was to take a complete Census of all the inhabitants of all the counties in the Territory. A Circular Letter, sent out on March 7, 1791, ordered "A Schedule of the Whole Number of Persons within the County of Washington in the Territory of the United States of America South of the River Ohio on the last Saturday in July, 1791".

The Census List for Washington County is in the county archives, although it is not found in the published papers of the South West Territory, issued in 1936 by the Department of State, and edited by Clarence E. Carter. Correspondence with Mr. Carter several years ago stated that this list was not found when he did this work. (One was forwarded to him to file in their records in Washington, D.C.

This 1791 Census shows that the total population for Washington County totaled 5862 persons. (See this list in the year for 1791.) Remember that by 1790, Sullivan in 1779, Greene in 1783, Davidson in 1783, and Hawkins in 1786, had all been formed out of the original mother county of Washington.

All throughout Governor Blount's administration of the Southwest Territory there were still more Indian depredations- with massacres of settlers both in the Watauga region and also in the newly settled Cumberland. Among these were John Sevier's Etowah Campaign in 1793, the Nickajack Expedition in 1794, and others, until the beginning of the Indian Treaties at Tellico Blockhouse, which were not concluded until several years after Tennessee Statehood (1796). All of these kept the settlers in a most disturbed condition. Many of the Militia companies saw active service during these years.

On March 3, 1791 President George Washington was authorized to raise six battalions of Levies for the campaign led by Gen. Arthur St. Clair against the Northwest Indians. In June or early July, three companies, totaling about 300 riflemen, were ready to march from Jonesboro, commanded by Major Matthew Rhea, who arrived at Fort Washington (Cincinnati) on July 19. Gen. St. Clair marched against the Indians on Nov. 4, and was disastrously defeated by them. This was the battle in which the brave Capt. Jacob Tipton (son of Col. John Tipton) of Washington County, was killed. The Muster Roll of this company was found in the British Archives in Ottawa, Canada. It listed many Washington County men.

The Lists for the 1790s furnish many interesting facts about life then. They began to list Stud Horses which were taxable; the location of the lands; Justices of the Peace were appointed for each company, who received the Taxes, yet these Justices were not allowed to collect them- they were paid to the Sheriff or a specially appointed Collector. The Clerk was to furnish a List which was arranged in alphabetical order- which was slow to be obeyed, for not until after 1800 do we find them alphabetized.

In May 1790, Patrollers, three to four for each District, were appointed, the duty of which was to "take all negro slaves passing out of their Master's premises without a pass, and to punish by whipping....." This likely gave rise to the old song "The Pattyroller will get you if you don't watch out". The court house seems to have been unfinished for many years, for in 1799 the General Assembly of Tennessee, on Oct. 23, passed an Act authorizing an additional Tax in Washington County "to complete the public buildings". This was to be collected in 1800 & 1801. (See the Tax Lists.)

On Oct. 27, 1797 the General Assembly ordered that the Poll Tax could be paid with producing the scalps of twenty-five squirrels for each Poll, with the scalps of two crows to equal one squirrel. To secure this credit the scalps had to be checked with the Captain of the company. In the 1798 Lists we find Scalps in one column, and on Capt. Charles Robertson's List we find "Squirrels".

An Act of the General Assembly passed on Oct. 28, 1797 ordered that "Each Justice of the Peace to Take in and make out in writing an accurate and complete List of the number of Free Taxable Inhabitants, who on Sept. 1 did live in the District of each Justice appointed to take the List of Taxable Property & Polls.....and turn into the Court before the last day of December next.....He shall make out two accurate copies of this List- one to be kept in the County, and the other to be transmitted to the Secretary of State on or before the 1st day of February 1799.....Each Justice to be allowed one dollar and fifty cents for every one hundred Taxable Inhabitants enumerated as directed by this Act, which sum shall be appropriated at the next session of the General Assembly". (This List was to be used as a Register of the voters used in voting for members of the General Assembly at the following election.) In the 1798 Lists we find many of these Lists as well as the Lists of Taxables.

In 1800 there was found no List of the Captains Companies, but there is the Complete Total Compilation, with the names of Captains given. For 1801 the same Captains were named- with one exception- and the complete Lists of the Taxables were found, so it seemed that this published account should include these for the year 1801. (No minutes are available for either 1800 or 1801.) Although the Federal Census for 1800 has been destroyed, we found that the total population in 1800 for Washington County was 6379 persons.

The Federal Census was first taken in 1790 and has been taken every ten years thereafter. Tennessee would be included in the Salisbury District of North Carolina in the 1790 Census. These Census records were stored in Washington, D.C. in the Department of Commerce Archives located in a basement. In 1921 a most disastrous fire destroyed almost all of these records. Those of the State of Tennessee are missing for 1800 and 1810 (with one exception- that of Rutherford County). All of those for East Tennessee for 1820 are missing, either burnt up in the fire, or later torn out by greedy researchers who had access to the original records. So the year 1830 is the first complete Census for the entire state of Tennessee.

Thus one can readily see the extreme importance of these Lists of Taxables discovered in the Washington County basement archives. They are the only records available of those early inhabitants. This area served as a funnel through which those pioneers migrated, many of them going farther west to settle other regions. Washington County has been fortunate in that it has had no consuming fire, but it has had three court houses, when the archives were cleared out and many records thrown away to make room for more. So it is nothing short of a miracle that these early Lists of Taxables have been preserved, even in their incompleteness.

In 1933, while working one day in the basement archives, Nancy E. Jones Stickley and this compiler found the 1778 List of Taxables in a coal skuttle, where it had most likely been tossed as waste paper. It is in the form of a small pamphlet, with pages hand-sewn together, and written in the Spencerian long-hand style of the first Sheriff- Valentine Sevier (brother of John Sevier). It is his copy of those lists which the Assessors turned in to him of those inhabitants of the Washington County of 1778, which extended from the Virginia line to the great river- Mississippi.

From time to time other lists were discovered among the loose records. Then in 1935-36 this compiler was fortunate to enlist help through the Tennessee Emergency Relief Administration, with Project #90-E4-54 with six weeks of work, and later continued through the Works Progress Administration, Project #65-44-258 for another eight weeks. This later project was personally signed and commended by the late Franklin D. Roosevelt, and was the first which furnished work for women teachers and secretaries during the depression of the mid-1930s. At various times, there were ten women and two men working under my supervision. Entitled "Indexing & Copying Old Records", this basement vault was literally cleaned up and records filed in the County Court Clerk's office. During this period all loose records were sorted and classified, and a complete Inventory made of all books there. Some 2215 marriage records (both bonds and licenses)-200 of which antedate 1800- were found and filed in the regular Marriage Files, copied into Marriage Book #0, and indexed for both men and women's names. Among the volumes compiled were- 1) A Master Index of the Estates of Washington County 1778-1900 - This was made for both the loose records and for the Inventory & Settlement Books, of which there is a complete file; 2) A Volume of Miscellaneous Records, containing all those records excepting those in the other two volumes; and 3) Washington County Lists of Taxables, 1778-1860 (in which there are many missing links). This last volume is of loose pages, copied in long hand and bound in an old second hand ledger file donated by a kind printer, Mr. Pete Muse. These Volumes are in the County Court Clerk's Office in Washington County, available to researchers today.

Since that time it has been the great ambition of this compiler and the late Nancy E. Jones Stickley, who died in December 1962, to publish these early Lists of Taxables. In 1951 this was about to be realized when, due to the sudden illness of the latter, it was postponed. About three years ago, with the aid of another historian, Miss Inez E. Burns of Maryville, Blount County, Tennessee, these Lists of Taxables have been arranged alphabetically, which will greatly facilitate their use by researchers, and today we are offering this volume-

"WASHINGTON COUNTY LISTS OF TAXABLES 1778-1801"
by
Mary Hardin McCown, Nancy E. Jones Stickley & Inez E. Burns

The first section contains an Abstract of the Minutes of the Court of Pleas & Quarter Sessions of Washington County, 1778-1801- governed successively by North Carolina, State of Franklin, North Carolina, Territory of the U.S. South of the River Ohio, and Tennessee. This Abstract will help to fill in some missing links. All Lists have been copied verbatim and are arranged in alphabetical order.

We dedicate this volume to those hardy pioneers who first came down our streams, cleared these hillsides, and cultivated these valleys. It is they to whom we are indebted for the wonderful heritage and the beautiful and historic Washington County which we today enjoy.

November 17, 1963
Johnson City, Tennessee

Mary Hardin McCown
Mary Hardin McCown (Mrs. L.W.)

"Life is a story in volumes three -
The Past; the Present; the Yet-to-Be.
The first we've written and laid away;
The second we're writing from day to day;
The third and last of the volumes three
Is hidden from sight - God holdeth the key."

WASHINGTON COUNTY, NORTH CAROLINA (Now Tennessee)

Court of Pleas & Quarter Sessions.
Abstracted Re- LIST of TAXABLES.

Note: This Abstract has been made from the Minutes which are in the Washington County Court House in Jonesboro, Tennessee; with additions from an Abstract made in 1950-51 from the original records which are in the Tennessee State Archives in Nashville; with additions from those records of Washington County Minutes publishe in the American Historical Magazine; and finally with some few notes taken from the records published in Kate White's "Kings Mountain Men".

"James Bradley- BOND for Appearance February Court 1778- Know all all men by these presents that we JAMES BRADLEY and JNO. GIBSON of Washington Couty and State of North Carolina farmers are holden and firmly bound unto the said state of North Carolina in the just sum of fifty pound good and lawfull money to be paid to the said state of levied of their goods and chatle-

The condition of the above obligation is sutch that if the above Bound JAMES BRADLEY do appear at the next Court held at Wattaga for the North State of Carolina in Washington Countey which said Court is to begin the 23 day of february 1778 and if the said breadly Do Appear at said Court and before the Justices of s'd Coart and there abid till leggaly discharged by the said Coart the above obligation is to be void and if no efect otherwise to Remain in full force and virtue acording to Law.

acknowledged before me
february the 26 Day 1778
Joseph Willson

as witnes our hand
James (X) Breadly
his
mark
Jno. Gibson"

(Found in the <u>loose records</u> in basement vault, 1936.)

At a court begun and held for the county of Washington, 23rd day of February, 1778- Present-

John Carter, Chairman

ESQ-

John Sevier	John McMahon
Jacob Womack	Benj. Gist
Robert Lucas	John Chisolm
John Shelby	Joseph Willson
George Russell	William Cobb
William Been	James Stuart
John McNabb	Richard White
Thos. Houghton	Benj. Willson
Andy Greer	Valentine Sevier

<u>Tues. 24th Feb 1778-</u> John Sevier, Clerk; Valentine Sevier, Sherriff; James Stuart, Surveyor; John Carter, Entry Taker; John McMahon, Registrar; Jacob Womack, Stray Master.

Wed. Feb. 25, 1778 - Ordered -- James Maulden, Josiah Hoskins, & John Higgins be apptd to assess all the taxable property of the people living above the Iron Mt. in this county & make return thereof to Benj. Willson, Esq. Ordered that-- Benjamin Cobb, Solomon Smith, & William Asher be apptd to assess all the taxable property of the people-----(Note: Omitted a line).

Thurs. Aug. 27, 1778 (given as May 26 & 27 in American Hist. Mag) - Ordered that the Collectors for the several districts in this county collect the following sums to wit:

For every hundred pounds worth of property as by Gen Asst	16/8
James Charter- For building court house, prison & stocks	2/6
Thos Houghton- For building court house in Salisbury	4d
For contingent charges of the county	11d
Total	1-0-6

Amounting in the whole to 20 shillings & 16 pence.
J Carter & Thos Houghton dissents.

Fri. Aug. 28, 1778 (Given as May 28 in AMH Mag) - Moved that Thos Houghton Esq collect the monies due from the several districts of which Jno McNabb, Benj Willson & John Chisolm maid returns of to this court. Also that Benj Gist collect for the districts that Zach Isbell, Jacob Womack & Wm Been maid returns of. Thos Houghton entered himself, Chas Robertson & Joseph Tipton, his security in bond for the sum of £ 3000-0-0 for it. Benj Gist entered himself into bond with Chas Robertson & Thos Houghton, his sec. in the sum of £ 3000-0-0 for performance of same.

Nov. 23, 1778 - Court at house of Matthew Talbot.

Nov. 27, 1778 - Assessors Henry Lile, Wm McNabb & Saml Henry be allowed £ 6 for their services. Each man for his trouble.

Nov. 27, 1778 - Valentine Sevier entered himself, John Carter & Chas Robertson, his sec. in the sum of £ 3000-0-0 for the faithful discharge of the public monies that may be delivered into his hands from the different Tax Gathers for the year 1778.
--John Sevier entered himself & John Carter & Chas Robertson his sec. in the sum of £ 1000 for the faithful discharge as County Trustee.
--Cleavers Barksdale apptd Dep Sheriff for 1779.

Feb. 23, 1779 - Ordered -- That Richard Willson serve as Constable in Capt Hoskins District. John Reding, Constable for P Smith.

May 24, 1779 - On motion of Ephraim Dunlap, State Attorney, that a Sheriff be apptd....court nominated Valentine Sevier, Sheriff.... gave bond and security.

May 25, 1779 - Ordered -- Ephraim Dunlap, State Attorney be allowed for his services- Agreed- Thos Houghton dissents....Allowed £ 133-6-8 for year 1778....

May 26, 1779-Wed- Ordered -- That James Roddy, Ligh Hoskins & Jesse Hoskins be apptd Assrs of taxable property lying above the Iron Mts & make returns to Richard White, Esq.

(X)--That Matthew Talbott, Senr, Andrew Taylor & Cleavers Barksdale be Assrs below the Iron Mt, including the waters on north side of Brush Creek & Watauga, also that on north side of Wattauga & make return to Thos Houghton, Esq.
--That William Been, Junr, Jaret Fitzgerald & Pharoah Cobb assess all below Brush Creek extending as far as Brown's line, & on down to county line, & make returns to Wm Cobb, Esq.
--That Jacob Brown, John Woods, & Jona. Tipton assess all below the Iron Mt as low down as Big Limestone extending as far north as Brown's line, also all on south side Chucky (Mill) Creek to J. Seviers- & make returns to Wm Clark, Esq.
(X)--That Henry Earnest, Leahy (Ashal) Rawlins & Saml Lyle assess all below the Big Limestone on north side of Chucky & all below J. Sevier's Mill creek on south side Nola Chucky & make returns to Joseph Willson, Esq.
--That John Robertson, Bradley Gambel, James Abbott & Valentine Little serve as Constables.

Thurs. May 27, 1779 - Ordered -- That Sheriff be allowed for ex-officio services for 1778---sum of L 130.
--William Ward says he attended 4 days as Constable in 1778.
--John Sevier, Jesse Walton & Zach Isbell entered themselves in recognizane to the Governor with Valentine Sevier, Andrew Greer, & Chas Robertson, their sec. in sum of L 250,000 for faithful discharge as Commissioners of Confiscated Estates.

Tues. Aug. 23, 1779 - Ordered -- That return made by Wm Cobb, Esq be received. -- That return made by Joseph Willson, Esq be received. -- That return made by Thos Houghton, Esq be received. -- That Joseph Campbell be discharged from paying public or county tax.

Wed. Aug. 24, 1779 - Ordered -- Opinion of the court that Assessors be allowd sum of ten dollars a day for their trouble...also Constables be allwd ten dollars a day for notifying the people to give in their taxes.
--James Jones made oath he served 4 days as Constable. Allwd.
--Maj Jonathan Tipton made oath he served 4 days, Assessor. Allwd.
--Saml Lyle made oath he served 3 days, Assessor. Allwd.
--Clevers Barksdale & Andrew Taylor made oath they served 18 days each as assessors.
--Josiah Hoskins, James Roddy & Jesse Hoskins made oath they served 8 days each Assessors on Roans Creek. Allwd.

Thurs. Aug. 26, 1779 - Ordered -- Sheriff collect from Wm More fourfold his taxable property...appraised by best information that John Woods, Jacob Brown & Jonathan Tipton could get...sum of L 8000.
Ordered -- Sheriff collect following taxes for 1779:

Public Tax for every L 100.......	L 1- 5- 0
County " " " "	5- 0
District " " " "	-- 4d
	L 1-10- 4
Court House, prison & Stocks.....	2- 6
	L 1-12-10

--That Richard White's return be received. Allwd.
--Valentine Sevier, Jesse Walton, Andrew Greer & Wm Clark Esq, entered themselves as sec. for Valentine Sevier, Sheriff, for 1779 for L 40,000.

Nov. 22, 1779 - Henry Earnest made oath he served 5 days as assessor. Allwd.
--Benjamin Cobb & Solomon Smith...allwd 4 dollars a day for 4 days as assessors in 1778.
--John Higgins, Josiah Hoskins & James Maulden allwd 4 dollars a day for 2 days in 1778 for assessing.

Nov. 23, 1779 - Aseal Rawlins made oath he served 5 days as assessor. Allwd 10/8.

Feb. 20, 1780 - Jarot Fitzgerald made oath he served 4 days, assessor. Allwd.
--Pharoah Cobb made oath he served 4 days, assessor. Allwd.
--Valentine Little made oath he served 2 days as Constable. Allwd.
Ordered -- That Clerk deduct out of John Carter's assessment all such lands as is give to the court in said Carter Inventory & direct sheriff not to collect the same.

Wed. May 24, 1780 - Ordered -- That James Roddy, John Higgins & Richard Willson be apptd Assessors of Roans Creek District...Andrew Willson as Constable, & Richard White be apptd to receive the Inventories of same.
--That John Shelby, Esq be apptd to receive the Inventories of taxable property of Cpt McNabb & Col Val Sevier's companies, that Saml Colberson, Robt McAfee & Ralph Humphreys, assessors, & Emanuel Carter apptd Constable for same.
--That George Russell, Esq be apptd to receive the Inventories of Capt Been's Co; that Thos Hardeman, John Russell & Arthur Cobb be assessors, & Bradley Gambril be Constable for same.
--That Jesse Walton Esq apptd to receive the Inventories of Capt Brown's, Williams', Isbell's & Patterson's companies; that John Nave, Alexander Moore & William Murphy be assessors; and John Bond be Constable for same.
(X)--That Joseph Willson be apptd to take the Inventories of Capt Trimble's, Willson's, Gist's, Stevson's, Davis' companies; that Saml Moore, John Alexander & Adam Willson be assessors; and Thos Brandon be Constable for same.
--Ordered that William Moore's Inv & Jno Woods be received.
--That Jacob Brown & Jonathan Tipton's only sum due be collected & no more.

May 25, 1780 - Ordered -- That John Sevier be apptd Trustee for county.--That Jesse Walton, James Stuart & Thos Houghton, Esq. be apptd to settle with Sheriff & Trustee for the Tax Collections for 1778 & 1779- & make return to the Court.

Aug. 27, 1780 - Rec from James Roddy £ 3 for copy of allowance for assessing in 1779.
--Ordered that Maj Jesse Walton make return of Inventory wherein he was apptd, last court.
--Thos Hardeman, John Russell & Wm Stone, Assessors - made return of their Inventories & recorded.

Wed. Aug. 29 (30), 1780 - John Russell made oath he served 4 days assessing and is allowed $60 per day.
--Isaac Lain served as Constable in place of Bradley Gambril.

--The court is of opinion that constables be allowed sixty dollars per day for their services.
--Isaac Taylor, son of Andrew, served as Constable in place of Emanuel Carter.

Nov. 27, 1780 - Court held at Court house. (Note: This is first court after Battle of Kings Mountain.)
Charles Robertson, Chairman -
--Clevers Barksdale entered himself, Charles Robertson & Jessee Walton, as sec. in sum of 3,000 £ as Sheriff for year 1780.
--John Sevier entered himself, & Charles Robertson as Sec in sum of 5,000 £ as Trustee for year 1780.

Nov. 28, 1780 - List of Taxables for Roans Creek District returned by Richard White & received.
--William Murphy, John Nave & Alexander Moore, Assrs, made return & recorded.
--William Murphy & John Nave made oath they served 5 days & allwd.

Feb. 1781 - Memo- Wm Ritchie gave in his list 150 acres- which is given in by James Stuart- do not tax Ritchie with same.

Tues. May 29, 1781 - At Court House.
--Ordered that sheriff receive 5 sh per £ 100 for Tax Property for years 1780 & 1781.
--Ralph Humphreys, Robt McAfee & Saml Culbertson Assrs made returns & recorded.
--Cleavers Barksdale apptd Sheriff for 1781 - Entered bond with Chas Robertson & Edmund Williams as sec.
--Bradley Gambril made oath he served 2 days as Constable. Allwd.

Wed. May 30, 1781 - Thomas Brandon made oath he served 10 days as Constable in Joseph Willson's District & allwd.
--Cleavers Barksdale apptd to collect the public & county levy for 1780 & entered himself with Ralph Humphreys, Andrew Greer, Saml Williams & Ephraim Dunlap as Sec...in sum of £ 200,000.
--Ordered that Valentine Sevier be allwd as ex-officio services for 1780...allwd £ 4000.
--Justices & Assrs apptd for year 1781 -
1st Distr- Richard White, Esq.
Assrs- James Roddy, Jesse Hoskins & Corn. Bowman
2nd Distr- Thomas Houghton, Esq.
Assrs- Wm Cocke, James Henry & Andrew Taylor
3rd Distr- Wm Cobb, Esq.
Assrs- Thos Hardiman, Thos Jonakin & Wm Coxe
4th Distr- Wm Clarke, Esq.
Assrs- John Woods, Michael Woods & Jacob Brown
5th Distr- Joseph Willson, Esq.
Assrs- Anthony Moore, Robt Wier & Abraham Hoskins
--Constables to notify the people -
1st Distr- Andrew Willson; 2nd Distr- Isaac Taylor, son of Andrew; 3rd Distr- Wm Frame; 4th Distr- Wm Meek & Joseph Reed; 5th Distr- Wm Moore & Abraham Hill.

Mon. Aug. 27, 1781 - Daniel Dunn, infirm man & object of charity, exempt from Tax.

Tues. Aug. 28, 1781 - Thomas Talbott took oath for public office- as Dep Sheriff under Clevias Barksdale for 1781..

Feb. 25, 1782 - John Woods, Michael Woods & Jacob Brown assrs- made returns & recorded.
--Court apptd Thos Houghton & Wm Webb to settle with Sheriff & make return to next court.

Feb. 26, 1782 - Thos Hardiman, Wm Cox & Thos Jonakin made returns & recorded.
--The court allwd John Sevier to render Inventory of his estate for year 1780 & recorded.
--Robert Irwine, Robt Weir & Anthony Moore made returns & recorded.

May 27, 1782 - At court house.
--Wm Cocke, Andrew Taylor & James Henry assrs, for 1781 made returns & recorded.
--Clevias Barksdale apptd Sheriff for 1782- & entered himself & Chas Robertson, Wm Cocke & Eph Dunlap as sec in sum of £ 5000-specie.
--John Sevier, Wm Cocke & Valentine Sevier entered themselves with Andrew Greer, Wm McNabb & Saml Williams as sec in sum of £ 5000 specie for 1782 as Commissioners of Confiscated Property.
--John Sevier reports he has sold 2 slaves of estate of Thomas Barker for £ 3400 & has the money to turn in.
--Court allwd Clevias Barksdale Sheriff for 1781 £ 50 for ex-officio services.
--Ralph Humphreys, Robt McAfee & Saml Culbertson assrs made returns & recorded.
--Ordered that Richard Minton serve as Constable for John B McMahon.
-- " " Thomas Brummitt " " " " Wm Meeks.
-- " " James Denton " " " " Joseph Whitson.
--Return from Roans Creek Distr- made by assrs & recorded.
--Returns from 3rd Distr- made by assrs & recorded.
--James Denton made oath he served 2 days as Constable- & allwd.
--Thomas Brummitt " " " 5 " " " " "
--James Rusell " " " 3 " " " " "
--Ordered that constables for 1781 be allwd $300 per day.
--Jacob Brown made oath he served 3 days as assrs in 1779 & 3 days in 1781 & allwd $300 per day.
--John Nave made oath he served 3 days as assrs. Allwd.

May 28, 1782 - Apptd to take the List of Taxables for 1782 -
1st Distr - Assessors- James Roddy, Cornelius Bowman, Joseph Ford; Richard White, Esq; & Andrew Wilson, Constable.
2nd Distr - Assessors- Landon Carter, Valentine Sevier & Andrew Greer; Thomas Houghton, Esq; & Joseph Whitson, Constable.
3rd Distr - Assessors- Mark Mitchell, Pharoah Cobb & Jesse Been; George Russell, Esq; & Wm Grisham, Constable.
4th Distr - Assessors- Jesse Bonds, Isaac Mayfield & Wm Murphy; Charles Robertson, Esq; & Wm Meeks, Constable.
5th Distr - Assessors- Peter Kirkindale, Wm Ritchey & Saml Wier; Danl Kennedy, Esq; & Jesse Gentry, Constable.

Nov. 4, 1782 - Danl Kennedy, Joseph Willson & John Newman, Esq assrs for 1782 made returns & recorded.
--Landon Carter, Andrew Greer & Valentine Sevier, Assrs made return & recorded.

--James Roddy, Cornelius Bowman & Joseph Foard Assrs, made returns & recorded.
--Wm Murphy, Isaac Mayfield & Jesse Bounds Assrs, made returns & recorded.
--Wm Murphy, Isaac Mayfield & Jesse Bounds made oath they served 3 days assessing & allwd.

Sat. Nov. 9, 1782 - Court levied County Tax for 1782 of 1 sh on each £ 100 Taxable property & Poll Tax to pay in proportion.
--Saml Wier, Peter Kirkindall & Wm Ritchey made returns for 1782 & recorded.

Mon. Feb. 3, 1783 - Wm Ritchey made oath he served 7 days in 1782- Allwd.

Wed. Feb. 1783 - Joshua Houghton, Jr. apptd Collector for 2nd Distr.
--James Sevier, Collector for 4th Distr.
--Daniel Kennedy, Collector for 5th Distr- made bond of £ 400.
--Thos Talbott apptd County Commissioner for specific property tax for 1783.
--Thos & Wm Talbott, Collectors for 1st & 3rd Districts.

May 5, 1783 - Capt Robt McAfee made oath he served 4 days in 1782- Allwd.
--Capt Saml Weir made oath he served 6 days in 1782- Allwd.
--Justices apptd to take the Inventories in 1783:
  1st Distr- Richard White, Justice
    Andrew Willson & John Thurman, Constables
  2nd Distr- Jno McNabb, Justice
    Wm Reeves & Joel Callahan, Constables
  3rd Distr- Wm Cobb, Justice
    John Brummitt & ~~Danl Henderson~~, Constables
  4th Distr- Zach Isbell, Justice
    Danl Henderson, Constable
  5th Distr- Joseph Willson, Jr., Justice
    Joseph Pearce, Constable
--Col Charles Robertson, Thos Houghton & Landon Carter, Assessors.
--James Denton made oath he served 5 days as Constable. Allwd.
--Andrew Hannah apptd Constable in place of Jesse Gentry.
--John Thurman " " " " " James Denton.
--Court ordered- Deduct from Robt McAfee's Assments for 1780 & 1781 property by him of James McAfee- for it was assessed in county of Lincoln.

Aug 4, 1783 - Joshua Houghton, Jr, Collector for 2nd Distr, made returns on several persons who have removed from sd district..... court orders persons be collected by others...
--Saml Moor made oath he served 5 days in 1780.
--Pharoah Cobb made oath he served 4 days in 1780 & 2 days in 1781.
--Saml Culbertson made oath he served 4 days in -----. 1782.
--The Court allows Assessors for the year 1782-- 12 sh per day each.
--Valentine Sevier, Andrew Greer & Landon Carter allwd 3 days for 1782 as Assrs.
--Pharoah Cobb allwd for assessing for 1780 4 days & 3 days for 1781.
--Thomas Gibson released from Poll Tax for 1783.

Nov. 3, 1783 - Peter Parkinson apptd Constable in John Carter's Distr.
--The Court allws the Assessors for year 1783 16 sh each per day.

Feb. 2, 1784 - Court ordered that County Tax for 1783 be 1 sh on each £ 100 - Poll Tax to pay in notwithstanding.
--Daniel Kennedy, Collector for 5th Distr, made return.
--Andrew Greer, Esq apptd Collector for year 1783- for county & public taxes- with Wm Cocke & Wm Ward as sec.

Aug. 3, 1783 Tues. - Moses Embree says- Isaac Embree was not of age 21 in 1783 when Poll Tax was levied against him...not to get sd Tax.
--Jesse Bounds says- James Bounds was not of age 21 in 1783.
--Susanna Humphreys says- Elisha Humphreys was not of age 21 in 1783.
--County Tax for 1783 is 2 sh for Poll & 8 pence per 100 acres of land for 1784.
--Justices apptd for 1784 -

1st Distr-	Richard White, Esq-	Andrew Wilson, Constable
2nd Distr-	James Stuart, Esq-	Benj Linderly, "
3rd Distr-	Chas Robertson, Esq-	John Collier, "
4th Distr-	John McMahon, Esq-	William Maston, "
5th Distr-	Joseph Willson, Esq-	Wm Carson, "

Aug. 1784 - Poll Tax for county- Each to pay 2 sh per Poll & 8 pence for every 100 acres of land for year 1784.
--Agnes Talbot, wife of Matthew Talbot relinquished all right of land of her husband, Matthew Talbott in Virginia.
--Robt Cowan, father says- John Cowan was under 21 years in 1783.
--The Court House to be built- John Chisolm, Esq- apptd to build it.
--Thomas Talbott apptd Sheriff for 1784.
--Alexander Greer apptd to repair & complete the prison on same terms as John Chisolm to build the court house. Court house to be 24'x24' and roof to be joint shingles hung with pegs.

Nov. 1784 - Wm McNabb apptd in place of James Stuart Esq to take Taxables in 2nd Distr.

Nov. 7, 1785 - Joshua Williams apptd Head Lawyer for Washington Co- with Edmund Williams & Christopher Taylor as sec. for £ 1000 each.
--Returns for 1785 -

2nd Distr- made by William Cox
3rd Distr- " " Abednego Inman
4th Distr- " " Joseph Willson on behalf of Alex McKee

Feb. 2, 1786 -

Mon. Feb. 1, 1787 - Court for Washington County, N C held at house of William Davis- with John Tipton, Clerk; Thomas Gourley, Dep Clk; Thomas Mitchell, Sheriff...These fill vacancies in county offices.

Tues. May 8, 1787 - John Tipton, Clerk; Thomas Gourley, Dep Clk; Jonathan Pugh, Sheriff; Alexander Moffat, Coroner.
--1- Distr- Richard White Esq to take Insolvent Taxables of Roan Creek & above Stone Mountain & above Capt. Parkinson's.
--2- William Turkey (?) Esq to take those in Capt Thornton's & Wm Campbell's old companies.
--3- Robert Love to take those in the Greasy Cove.

--4- Alexander Moffat to take those in Capt Brown's, Trimble's & Moore's old companies.
--5- James Stuart to take those in Capt McNabb's, Parkerson's & Hendrick's old companies.
--6- John McMahon to take those in Capt Rader's & Rife's old companies.
--7- Robert Allison to take those in William Hues' old company.
(X)--8- John Hammer to take those in Capt Fain's & Capt Coxe's companies on Boones Creek.
--They are to take all inhabitants, describing the free from the slaves.

Wed. May 9, 1787 - Jacob Tipton, Sheriff; William McNabb, former Ranger. They are to demand the records of the county from former Clerk, John Sevier, and to demand the key of the jail in Jonesboro from former Sheriff.
--Wm Nelson apptd to receive the fines as Commissioner.

Mon. Aug. 6, 1787 - Met at home of William Davis.

Tues. Aug. 7, 1787 - John Tipton resigned as Clerk- Thomas Gourley apptd Clerk pro tem with Gourley & Tipton as Sec..
(X)--John Hammer says he served for Samuel Bogart 2 days as Constable in Capt Fain's company...allwd 8 sh per day.
--Caleb Odells served 5 days in Capt Hendricks co...8 sh per day.
--Jonathan Pugh & Jacob Tipton each served 1½ days in Capt Brown's Co...8 sh per day.
--Saml Willson- 20 sh as constable in upper county on Roans Creek.
--James Denton, Constable, says served 8½ days in warning Taxables in Capt McNabb's, Parkinson's & Stone's old companies...8 sh per day.
--Ephraim King claims unable to pay Taxes as cannot support his family.

Nov. 5, 1787 - Thomas Gourley clerk- with Edmund Williams, Wm David & Robert English as Sec.

2nd Mon. Feb. 1788 - Jonathan Pugh, Sheriff, ordered to obtain the records from John Sevier, Esq. (Last record in that book.)

Mon. May 12, 1788 - Andrew Jackson, Esq- came into court & produced a license as an attorney with a certificate sufficently attested of his taking the Oaths necessary to sd office & was admitted to practice in this county court...(p-321 in sd book-Washington Co. N.C.)
--John McNairy, also admitted to practice in Washington County.
--Jonathan Pugh, dec- with Col John Tipton & Susanna Pugh as admrs.
--Peter Bowman exempt from paying Taxes.

May 13, 1788 - George Mitchell elected Sheriff.

May 14, 1788 - George Mitchell resigned as Sheriff- & Edmund Williams unanimously chosen as Sheriff...

May 15, 1788 - Estate of Jonathan Pugh, dec- is to be paid £ 15 out of County Tax for his ex-officio services as Sheriff.
--James Stuart allwd until next court to make return for 1787 of his Taxable property for 1787.
--Court house to be in Jonesboro, & court adjourned to sd place.

--Allwd Alex Moffat £ 3 for acting as Sheriff.
--Allwd George Mitchell £ 5 as Sheriff.
--County is to be divided into Districts:
Upper District- From the Iron Mt east to county line.
Middle District- From Iron Mt downwards, incl Capt Renno's, Gudger's, Rader's, Fain's, Gregg's & Stone's companies.
Lower District- All below above Districts.
--Assessors for 1787 -

Upper Distr-	Joseph Culton, Esq.
Middle Distr-	John Nelson, Esq.
Lower Distr-	Alex Moffat

--Assessors for 1788 -

Richard White, Esq-	Capt Johnson & Parkersin's Cos.
Landon Carter, Esq-	Capt Renno's Co.
Joshua Kelley, Esq-	Capt Hendrick's Co.
Robert Allison, Esq-	Capt Gregg's Co.
Col John Tipton, Esq-	Capt Cooper's Co.
Robert Love, Esq-	Capt Gudger's & Brown's Cos.
John Strain, Esq-	Capt Millikin & Rüfe's Cos.
William Barkley, Esq-	Capt Blair's & Campbell's Cos.
William Cox, Esq-	Capt Stone's & Shelby's Cos.
John Hammer, Esq-	Capt Pearson's Co.
John McMahon, Esq-	Capt Fain's Co.
Henry Nelson, Esq-	Capt Rader's Co.

Thomas Gourley, Clerk.

No Date - Thomas Evans exempt from Poll Tax.

Tues. Morning 1788 - Following Companies reported:

Taxables in Capt	Cooper's Co-	from John Tipton, Esq-
" " "	Gudger's Co-	" Robert Love, Esq-
" " "	Hendrick's Co-	" Joshua Kelley, Esq-

--County Tax to be 1 sh per Poll & 4 d on every 100 acres- 1787.
--John Harold exempt from Poll Tax for 1787.
--John Nolan to be paid 25 pounds for finishing the public building in Jonesborough.

Wed. Morning Aug. 1788 - Rec of Richard White- List for 1788.
--Wm McCloud allwd 3 days as Constable in Capt Shipley's Co, also 3 days in Capt Stone's Co...Allwd 8 sh per day; & 3½ days in Capt Pearce's Co.
--James Stuart gave in Tax property of Maj Thomas Stuart for 1788- as 1 wh Poll- 1 bl Poll- to be entered on List.

2nd Mon. Nov. 1, 1788 - James Ryan excused from paying Poll Tax for 1787- having paid it in Guilford Co; and not to collect Tax on land from James Ward until next Court.
--Ordered- Alexander Talbott be relieved from Poll Tax for 1787.
--Capt Rader allwd 3 days for 1788- also as Constable for 1787.
--Apptd John Hammer Esq in place of John McMakin Esq-(McMahon) in Capt Tullis Co.
--William Cocke Esq- asked to be made Clerk of Pleas & Quarter Sessions. Thomas Gourley, present Clerk.
--Thomas Gourley Clerk, allwd 15 pounds for ex-officio services to date.

Feb. 1789 - Samuel Bogart allwd 16 sh as Constable in Capt Tullis Co- for 1788.
--William Carson exempt from Poll Tax in 1787 acct of age, & not to collect from James Cash for 2 Polls in 1787.
--James Gregg allwd 20 sh as Constable in Capt Jonakin's Co for 1787.
--James Denton allwd, as Constable in Capt Cooper's Co in 1788.
--Excused John & George Kincheloe from paying Tax in 1787 & 1788, having paid it in Virginia then.

Mon. May 2, 1789 - Alexander Moffatt, Collector for county, notified by Edmund Williams, late Sheriff, to turn in account for Public Taxes- will save for judgement vs him in court.
--James Denton came at order of Edmund Williams, Sheriff, testified he duly notified Wm Davis & Caleb Odell, sec for Joseph Culton, one of Collectors for county to settle his collections & save judgement.
--Ordered that the late Registrar's books be delivered to Wm Stevenson, now Register of this county, & to take necessary steps for it.
--Edmund Williams, Sheriff, received 20 pounds for his services as Sheriff for 1788.
--Benjamin Blackburn released from Poll Tax as over age- 1787.
--Michael Harrison elected Sheriff- with John Carter Dep Sheriff.
--William Stevenson, Register, David Brown, coroner, Joseph Brown as Dep Surveyor.
--William Frame allwd for 1½ days as Constable in Capt Hughs Co- 1787.
--Ordered- That same Justices who took Taxables in 1788, take for 1789.
--Ordered- Taxes for 1789 shall be levied as directed by Act of Gen Assembly: County Tax- 1 sh per Poll & 4 d each 100 acres
State Tax- 12 d on every Poll.
Viz: 2 sh in cash, 2 sh in certificate & 12 sh per Poll.
--Edmund Williams be apptd Dep County Clerk.
--Alexander Moffat to collect the Tax for 1788 for same district he did in 1787.
--Nicholas Hail - Coll for Middle District
--Joseph Ford - Coll for Upper District

Aug 2nd Mon. 1789 - Samuel Bogart served as Constable in Capt Tullis Co. 2 days.
--Elisha Walden exempt from payment of Public Tax...over age.
--Jane Nelson be exempt from Tax on Negro named Woody- for reason shown court.
--All persons get refund for Taxes paid over 12 sh per Poll for 1787.
--Ordered that Wm Parker & Alex Greer be allwd 95 pounds for erecting the prison in county- to be paid from Public Taxes.
--Joseph Ford to be Collector for Upper Distr- with Peter Parkinson as sec & Jacob Smith.
--John Metlock released from Taxes for 1788.
--Taxes for 1788 & 1789 to be: 12 sh on each Poll & 4 d on each 100 acres land... Andrew Greer, Joseph Brittain, John Webb, Comm.

Nov 2nd Mon. 1789 - William Nodding released from Poll Tax for 1788.
--Rev John Cossons property for 1789- 250 acres- 1 wh Poll.
--Adam Willson released from Tax on Negro George for 1788.
--Edmund Harrison apptd Dep Sheriff.
--Andrew Thompson apptd Constable in Capt Millikin's, Campbell's & Stephen's Cos.
--George House made oath he served 2 days as Constable in Capt Campbell's Co for 1789.

--Lewis Jones released from Poll Tax.
--Wm Findley released from Taxes.
--Elijah Cooper apptd Ranger for county.

Feb 2nd Mon. 1790 - John Wear, Esq to notify Taxables in Capt Bounds Co to make return for 1789 & clerk to annex it to Collector's List for year.
--Elijah Cooper, Stray Master for the county.
--John Webb apptd Constable for Greasy Cove Distr- James Love & George Mitchell as Sec.
--George Davis gave in his Tax for 1789- viz: 100 acres land & 1 Wh Poll.

May 2nd Mon. 1790 - Following to take the Taxables for 1790:

	Wm Moreland, Esq-	All above the Iron Mt.
(X)	Andrew Greer, Esq-	In Capt Greer Distr-
	Joshua Kelley, Esq-	For Capt Maxwell's Co.
	John Tipton, Esq-	For Capt Davises Co.
	Robt Love, Esq-	For the Greasy Cove
	Henry Nelson, Esq-	For Capt Young's Co.
	John Hammer	For Capt Tullis Co.
	Joseph Brittain	For Capt Stone's & Shipley's Co.
	Wm Pursley	For Capt Murray's Co.
	John Campbell	For Capt Harrison's Co.
	John Strain	For Capt Campbell's Co.
(X)	John Millikin	For his own Co.
	Abednego Inman	For Capt Wyley's Co.
(X)	Alex Moffet	For Capt Hanley's Co.
(X)	John Wear	For Capt Bounds Co.
	----Dyer	To take all east of the Iron Mt.

--Wm McCloud allwd 8 sh per day as Constable in Capt Stone's Co 3 days, in Capt Shipley's Co 3 days, Capt Pearce's Co 3½ days, for 1788 & same for 1789.
--Michael Harrison apptd Sheriff for 1790.
--Tax for 1790- 12 sh on every Poll & 4 d each 100 acres land, exclusive of Tax for prison & court house for 1790.
--The following Patrollers be apptd in following Distr-

1- Capt Greer's & Maxwell's Co.- Wm Ward, George McCormack, Isaac Tipton & John Carter
2- Capt Davises & The Greasy Cove- Capt Love, Wm Davis, Thomas Gourley, Thomas Love & John Webb
3- Capt Tullis & Capt Stone's Co.- William Nelson, Pharoah Cobb, Russell Bean & Robt Stone
4- Capt Young & Capt Wyley's Co.- Christopher Taylor, James Allison, Thomas Rodgers & Thos Young
5- Capt Shipley's & Capt Murray's Co.- James Noland, Jesse Crouch, Richard Hale & Joseph Barron
6- Capt Harrison & Capt Campbell's Co.- James Carmichael, Abraham Campbell, David Shields & Joseph Martin.
7- Capt Millikin's, Henley's & Bounds Co.- Thomas Brown, Alexander Moffat & Wm Trimble

--Patrollers are to take up all Negro slaves passing out of Master's premises without a pass & punish by whipping, giving 39 lashes or less at own discretion....and to punish list by Captains of sd companies.

Aug 2nd Mon. 1790 - Daniel Baker allwd 1 day as Constable in Capt Hanley's Co.
--Capt Greer's Co to be N of Watauga River & Capt Maxwell's Co in area of road from Landon Carter's Mill to head of Indian Creek..
--James Denton, as Constable, served 3 days in 1789 in Capt Rennos Co; 2 days in Capt Davis Co, 1789; 2 days in Capt Young's Co, 1790; 2 days in Capt Davises Co, 1790.
--George House made oath he served 2 days as Constable.
--Ordered- Godfrey Carriger apptd overseer of Road from Sycamore Shoals to certain branch at Mountain above Carriger's- & those of Capt Greer's & Maxwell's 2 companies on south side of Wataga from Sycamore Shoals to be his gang.
--Ordered- Solomon Hendrix apptd overseer of Road from Joseph Tipton's to Brush Creek- & to warn all people within 2 miles of sd road.
--Ordered- Peter Range apptd overseer road from Brush Creek to the long ford on Knobe Creek, and warn all people within 3 miles to work road.
--Ordered- Thomas Brown & Obediah Bounds be Patrollers in Capt Jacob Brown's Co.
--Ordered- Andrew Caldwell & James King apptd same for Capt James Wyley.
--Ordered- Capt George North & Saml Irwin apptd for Capt North's Co.

(Minutes of Washington County Court of Pleas & Quarter Sessions are missing from Aug. 1790 until Feb. 1794 - but many of the Lists of Taxables are extant. These are given in the Tax Lists. MHMcC)

Mon. Feb. 4, 1794 - (1st page is missing, and no date- but later data gives date of Feb. term, 1794. MHMcC)

May 26, 1794 - Court of Pleas & Quarter Session, Terr S of River Ohio.
--Ordered- Joseph Crouch Esq- take Taxable property of Capt Morrison Co for years 1793 & 1794.
--Wm Ward allwd 3 days @ 8 sh each as Constable- 1 pound- 4 sh.
--John Carter Esq- released from Taxes.
--Nathan Shipley apptd Dep Surveyor.

May 29, 1794 - Godfrey Carriger, Jr allwd 4 days @ 8 sh per day as Constable - 1 pound & 12 sh.
--Ordered that George Gillespie, Sheriff, advance to Col Chas Robertson 100 dollars for 1793 to carry on public buildings.--Charles Robertson, ex-officio- while Sheriff.

Aug. 25, 1794 -

Nov. 17, 1794 - County Court Pleas & Quarter Session

Feb. 18, 1795 - County Court Pleas & Quarter Session

Fri. Feb. 20, 1795 - Inventories of Taxable Property Returned by: (X) Nicholas Carriger; (X) John Strain; (X) John Millikin; John Carter; (X) Reuben Thornton; (X) Joseph Crouch; (X) Joseph Brittain; Charles Robertson; Jesse Payne; (X) Joseph Young; James Stuart; Charles McCray, Esqs.

Feb. 21, 1795 - Ordered- That Tax for defraying contingent expenses of county for the year & that Tax be levied for repairing or erecting Court House, prison & stocks by late Act of Gen Assembly, be collected agreeable to same for present year 1795.
--James Sevier, Clerk, be allwd 15 pounds for services 1794.
--George Gillespie, Esq- Collector for public & county tax for 1795- and gave his bond.

May 19, 1795 - Inventory of Capt Handley's Co for 1794 & 1795 returned & recorded.

Aug. 7, 1795 - George Gillespie apptd High Sheriff.
--Rev Sam Doak be released from Tax on stud for 1795.
--James Polly released for Tax on stud, 1795.
--James Pollock pay Tax on 750 acres & not 300 acres.
--Ordered- Joseph Young Esq- Tax Taxables in Nath Taylor's Co for 1795.
--Ordered- That Landon Carter serve as County Trustee for 1 year.
--James Cash released from Poll Tax for 1795.
--Henry Oldham released from Tax on stud.

Aug. 19, 1795 - Garret Reasoner released from Tax on 1800 acres- & John Hyder released from Tax on 250 acres.

Feb. 15, 1796 -

May- 1796 - Lists of Taxables returned:

(X)	Capt Brown's Co-	by John Weir	for 1796
(X)	Capt John Millikin's Co-	by himself	" "
(X)	Capt Handley's Co-	by John Wear	" "
	Capt Deacon's Co-	by John Strain	" "
(X)	Capt Morrison's Co-	by William Nelson	" "
(X)	Capt Calvert's Co-	by John Adams	" "
(X)	Capt Young's Co.-	by Joseph Young	" "
(X)	Capt Longmire's Co.		" "
(X)	Capt Shipley's Co.	by Joseph Brittain	" "
(X)	Capt Melvan's Co.	by Joseph Crouch	" "
(X)	Return of the Town Lots	by James Stuart	" "

--Apptd- Nathaniel Davis, Coroner for 1796.
- George Gillespie - Sheriff...pd $60 for 1796.
- John Adams, Ranger, for 1796.
- Charles McCray, Trustee
- Landon Carter allwd $131 for Trustee for 2 years.

Aug. 15, 1796 -

(The years 1797 & 1798 Minutes are missing from court house. MHMcC)

1798 - George Gillespie, Sheriff

(The end of Book #1 - Minutes of the Superior Court 1791 are in this book also. The Court of Pleas & Quarter Sessions Minutes were copied in this book when the original ones were taken to Nashville, 1880. MHMcC)

Book #2 - 1798

May 1798 - Wm Young apptd Constable.
--John Elleman as Constable, David Carson as Constable.
--Apptd John Strain, Treasurer.
--Charles Robertson allwd $46.00 as Jailor.
--George Gillespie, late Sheriff, allwd $60 for 1797.
--Charles McCray, allwd $39.34½ for bal due as County Treas.
--George Gillespie allwd $90.66 for Sheriff for 1797.
--John Sevier, apptd Trustee.
--Dufty Jacobs, allwd $154.00 (Jailor)
--Charles Robertson allwd $29.46 as Jailor.

Aug 1st Mon, 1798 -

Aug. 6, 1798 - Henry Saults apptd Constable.
--Burgiss Witt apptd Constable for 2 years.
--Francis Baxter apptd Constable.
--Richard Blair released from Taxes on 607 acres.
--Saml Johnston released from Tax on stud horse as did not have horse until 1798 in May.
--Noah Hawthorn apptd Constable.

Nov 1st Mon, 1798 - Richard Blair released from Tax on 697 acres.
--Gabriel Devault to keep a ferry on the Watauga at John Bean's Old Plantation.
--Barnabas Eagan released from paying .25 for his no. of scalps-he having paid the same.
--Dufty Jacobs, Jailor, allwd $29.91½.

Feb. 1799 - Daniel Bayless apptd Constable.
--Peter Jackson apptd Constable; also Samol Randolph.
--Ordered that Wm Clark be released from $1.25 County Tax for 1798.
--James Stuart, one of the poor of the county, allwd $50 per year for support. (Is this the Surveyor? MHMcC)
--Brice Blair, High Sheriff for 1798.
--James Templin released from Tax on stud for 1798.
--Daniel Bayless apptd Constable.
--James Sevier allwd $30 for ex-officio services as Clerk in 1798.

May 1st Mon, 1799 - Alexander Mathes apptd Commissioner in place of John Nelson to settle with the Sheriff for county monies.
--John Elleman resigns appt as Constable.
--John G Brown apptd Constable in Capt Robertson's Co.
--Thomas Copps apptd Constable.
--List of Taxables returned:
- (X) Capt Duncan's Co.
- Capt Biddle's Co.
- (X) Capt Moore's Co.
- Capt Morrison's Co.
- (X) Capt Norwood's Co.
- Capt Taylor's Co.
- Capt Shipley's Co.
- Capt Longmire's Co.

--Brice Blair, Sheriff, allwd $60 for 1798.

Aug 1st Mon, 1799 - John O'Brien apptd Constable in Capt Robertson's Co.
--Saml Shaw released from Tax on 200 acres land- reason given to the court.
--George Gillespie apptd High Sheriff.

(This is end of Minutes for Court of Pleas & Quarter Sessions, 1799. This same book, pp-141-346, contains Minutes of the Court of Equity for the District of Washington, Terr South of River Ohio, held in Jonesboro, Washington Co. Begins Feb 1791--1792, 1793, 1794, 1795, 1797, 1798, 1799. Nowhere have I found any Minutes for the Court of Pleas & Quarter Sessions for the years 1791--92--93. There are no Minutes for the years 1800 & 1801. The next book, #2, begins with 1802. In the List of Taxables for those missing years, we do find some lists of persons appointed to take the lists in the various Militia Companies, which is given with those lists. MHMcC 7-5-63)

(X) Lists so marked are given in the following pages.

WASHINGTON COUNTY LISTS OF TAXABLES

YEAR	CAPTAINS	RETURNED BY	
1778	Assessors- James Maulden) Josiah Hoskins) John Higgins)	--------- Benjamin Wilson, Esqr.	
	Henry Lyle) Samuel Henry) William McNabb)	--------- Jno. McNabb, Esqr.	
	Benja. Cobb) Solomon Smith) Wm Asher)	--------- John Chisolm, Esqr.	
	-------------)	--------- Wm Been, Esqr.	
	-------------)	--------- Michal Woods, Esqr.	
	Saml Williams) Robert Box) Frances Hughes)	--------- Zacha. Isbell, Esqr.	
	-------------)	--------- Jacob Womack, Esqr.	
	-------------)	--------- The Court	
		--------- Thomas Houghton, Collr.	
		--------- Benjamin Gist, Collr.	
1779	Assessors- Matthew Talbott, Senr) Andrew Taylor) Clevias Barksdill)	-- Thomas Houghton	(The First & Fifth (Districts of Wash- (ington County
	Henry Earnest) Asael Rawlings) Samuel Lyle)	--- Joseph Willson, Esqr.	("The Lower (District", Wash- (ington County
1780 & 1781	Assessors- Robert Irvine) Anthony Moore) Robert Wear)	-- Joseph Willson, Collr.	(Fifth District (Washington County

The property of the above Assessors was assessed by Daniel Kennedy, John Newman & Charles Allison.

Undated List - The same form as the List for 1780-1781. It is before 1783 when Greene County was formed. Begins with "Lanty Armstrong".

Undated List - The size and quality of the paper, the enumerations, and other similarities strongly indicate the date to be after the 1780-1781 Lists and before the 1787 single List found. It could be part of the 1780-1781 List, as only the Fifth District List was found. Begins with "Matthew Huston".

Undated Scrap #1 - A single sheet of paper, of similar size and quality as the Undated List, written in the same ink and scribe, with same spelling as the Undated List. Must be in the early 1780s.

Undated Scrap #2 - A single sheet of paper of similar size and quality as the Undated List, written in the same scribe and ink, and with the same spelling as the Undated List.

(Above scraps are combined with the "Lanty Armstrong" List.)

1787 Captain Fain - Returned by John Hammer, Esqr.

1790 List of the Justices appointed for the years 1790 & 1791

Capt. Biddle's Co. - For the years 1790, 1791 & 1792

Capt. Blair's Co. - Undated List, but same form as 1790

Capt. Chism's Co. - 1790 List taken in 1792

Capt. Depew's Co. - Undated List, but same form as 1790
(Also contained Capt. Blair's List)

Capt. Greer's Co. - Copied on back of Total Schedule for 1791

Capt. Hanley's Co. - Taken by John Were
(On the back is same company for 1791)

Capt. Maxfield's Co. - Scrap #1 & Scrap #2 for 1790 & 1791

Capt. John Millikin's Co.

Capt. Nelson's Co. - Undated List, but same form as 1790

Capt. Shipley's Co. - List for 1790 & 1791 (On the back of Capt Stone's List for 1790 & 1791)

Capt Stone's Co. - Taken by Joseph Britten
(1791 List on same sheet)

Capt. Tullis's Co. - Scrap- William Cobb's Taxable Property for 1790 & 1791

Capt. Richard White's Co.

Capt. E. Williams's Co. - Taken for 1790 & 1791

Undated List taken by Order of the Court, same form as 1790 & 1791

1791 Justices appointed in 1790 for 1790 & 1791 (See 1790 List)

Capt. Biddle's Co. - See 1790 List

Capt. John Chisolm's Co. - Taken by John Chisolm
Jan 28, 1792 for 1791

Capt. Hanley's Co.

Capt. John Millikin's Co. - Taken by self

Capt. George North's Co. - Taken by self

Capt. Shipley's Co. - See 1790 List

Capt. Stone's Co. - See 1790 List

Capt. Tole (Tullis) Co.

Capt. Richard White's Co.

Capt. Willey's Co.

Capt. Edmund Williams's Co. - See 1790 List
Scrap to be added for 1791

"A Schedule of the Whole Number of Persons within the County of Washington in the Territory of the United States of America South of the River Ohio on the last Saturday in July, 1791"

1792 Capt. Biddle's Co. - See 1790 List

Capt. Brown's Co. - Taken by Charles Robinson

Capt. Carriger's Co. - Taken by self (undated List which seems to be for 1792)

Capt. Depew's Co. - List is bound with Capt. Biddle's Co.

The Greasy Cove - Taken by Robert Love

Capt. Thomas Maxwell's Co. - On back of Capt. Tullis's Co. for 1792

Capt. Millikin's Co. - Taken by self

Capt. George North's Co. - Taken by Charles Robinson

Capt. Scott's Co.

Capt. Tullis's Old Co. - Undated, but likely 1792 List (On back of Capt Maxwell's Co List)

Capt Richard White's Co.

1792 Scrap #1 - James Allison's Personal List

Scrap #2 - Charles Robertson, Senr. Personal List

List of Taxes for the Year 1792

1793 Capt. Blair's Co, formerly Capt. Biddle's - Taken by John Strain (on same sheet as Capt. Depew's Co.)

Capt. Brown's Co.

Capt. Campbell & Thornton's Cos. - Taken by Richard White

Capt. Depew's Co. - Taken by John Strain - On same sheet as Capt. Blair's, formerly Biddle's Co.

Capt. Alexander Greer's Co.

Capt. Hale's Co. - List for 1794 on other side of sheet

Capt. Handley's Co.

Capt. Maxwell's Old Co. - Taken by Edmund Williams

Capt. Melvan's Co. - Taken by J. Britten (On back of Capt. Murry's Co. for 1793)

Capt. Millikin's Co.

Capt. Morrison's Co. - For 1793 & 1794 - Two Lists Taken by J. Britten

Capt. Murry's Co. - Taken by J. Britten (On back of Capt. Melvan's Co.)

Capt. North's Co.

Capt. Scott's Co.

Scrap #1 - James Allison's Return

Delinquents for 1793 - Returned by George Gillespie (Sheriff)

1794 Tax for the year 1794

Capt. Blair's Co. - Taken by John Strain Formerly Capt. Biddle's Co.

Capt. Brown's Co.

Capt. Carriger's Co.

Capt. Depew's Co. - In same booklet with Capt. Blair's Co.

Capt. Joseph Ford's Co. - On back of Capt. Thornton's Co.

1794 Capt. Hale's Co. - On back of Capt. Hale's Co. for 1793

Capt. Samuel Handley's Co.

Capt. Melvan's Co. - Taken by J. Crouch, J.P.

Capt. John Millikin's Co. - Taken by John Millikin

Capt. Morrison's Co. - See 1793 List

Capt. Murray's Co. - Taken by J. Britten, J.P.

Capt. North's Co.

Capt. Scott's Co. - Taken by James Stuart

Capt. Nathaniel Taylor's Co. & Edmund Williams's Personal List

Capt. Thornton's Co. - Taken by self
(On back of Capt. Ford's Co.)

Delinquents for the Year 1794

1795 Capt. Calvert's Co. - Taken by self

Capt. Nicholas Carriger's District - Taken by
Landon Carter, J.P.

Capt. Ford's District - Taken by John Carter, H.T.L.

Capt. Samuel Handley's District

Capt. Melvan's District

Capt. John Millikin's Co. - Taken by self

Capt. Morrison's Co. - Undated but most likely 1795

Capt. Murray's Co. - Taken by Joseph Britten, J. P.

Capt. Nathaniel Taylor's Co. - Taken 1794 but filed Feb 1795
Scraps- Capt. Taylor's Co.

Capt. Reuben Thornton's Co. - Taken by self

Capt. Joseph Young's Co. - Undated, but form similar to 1795
& Capt. Young's missing that year

Undated List - No Captain given - Form similar to 1795 Lists

Different Men's Taxes for 1795

Mistakes in Taxable Property for 1795 - Returned by
George Gillespie

1795 Scrap #1 - Joseph Britten's List - Personal

Scrap #2 - Landon Carter's List - Personal

Scrap #3 - James Charter's List - Personal

Scrap #4 - Wm Colyar's List - Personal

Scrap #5 - James Stuart's List - Personal

Delinquents for the Year 1795

1796 Capt. Brown's Co.

Capt. Calvert's Co.

Capt. Handley's Co.

Capt. Longmire's Co.

Capt. Melvin's Co. - Returned by Joseph Crouch

Capt. Millikin's Co.

Capt. Morrison's Co. - Returned by William Nelson, J.P.

Capt. Shipley's Co., late Capt. Murry's Co. - Taken by Joseph Britten, J.P.

Capt. Joseph Young's Co.

List of Town Lots of Jonesborough - Taken by James Stuart

1797 Capt. Biddle's Co.

Capt. Calvert's Co.

Capt. Duncan's Co. - Taken by J. Isaac Depew

Capt. Gann's Co.

Capt. Hannah's Co. - Taken by Henry Nelson

Capt. Longmire's Co.

Capt. Charles Robertson's Co.

Capt. Nathan Shipley's Co. - Taken by John Norwood, J.P.

Capt. York's Co. - Undated (most likely 1797 or 1798)

Capt. Joseph Young's Co.

1798 Capt. Biddle's Co. - Taken by John Alexander
Also List of Free Taxable Inhabitants

Capt. Calvert's Co. - Taken by John Waddell
Also List of Free Male Inhabitants

Capt. Joseph Duncan's Co. - Taken by Isaac Depew
Also List of Free Taxable Inhabitants

Capt. Nathan Gann's Co.

Capt. Hannah's Co. - List of White Poles taken by Jesse Payne

Capt. Longmire's Co. - Taken by Samuel Wood
Also List of White Poles, Joseph Britten, Ch.

Capt. Morrison's Co. #1

Capt. Morrison's Co. #2
Also List of Free Taxable Inhabitants
Taken by Wm Nelson, J.P.

Capt. John Norwood's Co. - List of Free Male Inhabitants
Taken by Joseph Crouch

Capt Robertson's Co. - Also List of White Poles
Taken by Joseph Brown

Capt. Shipley's Co. - Also List of Free Taxable Inhabitants
Taken by Joseph Britten

Capt. Joseph Young's Co. - List of White Poles
Taken by self

Persons who have not given in their Taxes

County Taxes for the Court House - 1798

1799 Justices to take the Taxable Property for the Year 1799

Capt. Calvert's Co. - Taken by James Stuart

Capt. Duncan's Co.

Capt. Gann's Co. Taken by John Wear

Capt. Hannah's Co.

Capt. Longmire's Co. - Undated, but likely for 1799

Capt. Moore's Co. - Taken by John Wear

Capt. Morrison's Co. - Undated, but likely 1799
Taken by John Hammer

1799 Capt. Norwood's Co. - Undated, but likely for 1799
Taken by Joseph Crouch

Capt. Robertson's Co.

Scrap #1 - Michael Harrison's List - 1799-1800-1801

Scrap #2 - Chaney Boren's List - 1799-1800-1801

1800 County Tax for the Year 1800

Poor Tax for the Year 1800

Amount of Tax Fees - Oct 1799 - Oct 1800

Amount of Taxes for the Year 1800

1801 Justices to take in the Taxable Property for the Year 1801

County Taxes ordered for the year 1801

Additional Taxes ordered for the year 1801

Poor Tax ordered for the year 1801

Capt. Matthew Aiken's Co. - Taken by James Gordon

Capt. Biddle's Co. - Taken by John Alexander

Capt. Calvert's Co. - Taken by Jacob Brown

Capt. Nathan Gann's Co. - Taken by James Stuart

Capt. Archebald Glasscock's Co. - Taken by Isaac White

Capt. Lane's Co.

Capt. Longmire's Co. - Taken by Robert Love

Capt. Morrison's Co. - Taken by John Hammer

Capt. John Norwood's Co. - Taken by Joseph Crouch

Capt. Charles Robertson's Co. - Taken by Thomas Brown

Capt. Squibb's Co. - Taken by John Adams

Capt. Henry Taylor's Co. - Taken by John Bayless

Capt. Wm Taylor's Co. - Taken by John Strain

Scrap #1 - Lawrence Glaze's List

1801 Scrap #2 - John Rhea's List - Taken by James Gordon, J.P.

The Amount of Taxes for the Year 1801

1778.
Valentine Sevier, Sheriff, Dr. to the County Court of --(torn)--

The Following Taxes Collected from the several --(torn)--

The County Aforesd. 1778. (To wit.)

Persons Names	Amt of There Estate	Sum to Pay	Total
Assest by James Maulden, Josiah Hoskins & John Higgans. Retd to Benjn Willson, Esqr.			
Abbott, Elijah	P.T.	1.0.6	
Arnold, John	P.T.	1.0.6	
Asher, Charles	130.0.0	1.6.7½	
Asher, Charles, Senr.	102.17.0	1.1.1	
Asher, John	P.T.	1.0.6	
Asher, Thomas	130.0.0	1.6.0½	
Asher, Wm	P.T.	1.0.6	
Brown, Zekel	P.T.	1.0.6	
Bunton, Andrew	465.10.0	4.13.11	
Certain, James	140.0.0	1.3.10½	
Certain, Jo---	P.T.	1.0.6	
Coleson, James	P.T.	1.0.6	
Collett, Richard	252.10.0	2.11.8	
Coward, James	138.10.0	1.8.2	
Curtis, David	206.4.0	2.2.3	
Curtis, Joshua	154.12.0	1.12.9	
Davis, John	343.10.0	3.10.6	
Denny, Samuel	170.8.0	1.15.0	
Durram, Nathn.	P.T.	1.0.6	
Flannary, William	465.11.2	4.13.9-3/4	
Garrott, Amos	P.T.	1.0.6	
Gentrey, Joseph	-	1.0.6	
Griffin, William	250.14.6	2.11.4	
Grimes, Henry	426.8.0	4.7.4½	
Grimes, John	P.T.	1.0.6	
Hatherley, Hueins	P.T.	1.0.6	
Hatherley, George	175.1.0	1.15.11	
Hatherley, Samuel	P.T.	1.0.6	
Hicks, David	253.12.0	2.12.10½	
Hicks, David P.T.	100.0.0	1.0.6	
Higgans, John	190.9.0	1.19.0	
Holdway, Timothy	P.T.	1.0.6	
Hoskins, E----	P.T.	1.0.6	
Hoskins, Jesse	417.16.0	4.-.9-3/4	
Hoskins, John	1001.16.0	10.5.4	
Hoskins, Josiah	181.0.0	1.17.1½	
Hoskins, Ning	295.0.0	3.0.6	
Maulden, A---on	338.10.0	3.9.3	
Maulden, James	499.0.0	5.2.3½	

Names	Amt of There Estate	Sum to Pay	Total
Morgan, Leonard	P.T.	1.0.6	
Oweings, James	137.10.0	1.8.2¼	
Polestone, Jonas	100.0.0	1.0.6	
Rains, Henry	P.T.	1.0.6	
Renolds, Wm.	189.10.0	1.16.0½	
Sawyer, William P.T.	100.0.0	1.0.6	
Shelly, Philip	534.1.0	5.9.7½	
Sweeton, Edward	119.4.0	1.5.0	
Tate, Samuel	1055.0.0	10.16.3	
Tidwell, George	P.T.	1.0.6	
Tidwell, John	P.T.	1.0.6	
Ward, Benjamin	356.10.0	3.12.0	
White, Richard	1346.0.0	13.15.6	
Willson, Benjamin, Esq.	224.0.0	2.6.1½	
Willson, Richd	295.2.6	3.0.7	
Wooldridge, Richard	841.11.0	8.12.4½	
	12127.7.2	143.9.3¼	

P-4 - Assest by Henry Lyle, Samuel Henry & William McNabb.
Retd to Jno. McNabb, Esqr.

Amt Brot Forward	£ 12127.7.2	£ 143.9.3¼
Arthurr, Matthew P.T.	100.0.0	1.0.6
Barksdill, Clevers	905.0.0	9.5.6
Brown, John P.T.	100.0.0	1.0.6
Brown, Wm. Ditto	100.0.0	1.0.6
Carter, Emanuel	360.0.0	3.12.9
Carter, John, Esqr.	3572.8.0	36.12.9
Casedy, John P.T.	100.0.0	1.0.6
Chamble, Jacob	191.4.0	1.9.4
Cocke, Wm.	870.0.0	8.18.4
Cooper, Patience	408.18.4	4.2.2
Culberson, Joseph	114.1.0	1.3.6
Culberson, Samuel	788.0.0	8.1.5¼
Cunningham, Christopher	626.12.6	6.9.4½
Cuninham, Chriso. Jr.	150.0.0	1.10.9
Denton, James	315.12.0	3.4.8
Denton, Joseph	376.14.8	3.17.1-3/4
Denton, Samuel	210.6.0	2.3.2
Doddy, Howell	310.8.0	3.3.8
Dugger, William P.T.	100.0.0	1.0.6
Dunging, Jeremiah	575.4.0	5.17.10½
Gilleland, John	255.0.0	2.12.3
Gooding, Drury	420.0.0	4.6.1
Greer, Joseph P.T.	100.0.0	1.0.6
Gris'm, James	185.0.0	1.16.11
Henry, James	649.8.3	6.13.2
Henry, Samuel Senr.	253.17.4	2.12.0
Hickey, David P.T.	100.0.0	1.0.6

Names	Amt of There Estate	Sum to Pay	Total
Hider, Michael	358.10.0	3.13.5	
Hodge, Ambrose P.T.	100.0.0	1.0.6	
Houghton, Joshua	2926.13.1	30.0.0	
Houghton, Thomas, Esq.	1431.14.0	14.13.7½	
Hughs, John	136.10.0	1.7.11½	
Jones, Lewis	369.14.0	4.1.10	
Kenner, John	380.0.0	3.17.10½	
Lain, Lewis P.T.	100.0.0	1.0.6	
Little, Jonas	560.0.0	5.13.10	
McNabb, Baptist	731.19.4	4.8.4	
McNabb, David P.T.	100.0.0	1.0.6	
McNabb, John, Esqr.	480.10.0	4.18.6-3/4	
McNabb, Wm, Esqr.	566.1.0	5.16.1	
Millican, James P.T.	100.0.0	1.0.6	
Moore, John	229.0.0	2.6.11½	
Nave, Teter	439.8.8	4.10.0-3/4	
Odull, John	242.0.0	2.9.6½	
Overall, William P.T.	100.0.0	1.0.6	
Parker, Wm.	446.13.4	4.12.3	
Pearce, James	295.13.4	3.4.8	
Reeves, George	174.4.0	1.15.10	
Reeves, Jorden	101.5.8	1.0.9½	
Reeves, William P.T.	100.0.0	1.0.6	
Robertson, Charles, Jr.	194.0.0	2.0.0	
Robertson, Julis	138.5.6	1.8.4	
Sevier, Robert	440.0.0	4.11.3	
Sevier, Valentine, Sr.	125.0.0	1.4.7½	
Sevier, Valentine	541.4.0	5.11.0-3/4	
Shelby, John, Esqr.	920.4.0	9.8.7¼	
Stuart, James	2014.4.0	20.13.0	
Talbert, Hail P.T.	100.0.0	1.0.6	
Talbert, Matthew	2050.0.0	21.0.3	
Talbert, Matthew, Jr. P.T.	100.0.0	1.0.6	
Taylor, Isaac	589.16.0	6.0.11	
Tipton, Joseph	310.0.0	3.3.6	
Ward, William	185.0.0	1.16.10½	
Wray, James	330.0.0	3.7.7½	
Young, Robert, Senr.	1815.0.0	18.12.0	
Young, Robert, Jnr.	385.0.0	3.19.1¼	
	Ŀ 47061.11.2	Ŀ 478.12.4¼	

P-7 - Assesst by Benja. Cobb, Solomon Smith, Wm Asher.
Retd to John Chisolm, Esqr.

Names	Amt of There Estate	Sum to Pay
Amt Brot Forward	Ŀ 47061.11.2	Ŀ 478.12.4¼
Bayley, William	192.0.0	1.19.9
Cawood, John in Viga.	10.0.0	0.2.1½
Chasons, Charles	574.0.0	5.17.10
Choate, Austin	234.0.0	2.8.0
Choate, Edward	523.0.0	5.5.0

Names		Amt of There Estate	Sum to Pay	Total
Choate, Richard		391.0.0	4.0.2	
Choate, Thomas		1280.0.0	13.2.4½	
Cobb, Arthur		1379.10.0	14.2.10½	
Cox, Abraham		878.1.6	9.0.0	
Cox, John		600.13.7	6.3.2	
Gris'om, Wm		465.0.0	4.15.3-3/4	
Hill, John		300.0.0	3.1.6	
Hutton, Samuel	P.T.	100.0.0	1.0.6	
Little, Mathias		200.16.0	2.1.2	
Little, Valentine		101.12.6	1.0.8½	
Mallock, James	P.T.	100.0.0	1.0.6	
Masengill, Henry, Senr.		628.0.0	6.8.9	
Masengill, Henry		260.9.0	2.12.4	
Matlock, John	P.T.	100.0.0	1.0.6	
Maxsey, Jesse		346.0.0	4.12.0	
Odull, Caleb		264.0.0	1.13.5	
Roach, Jorden		304.0.0	3.2.4	
Ryley, John		326.13.0	3.6.9	
Shells, Arnol.		476.15.0	4.17.9	
Smith, Samuel		654.12.6	6.14.3	
Stout, Hosea		198.0.0	2.0.8	
Top, Roger (Virga)		200.0.0	2.1.0	
Underwood, Samuel	P.T.	100.0.0	1.0.6	
Vawter, Jesse in Virga.		10.0.0	0.2.1½	
Weaver, Christian		300.0.0	3.1.6	
Webb, Jonathan		616.0.0	6.6.4	
		£ 59585.5.3		£ 606.4.7½

P-9 - Assest by ------------------
Retd to Wm Been, Esqr.

Amt Brot Forward		£ 59585.5.3	£ 606.4.7½
Abbott, James		176.0.0	1.16.0
Adcocks, Leonard		100.0.0	1.0.6
Anthony, William	P.T.	100.0.0	1.0.6
Bayley, John		227.0.0	2.6.6
Bean, Jesse		254.0.0	2.12.7
Been, John		311.17.0	3.4.0
Been, Robert		150.0.0	1.10.9
Been, Wm, Esqr.		1254.16.0	12.17.3
Benn, Wm, Junr.		257.2.0	2.12.2
Bridges, Edward	P.T.	100.0.0	1.0.6
Calliham, Joel		150.0.0	1.10.9
Calliham, John		224.16.0	2.11.2
Carrole, Delany	P.T.	100.0.0	1.0.6
Cavil, Alexr.		217.7.0	2.4.6
Chis'm, John		353.9.4	3.12.5-3/4
Choate, Christopher		209.0.0	2.2.10½
Clark, John		217.6.3	2.4.0
Clark, Henry		904.16.0	9.5.5

Names		Amt of There Estate	Sum to Pay	Total
Cobb, William & Pharoh		2001.0.0	20.10.2½	
Cooper, James		120.0.0	1.4.7½	
Crawford, John	P.T.	100.0.0	1.0.6	
Davis, Nathan		172.0.0	1.15.10	
Davison, Joseph	P.T.	100.0.0	1.0.6	
Dillingham, Vachworth		1147.0.0	11.15.7	
Dixon, Clement, Senr.	P.T.	100.0.0	1.0.6	
Drake, Benjamin		523.7.0	5.6.6	
Drake, John		199.12.0	2.0.11	
Dunkin, Charles		120.19.6	1.5.8	
Duncome, Elizabeth		157.12.0	1.12.2	
Duncome, John	P.T.	100.0.0	1.0.6	
Duncome, Joseph		151.8.0	1.11.1	
Dunkin, John	P.T.	100.0.0	1.0.6	
Fain, Samuel		157.16.0	1.12.5	
Fletcher, Richd.		223.12.0	2.6.0	
Fletcher, Thomas		134.0.0	1.6.7½	
Gambrel, Bradley		102.4.0	1.0.11½	
Gotcher, Henry		132.16.0	1.6.1½	
Gray, George		516.12.0	3.4.11	
Hickky, Henry		250.0.0	2.11.9	
Hollis, James		347.18.9	3.11.9	
Hufman, Jacob	P.T.	100.0.0	1.0.6	
Hufman, Peter	P.T.	100.0.0	1.0.6	
Hunt, Uriah	P.T.	100.0.0	1.0.6	
Jonachin, Thomas		327.8.0	3.6.1	
Kelley, James		225.0.0	2.5.3½	
Laird, Moses		474.16.0	4.17.4	
Lucas, Robert, Esqr.		1192.16.8	12.6.0	
McMahon, John B.		283.5.0	2.18.0½	
McMahon, John B.		153.2.0	1.11.5	
Martin, George		140.0.0	1.8.7	
Masengill, Michael	P.T.	100.0.0	1.0.6	
Moray, Morgan		134.4.0	1.7.6½	
Mitchell, Joab		325.0.0	3.4.7½	
Parker, Charles	P.T.	100.0.0	1.0.6	
Renfro, Peter		471.14.0	4.17.4	
Rice, John		163.4.0	1.13.5	
Richardson, George	P.T.	100.0.0	1.0.6	
Richardson, Henry		115.3.6	1.3.8	
Richardson, Mary		450.0.0	4.12.3	
Russell, George, Esqr.		244.12.0	2.10.0	
Russell, George		114.0.0	1.2.4½	
Russell, John	P.T.	100.0.0	1.0.6	
Russell, John		265.8.0	2.14.9	
Stringer, William	P.T.	100.0.0	1.0.6	
Thompson, Absolum		173.12.0	1.16.0	
Thompson, Andrew	P.T.	100.0.0	1.0.6	
Thompson, Andrew	P.T.	100.0.0	1.0.6	
Thompson, Charles		107.0.0	1.2.0	
Titsworth, Isaac		316.12.0	3.4.10	
Titsworth, Thomas		203.0.0	2.1.7	
Vance, John		117.10.0	1.3.11	
Walker, Danl.		121.0.0	1.4.9	

Names		Amt of There Estate	Sum to Pay	Total
Walker, James		125.0.0	1.4.7½	
Walker, Richard		138.0.0	1.8.2	
Ward, Demsey		171.10.3	1.15.3	
Wheeler, John	P.T.	100.0.0	1.0.6	
White, John	P.T.	100.0.0	1.0.6	
Whitter, James		121.3.8	1.4.4	
Williams, Tho.	P.T.	100.0.0	1.0.6	
Young, Wm.		187.12.0	1.18.5	
		Ŀ 80017.5.2	Ŀ 807.11.9¼	

Assesst by --------------
Retd to Michl. Woods, Esqr.

P-13 Amt Brot Forward		Ŀ 80017.5.2	Ŀ 807.11.9¼
Atkins, Charles	P.T.	100.0.0	1.0.6
Bayley, Robert	P.T.	100.0.0	1.0.6
Bond, Jesse	P.T.	100.0.0	1.0.6
Brown, Jacob		1171.0.0	12.0.6
Brown, John	P.T.	100.0.0	1.0.6
Cannon, Wm	P.T.	100.0.0	1.0.6
Chosewood, Alexr.	P Tax	100.0.0	1.0.6
Crawford, Samuel		126.2.0	1.5.10
England, Charles	P.T.	100.0.0	1.0.6
England, John	P.T.	100.0.0	1.0.6
England, Joseph		214.2.0	2.4.0
English, Joseph		25.0.0	1.0.6
English, Wm		130.10.0	1.6.8
Gibson, Benja.	P.T.	100.0.0	1.0.6
Gibson, Humphrey		142.2.0	1.9.1
Isbell, Godfrey	P.T.	100.0.0	1.0.6
Isbell, Zacha.		30.0.0	0.6.3
Johnston, Benjamin	P Tax	100.0.0	1.0.6
Johnston, Wm	P Tax	100.0.0	1.0.6
Jones, James	P Tax	100.0.0	1.0.6
Jones, Philipp	P Tax	100.0.0	1.0.6
Leech, Joseph	P Tax	100.0.0	1.0.6
Lewis, Surrel	Ditto	100.0.0	1.0.6
McAdams, James	Ditto	100.0.0	1.0.6
Nave, Henry	P.T.	100.0.0	1.0.6
Nave, John		559.8.4	5.14.0
Oneal, John	P.T.	100.0.0	1.0.6
Pinson, Aaron	P.T.	100.0.0	1.0.6
Pinson, Joseph	Ditto	100.0.0	1.0.6
Pinson, Thomas	Ditto	100.0.0	1.0.6
Reding, John	Ditto	100.0.0	1.0.6
Roase, Hosea		119.3.4	1.4.6
Shurley, Edward	P.T.	100.0.0	1.0.6
Shurley, John	Ditto	100.0.0	1.0.6
Shurley, Thomas	Ditto	100.0.0	1.0.6
Smith, Edward	Ditto	100.0.0	1.0.6

Names		Amt of There Estate	Sum to Pay	Total
Smith, John	P.T.	100.0.0	1.0.6	
Thornton, Wm.	Ditto	100.0.0	1.0.6	
Tipton, Jonathan		104.1.0	1.1.4	
Tipton, Jonathan	P.T.	100.0.0	1.0.6	
Trevillian, Richd.		158.0.0	1.12.5	
Vaich, Jeremiah	P.T.	100.0.0	1.0.6	
Webb, Martin		102.0.0	1.1.0	
Woods, Michael		358.8.0	3.13.5	
		L 86356.19.10		L 873.6.9¼

Assesst. by Saml. Williams, Robert Box & Frances Hughes.
Retd to Zacha. Isbell, Esqr.

P-16 Amt Brot Forward		L 86356.19.10		L 873.6.9¼
Baits, Henry, Senr.	P.T.	100.0.0	1.0.6	
Baits, Henry, Jr.	P.T.	100.0.0	1.0.6	
Bond, Charles	Ditto	100.0.0	1.0.6	
Border, Michael		186.6.8	1.18.0½	
Box, Edward	P.T.	100.0.0	1.0.6	
Box, James	P.T.	100.0.0	1.0.6	
Clark, William, Esqr.		619.0.0	6.6.10	
Clauson, William	P.T.	100.0.0	1.0.6	
Conway, Philip	P.T.	100.0.0	1.0.6	
Dunham, Joseph		358.12.0	3.13.5	
Earnest, Henry		186.1.0	1.18.0½	
English, Joseph		240.0.0	2.9.3	
Evans, John	P.T.	100.0.0	1.0.6	
Evans, Thomas	P.T.	100.0.0	1.0.6	
Hair, Daniel	P.T.	100.0.0	1.0.6	
Hightower, Oldum	P.T.	100.0.0	1.0.6	
Holley, Jonathan	Ditto	100.0.0	1.0.6	
Ireby, Isom	Ditto	100.0.0	1.0.6	
Isbell, Zachariah, Esqr.		412.13.0	4.4.0½	
Murphy, Patrick	P.T.	100.0.0	1.0.6	
Price, Thomas		293.10.0	3.0.6	
Reed, George	P.T.	100.0.0	1.0.6	
Rice, Edward	P.T.	100.0.0	1.0.6	
Rice, Leonard	Ditto	100.0.0	1.0.6	
Seduxas, Emanuel	Ditto	100.0.0	1.0.6	
Sevier, John		1872.8.8	19.4.0	
Sherrill, Philip		Tax 4 Fold	3.6.8	
Sherrill, Samuel		277.0.0	2.16.9½	
Sherrill, Samuel, Jr.	P.T.	100.0.0	1.0.6	
Underwood, George		174.0.0	1.15.6	
Vance, John	P.T.	100.0.0	1.0.6	
Waddell, John	Ditto	100.0.0	1.0.6	
Walton, Jesse, Esqr.		592.5.0	(	
do	do	690.5.0	(13.2.10½	
Williams, Benjamin		Tax 4 Fold	3.6.8	

Names		Amt of There Estate	Sum to Pay	Total
Williams, Joshua	P.T.	100.0.0	1.0.6	
Wood, John		218.18.8	2.4.10	
		₤ 94677.19.10		₤ 965.15.1-3/4

Assest by ----------------
Retd to Jacob Womack, Esqr.

P-18 Amt Brot Forward		₤ 94677.19.10	₤ 965.15.1-3/4
Allison, Charles		255.0.0	2.11.9
Allison, John		269.0.0	2.15.4
Allison, Robert		256.4.0	2.12.6
Allison, Wm		125.0.0	1.4.7½
Anderson, Barnaba	P.T.	100.0.0	1.0.6
Angland, Adren	P.T.	100.0.0	1.0.6
Arrington, Charles		845.0.0	8.13.3
Bacon, Michael		160.0.0	1.12.10
Barker, Thomas		1052.16.0	10.15.8
Bird, Jonathan	P.T.	100.0.0	1.0.6
Blackburn, Robert		146.0.0	1.10.1
Blackwell, John	P.T.	100.0.0	1.0.6
Blair, Hugh		165.10.0	1.13.11
Bradley, James	P.T.	100.0.0	1.0.6
Brown, Thomas		241.0.0	2.9.4½
Buchanan, James		271.15.0	2.15.7½
Bullard, John		308.6.0	3.3.2
Bullard, Joseph		636.1.0	6.9.2
Burleson, Aron		310.0.0	3.3.7
Burleson, Thomas		166.0.0	1.14.1
Campbell, Alexr.		130.1.4	1.5.7½
Campbell, David		129.16.0	1.5.8
Campbell, William		123.4.0	1.4.7½
Carrack, John		308.2.0	3.3.3
Chambers, David		215.0.0	2.4.2
Chambers, John	P.T.	100.0.0	1.0.6
Chambers, William	P.T.	100.0.0	1.0.6
Coal, Solomon	P.T.	100.0.0	1.0.6
Craduck, David	P.T.	100.0.0	1.0.6
Denton, Jonathan		168.10.9	1.17.7½
Dunham, Daniel		221.2.0	2.6.3½
Dunham, Henry		406.4.8	4.3.3
Dunham, John		257.3.8	2.12.0
Dunham, Reubin		226.10.0	2.5.4
Edwards, Evan		401.16.0	4.2.5
English, James		532.19.8	5.8.1
Fowler, Joseph		171.14.8	1.14.10½
Gentry, Charles		233.0.0	2.6.9½
Gentry, Robert		173.10.0	1.15.6
Gest, Benja.		211.0.0	2.3.3½
Gest, Joseph		141.0.0	1.8.9
Gibson, John		825.0.0	8.8.1½

Names		Amt of There Estate	Sum to Pay	Total
Gillihan, John		169.13.10	1.14.9	
Gillaspy, Thomas		342.12.0	3.9.8	
Gozach, Sandofer		144.10.8	1.9.6	
Grymes, James		367.3.4	3.15.3	
Hamilton, Francis	P.T.	100.0.0	1.0.6	
Hamilton, Isiah		164.16.4	1.13.9	
Hamilton, Jacob	P.T.	100.0.0	1.0.6	
Handley, Samuel	P.T.	100.0.0	1.0.6	
Hobson, Edward		1548.0.0	15.17.8	
Howard, John		250.0.0	2.11.3	
Hudson, George	P.T.	100.0.0	1.0.6	
Hughes, David		234.4.0	2.7.0	
Hutton, William		173.16.0	1.15.2	
Johnson, Isaac		325.2.4	3.6.8	
Jones, Henry	P.T.	100.0.0	1.0.6	
Karr, George	Ditto	100.0.0	1.0.6	
Kenedy, Daniel		265.19.2	2.14.7	
Lyle, Samuel		204.7.4	2.1.10	
McCartney, Charles		133.0.0	1.6.3	
McCartney, James		156.0.0	1.12.0	
McCord, David		254.0.0	2.12.1	
McNamee, Peter		205.6.0	2.2.1	
Magahah, Farill	P.T.	100.0.0	1.0.6	
Martin, Andrew		113.0.0	1.3.2	
Martin, Joseph		186.2.0	1.17.3	
Martin, Josiah		372.16.0	3.16.7	
Michael, James	P.T.	100.0.0	1.0.6	
Miller, James		207.11.0	1.2.0	
Moore, Moses		132.0.0	1.6.1	
More, Moses		145.0.0	1.9.9	
Mulchy, Phillip		453.16.0	-----	
Morrison, John		262.0.0	2.13.9	
Murray, James	P.T.	100.0.0	1.0.6	
Murrow, Alexr.		173.16.0	1.15.2	
Nelson, Elisha	P.T.	100.0.0	1.0.6	
Nelson, Southey	P.T.	100.0.0	1.0.6	
Nelson, William		240.0.0	2.9.3	
Patterson, John		227.0.0	2.6.9	
Pinson, Aaron		256.4.4	2.12.3	
Pinson, John	P.T.	100.0.0	1.0.6	
Posey, David		169.10.0	1.14.9	
Pyburn, Benjamin		311.8.0	3.3.10	
Randol, James		114.9.0	1.3.5	
Rawlings, Asael		308.6.0	3.3.2	
Ritchie, John		145.6.0	1.9.9	
Ritchie, William		224.12.4	2.6.1	
Roberts, Edmund	P.T.	100.0.0	1.0.6	
Robertson, ------		148.10.0	1.10.7	
Robertson, John	P.T.	100.0.0	1.0.6	
Scott, Thomas		113.0.0	1.3.2½	
Sherrill, Adam		165.16.0	1.13.8	
Shurley, Robert		154.0.0	1.11.7	
Stephenson, James		151.8.0	1.11.0	
Story, William		121.15.0	1.5.8	

Names		Amt of There Estate	Sum to Pay	Total
Taylor, Christopher	P.T.	100.0.0	1.0.6	
Trimble, John		148.16.0	1.10.4	
Trimble, William		215.0.0	2.4.0	
Weaver, Samuel		332.16.0	3.---	
Wilson, ------		336.19.6	3.8.0	
Williams, Jarret		189.0.0	1.17.10	
Webb, John	P.T.	100.0.0	1.0.6	
Willson, Adam		525.16.0	5.6.9½	
Willson, Isaac		344.0.0	3.10.6	
Willson, Joseph		425.15.2	4.6.3½	
Willson, Robert		140.0.0	1.8.8	
Womack, Jacob		671.8.0	6.17.7½	
Woods, Bartholomew		232.0.0	2.6.7½	
Wray, Joseph	P.T.	100.0.0	1.0.6	
			L 120859.1.7	L 1231.14.2-3/4

P-22 - Assest by ---------
Retd to Court.

Names		Amt of There Estate	Sum to Pay
Amt Brot Forward		L 120859.1.7	L 1231.14.2-3/4
Ashurst, William		266.0.0	2.14.0
Bird, Amos		1093.0.0	------
Clark, Nathnl.		326.14.0	3.7.8
Clark, John		553.5.0	-----
Cobb, Benjamin		2006.13.4	20.11.3
Cole, Joseph	P.T.	100.0.0	1.0.6
Cornealious, William		192.10.0	1.18.5
Crawford, James		699.5.0	7.0.0
Cross, Henry	P.T.	100.0.0	1.0.6
Dunham, John		130.0.0	1.6.9-3/4
Ervin, Alexr. in Burk		150.0.0	1.10.9
Fauling, William, Dec.		1399.4.0	14.6.9-3/4
Greer, Andrew, Esqr.		4865.0.0	49.17.4½
Holley, Francis	P.T.	100.0.0	1.0.6
Holley, Jacob		135.0.0	1.7.8½
Holley, John		753.0.0	7.14.4½
Holley, John, Jr.		263.19.0	2.13.11½
Honycutt, Austin		352.0.0	3.12.2
Honycutt, John		1257.17.2	12.17.9
Howard, James in Burk		75.0.0	0.15.4½
Hughes, Francis		1155.5.5	11.6.10
Keith, Daniel	P.T.	100.0.0	1.0.6
Lyle, Henry		1891.5.8	19.7.8
McCord, James		125.0.0	1.5.7
McFarling, John		147.5.0	1.10.2
Malone, John	P.T.	100.0.0	1.0.6
Morris, Gideon		936.4.0	9.11.0
Morris, Shadrick	P.T.	100.0.0	1.0.6
Pebley, John	P.T.	100.0.0	1.0.6
Phillips, Charles	P.T.	100.0.0	1.0.6

Names	Amt of There Estate	Sum to Pay	Total
Prator, John	148.0.0	1.10.4½	
Robertson, Charles, Esqr.	2382.13.4	24.8.4	
Robertson, David P.T.	100.0.0	1.0.6	
Smith, Ezekiel	792.0.0	8.2.5	
Smith, Solomon	256.4.6	2.12.6	
Stuart, John	692.6.0	7.1.10	
Thomas, Isaac	942.12.0	9.13.2	
Whood, William	181.17.0	1.17.4½	
Williams, Samuel	873.4.0	8.19.0	
--------, Alexander	----	---	
		£ 146801.6.0	£ 1497.12.10

Pd Contra-

By Arthur, Matthew	Ret by	Thos Houghton Colr.	1.0.6
" Bayley, John	" "	Benj. Gist Colr.	---
" Bradley, James, Ded.	" "	" " "	---
" Bridges, Edward, Delgt.	" "	" " "	1.0.6
" Brown, Ezekiel	" "	Thos Houghton Colr.	1.0.6
" Carroal, Delany	" "	Benj. Gist Colr.	1.0.6
" Chambers, William	" "	" " "	1.0.6
" Coal, Joseph	" "	" " "	1.0.6
" Collett, Richard	" "	Thos Houghton Colr.	1.0.6
" Coward, John	" "	" " "	0.2.0½
" Cradduck, David	" "	Benj. Gist Colr.	1.0.6
" Cross, Henry	" "	" " "	1.0.6
" Denney, Samuel	" "	Thos Houghton Colr.	1.15.0
" Dixon, Clement, Senr	" "	Benj. Gist Colr.	1.0.6
" Draike, Benjamin	" "	" " "	5.6.6
" Duncome, John	" "	" " "	1.0.6
" Durram, Nathaniel	" "	Thos Houghton Colr.	1.0.6
" Hair, Daniel	" "	Benj. Gist Colr.	1.0.6
" Hobson, Edward	" "	" " "	15.17.8½
" Holdway, Timothy	" "	Thos Houghton Colr.	1.0.6
" Howard, James	" "	Benj. Gist Colr.	0.15.4
" Hufman, Jacob	" "	" " "	1.0.6
" Hufman, Peter	" "	" " "	1.0.6
" Ireby, Isam	" "	" " "	1.0.6
" Lain, Elias	" "	Thos Houghton Colr.	1.0.6
" Laird, Moses	" "	Benj. Gist Colr.	4.17.4
" Malone, John	" "	" " "	1.0.6
" Morgan, Leonard	" "	Thos Houghton Colr.	1.0.6
" Parker, Charles	" "	Benj. Gist Colr.	1.0.6
" Philipps, Charles	" "	" " "	1.0.6
" Rains, Henry	" "	Thos Houghton Colr.	1.0.6
" Vawter, Jesse	" "	" " "	0.2.0½
" Webb, John	" "	Benj. Gist Colr.	1.0.6
" Williams, Joshua	" "	" " "	1.0.6
" Williams, Thomas	" "	" " "	---

Amt Brot Forward	£ 146,801.6.0	£ 1497.12.10
That was omitted in adding	1,900.0.0	
Total	£ 148,701.6.0	

NOTE: This List of Taxables for the year 1778 is the assessed valuation of all the Taxable Property of the inhabitants of Washington County. This extended from Burke County, North Carolina to the Mississippi River. The several Assessors made returns to seven Collectors who were named by the first Court. These Lists were return to Valentine Sevier, Sheriff, who (according to North Carolina law) was the officer into whose hands the public monies were delivered.

Valentine Sevier's copy of this 1778 List is in the form of a hand sewn booklet. The handwriting is Spencerian style, very legible and the ink is still vivid and easily deciphered. This was discovered by the compiler in 1933, where it had been tossed into a trash skuttle by someone utterly unaware of its importance. MHMcC.

A List of Taxable -----(torn off)-----
To Thomas Houghton, Appraiser -----(torn off)----- of Washington County to receive the same with proprietors names delivering the same on oath, as also, the Assessment thereon for the year 1779.

To which is placed the Sum Total of each particular persons Taxable Property, with the amount of the Tax on the Whole Sum.

ASSESSORS: Messrs. Matthew Talbot, Senr., Andrew Taylor & Clevias Barksdill; Assessors appointed by the Court of our said County to assess Land & Horses belonging to the Inhabitants of the First & Fifth Districts of the same with an Account of their Taxable Property, the whole attested by them, and their Receivers, etc.

KEY TO COLUMNS: (1) List of Names, (2) No. of Sites, (3) Acres, (4) Value, (5) Horses, (6) Value, (7) Cattle, (8) Value, (9) Ready Money, (10) Negros, (11) Age, (12) Value, (13) Total Sum

(1)	(2)	(3)	(4)	(5)	(6)	(7)	(8)	(9)	(10)	(11)	(12)	(13)
Allin, William	-	-	-	6	625	8	80	4.0.0	-	-	-	709.0.0
Allin, Zachariah	-	-	-	1	225	13	130	17.8.9	-	-	-	373.8.6
Allison, John	1	200	200	2	250	-	-	6.8.0	-	-	-	456.8.0
Ashurst, William	1	300	200	5	625	19	190	16.7.8	-	-	-	1031.7.8
Bailey, William	-	-	-	6	525	5	50	30.0.0	-	-	-	606.0.0
Barksdell, Cleveis	1	323	600	4	500	12	120	71.4.0	3	10-40 yrs	@ £2100	3470.0.0
								78.16.0	(bond at Int.)			
Bassett, William,	single man - Poll Tax -										Tax equal to	400.0.0
Bearden, John	-	-	-	1	2	5	50	1.12.0			Poll Tax on	100.0.0
Brown, John, Senr.	1	200	100	2	200	3	30	0.8.0	-	-	-	330.8.0
Brown, Joseph, single		-	-	2	20	2	20	-	-	-	Poll Tax on	400.0.0
Brown, William, single		-	-	3	300	3	30	10.0.0	-	-	Poll Tax -	400.0.0
Bundy, Simon	-	-	-	2	150	4	40	2.16.0	-	-	-	192.16.0
Burk, John	1	200	200	4	350	10	100	125.0.0	-	-	-	775.0.0
Burner, Daniel	1	150	100	3	30	-	-	-	-	-	-	130.0.0
		(Unimproved)										
Campble, Solomon	1	100	150	5	525	7	70	0.13.0	-	-	-	945.13.0
	(The dwelling)											
	1	100	200	(In Wilkes Co.)								
Carder, Thomas	-	-	-	3	151	-	-	33.1.0	-	-	-	184.1.0
Carter, Emanuel	1	400	400	3	425	13	130	100.0.0	-	-	-	1155.0.0
	(Manor Plantation)			1	100	(Breeding mair) (up to Apr. 1)						

Carter, John, Esqr. 1 640 2000 7 1800 42 420 400.0.0 - - - 20455.0.0
(Manor Plantation, entered in name J.C.) 125.0.0 (bond on interest)
2 10-40 @ Ƚ 1400
1 boy 6 yrs Ƚ 400
1 boy 3 yrs Ƚ 150

1 400 400
(In Carter's Valley - Entered in name of J.C. for Elen Hains)
1 250 250
(In Carter's Valley - " " " " " " Jno. McNitt Alexander)
1 640 640
(No. fork Holstn. - " " " " " " William Smith)
1 500 500
(No. fork Holsten - " " " " " " Wm. Jones)
1 300 300
(No. fork Holsten - " " " " " " William Clanton)
1 500 500 " " " " " " Jas. Ransom
1 640 640 " " " " " " Edward Clanton
1 300 300 " " " " " " William Clanton
1 640 640 " " " " " " " "
1 200 200 " " " " " " Robert Pebels
1 600 600 " " " " " " William Jones
1 640 640 " " " " " " Thos. Gibbons
1 200 200 " " " " " " Jonas Little
1 400 400 " " " " " " Jno. McNitt Alexander
1 540 540 " " " " " " Jonas Little
1 500 500
(On Big Creek - " " " " " " David Johnson)
1 640 640
(On Big Creek - " " " " " " William Johnson)
1 500 500
(The old French Fort - " " " " " " John Hurd)
1 400 400
(On Cain Creek - " " " " " " Allin Jones)
1 600 600
(On Big Creek - " " " " " " Gideon Harriss)
1 300 300
(The Beaver Dam)
1 640 400
(Doe River - " " " " " " Wm. Jones)
1 300 150
(Flag Pond - " " " " " " " "

1 340 340 Entered in name of J.C. for William Bailey Smith
1 300 300 " " " " " " " " "
1 300 300
(No. side Holsten - " " " " " " Robert Colwell)
1 300 300
(Big Creek - " " " " " " " "
1 340 340
(No. side Holsten - " " " " " " " "
1 300 300 " " " " " " James Ransom
1 640 700
(Stony Creek - " " " " " " John Sevier)
1 300 300
(Stony Creek - " " " " " " " "
1 640 640
(Goos ponds - " " " " " " Robert Pebels)

Carter, Landon 1 300 300 4 900 - - 20.0.0 - - - 1660.0.0
(On the so. side of Holston River oppost. Fredrick Calvits)
1 440 440
(Including Frederick Calvits plantation on no. side of Holston)

Cashady, John - - - 2 250 5 50 3.1.0 - - - 303.1.0
Chamble, Jacob 1 200 300 6 475 5 50 8.5.0 - - - 833.5.0
Charter, James 1 300 300 2 300 - - 0.11.0 - - - 600.11.0
Choat, Ann, relict of Thomas Choat 1 200 500 18 1960 20 200 111.0.0 1 grown Ƀ 700 3461.0.0
(Manor Plantation)
Choat, Austin - 165 300 4 275 6 60 4.0.0 - - - 739.0.0
(The manor plantation)
Cobb, Benjamin 1 323 900 24 2485 35 350 13.0.0 3 grown Ƀ2100 5848.0.0
(The manor plantation) under 40 yrs
Cocke, William 9 3520 6635 3 900 - - - 4 10-40 Ƀ2800 10885.0.0
(Including the manor Plantation) 1 5 yrs Ƀ 400
1 3 yrs Ƀ 150
Colbotth, Henry - 331 430 4 475 2 20 20.8.0 - - - 945.8.0
(Of the manor Pl & Joining)
Cooper, Patience 1 400 600 5 445 6 60 - - - - 1105.0.0
(Manor Plantation)
Cox, John - 100 200 3 675 - 80 37.12.0 - - - 992.12.0
(Manor Plantation)
Cox, William - - - - 1200 - - 404.10.0 - - - 1604.10.0
(Also for year 1778, unlisted but ought to have paid sd yrs Tax)
Craguner, Patrick 1 170 100 4 510 3 30 0.4.0 - - - 640.4.0
Craig, Robert 1 @ 20 sh per acre (assessed by court)
(The above not entered for want of no. of acres of land from Entry Taker)

Crawthers, John	1	100	25	2	100	8	80	1.0.0	-	-	-	206.0.0
	(Home house)											
Cross, Benjamin	1	640	500	3	300	3	30	-	-	-	-	830.0.0
	(The manor Plantation)											
Culbertson, Samuel	2	900	700	9	1275	30	300	10.0.0	-	-	-	2285.0.0
	(100 of above is part of entry of 300 acres)											
Cunningham, Christopher, Senr	1	600	1200	5	650	16	160	0.1.0	-	-	-	2010.0.0
	(The manor plantation)											
Cunningham, Christopher, single	1	240	200	3	200	-	-	8.12.0	-	-	-	408.12.0
Davis, Samuel	2	340	100	1	75	1	10	-	-	-	-	185.0.0
Davis, William	2	840	1000	3	200	23	230	-	-	-	-	1430.0.0
	(Joseph Tipton's old place)											
Denton, James	1	500	1000	6	700	7	70	3.4.0	-	-	-	1313.4.0
	(Manor Plantation)											
Denton, Joseph	1	640	700	9	950	16	160	0.12.0	-	-	-	1810.12.0
	(Manor Plantation)											
Denton, Samuel, Jr.	(Single man)			2	375	-	-	5.12.0		Pole Tax on		₺ 400.0.0
Denton, Samuel, Sr.	1	529	700	3	400	8	80	3.6.0	-	-	-	1183.0.6
	(Manor Plantation)											
Depreast, Randol	1	100	50	1	80	1	10	3.8.0	-	-	-	142.8.0
Doddy, Howell	-	-	-	3	200	4	40	17.5.6	-	-	-	257.5.6
and for Isaac & Jacob Linckhorn	1	150	600	-	-	-	-	-	-	-	-	600.0.0
Duggard, William	(Single man)		-	2	125	3	30	6.4.8	-	-	-	400.0.0
Dunghan, Jeremiah	2	800	2000	3	500	7	70	2.0.0	-	-	-	2590.0.0
	(Including the manor plantation, mill, and joining the whole)											
Dunlop, Ephraim	5	1700	1700	-	-	-	-	-	-	-	-	1700.0.0
Earley, Thomas	-	-	-	2	200	1	10	1.4.0	-	-	-	211.4.0
				(Breeding mairs)								
Finn, Jesse	-	-	-	2	425	2	20	8.11.8	-	-	-	453.11.8
Forgeson & Hodges	1	500	800	-	-	-	-	-	-	-	-	800.0.0
	(Arthur Cobb's old place)											
Gibson, Jordan	-	-	-	-	-	-	-	-	2	10-40	₺1400	1550.0.0
									1	under 5	150	
Gilliland, John	3	1040	600	7	1050	6	60	8.2.0	-	-	-	1718.2.0
Greer, Alexander	-	-	-	2	450	-	-	32.16.0	-	-	-	482.16.0
Greer, Andrew, Esqr	3	1505	4250	50	6410	49	490	2641.0.0	1	prime of life		14641.0.0
									1	ab 50 @ ₺ 850		
Greer, William	-	-	-	2	325	1	10	-	-	-	-	335.0.0
Grissom, James	1	150	200	4	625	9	90	5.12.0	-	-	-	920.12.0

Grissom, William	-	-	-	12	2250	14	140	1.5.0	-	-	-	2391.5.0
Hail, Mesack	1	392	300	3	300	9	90	14.16.0	1	over 50	£150	1054.15.0
	(Manor Plantation)											
	1	200	200	Joining ye above								
Hainey, Barney	-	-	-	1	100	3	30	-	-	-	-	130.0.0
Hainey, John	-	-	-	1	100	2	20	1.4.0	-	-	-	121.4.0
Hainey, Thomas	(Single man, taxed on £ 400.0.0)-							3.15.8	-	-	-	400.0.0
Haislip, Robert	(Single, failing to give in his list of taxable property for 1779, the Assessors have found 1 horse worth £ 150 -- Fourfold Tax on £ 400.0.0)											
Henry, Hugh	1	200	400	1	174	-	-	2.8.0	-	-	-	577.8.0
	(William Petterson's mair)											
Henery, James & Wm	2	750	1400	14	2650	12	120	269.8.0	-	-	-	4439.8.0
Henry, Samuel	1	500	450	3	375	6	60	3.4.0	-	-	-	1313.4.0
	(The dwelling place)											
	1	200	400	(Unimproved)								
	1	150	25	(On Dry Creek)								
Hickey, David	2	200	400	3	330	4	40	0.2.0	-	-	-	770.2.0
	(Each in Carter's Valley)											
Hinton, Wm Robert	-	-	-	10	855	-	-	6.16.0	1	woman @	£ 700	1711.12.0
(This is supposed to be taxed in Virginia, Henry Co, and the tax)									1	child @	£ 150	
(if pd there, so much to be deducted from this tax on receipt)												
Hooss, Joseph	-	-	-	6	750	2	20	3.0.0	-	-	-	773.0.0
Houghton, Joshua Sr	1	640	1500	8	1050	15	150	170.5.8	1	45	£ 400	8970.5.8
	(Manor Plantation)								1	43	£ 400	
	1	400	500	(Where Joshua Houghton, Jr lives)					5	10-40	£3500	
									2	5	£ 800	
	1	600	200	(Back Land)					2	under 5	300	
Houghton, Joshua Jr	1	200	50	6	590	3	30	612.16.5	1	25	£ 700	2132.16.5
	(Back land unimproved)								1	girl 2 yr	150	
Houghton, Thomas	1	568	1000	5	435	15	150	720.12.8	1	22 @	£ 700	3605.12.8
	(Manor Plantation)								1	45 @	£ 400	
	1	640	50	(In Burke County)					1	4 @	£ 150	
Hughes, David	1		50	3	450	-	-	12.0.0	-	-	-	537.0.0
	(Below ye Tug Creek on Holsten River)							25.0.0	(Bond on interest)			
Hughes, John	2	300	440	5	550	4	40	1.5.0	-	-	-	1031.5.0
Hurd, John	-	-	-	6	625	5	50	0.8.8	-	-	-	765.8.0
Hutton, Samuel	-	-	-	2	125	4	40	5.13.0	-	-	-	170.13.0
Hyder, Michl	1	260	500	8	975	13	130	49.4.0	-	-	-	1654.4.0
	(The manor Plantation)											
Jobb, David	-	-	-	5	750	2	20	55.4.6	-	-	-	825.4.6
Jones, Lewis	1	300	400	9	1025	7	70	1.6.8	-	-	-	1496.6.8
	(The manor Plantation)											

Keener, Francis	-	-	-	5	750	3	30	58.0.0	1	under 5		2538.0.0
								(Up to Apr 1)	1	over 50	@ £ 300	
									2	10-40	@ £1400	
Knowland, John	3	400	300	6	400	5	50	11.14.0	-	-	-	761.14.0
	(Includes the manor Plantation)											
Linckhorn, Isaac & Jacob (See Howell Doddy)												
Lammon, Abraham	(A Dunkard & single man)					-	-	-	Taxed a threefold tax on			400.0.0
Lammon, John	1	150	200	2	75	4	40	2.0.0	"	"	"	317.0.0
	(A Dunkard - Part of an entry made by Arnold Shells)											
Laster, Augustine	-	-	-	3	500	-	-	35.8.8	-	-	-	535.8.8
Lemmon, William	1	200	100	1	75	3	30	1.0.0	-	-	-	306.0.0
	(1 stray mair & colt @ £ 100)											
Lewis, Aaron	7	1050		-	-	-	-	-	-	-	-	775.0.0
	5	500	775 (total)									
Lile, Henry	1	640	1500	28	3080	23	230	110.2.10	1	3 yrs	@ £ 150	5470.2.10
	(Manor Plantation)											
	2	400	400									
Little, Andrew	1	300	750	4	325	12	120	25.12.0	-	-	-	1220.12.0
	(Manor Plantation)											
Little, Jonas	1	300	600	7	1025	16	160	11.4.0	-	-	-	1946.4.0
	(Manor Plantation)											
				1	150							
Little, Matthias	1	100	100	2	425	-	50	0.16.6	-	-	-	575.16.0
Little, Thomas	(Single)		-	3	350	-	-	0.10.8	-	-	Poll Tax on	400.0.0
Little, Valentine	1	100	200	4	500	-	-	8.18.0	-	-	-	728.18.0
	(Unimproved)											
	½	150	20	(Entered in Martin Shules name)								
--(torn off)---	1	-	1400	17	2225	19	120	33.16.0	3	10-40	@ £2100	6628.16.0
	(Where Robert Lucas is now living on)								1	under 5	@ 150	
Lusk, Robert	1	260	300	2	300	5	50	4.16.0	-	-	-	654.16.0
	(Manor Plantation)				(Mairs)							
Lyle, David	1	300	150	2	400	-	-	62.13.0	-	-	-	612.13.0
Macklen, William	-	-	-	2	300	-	-	-	2	ab 50	@ £ 300	4800.0.0
									5	10-40	@ 3500	
									1	7 yrs	@ 400	
Madcap, William	(Single)		-	-	-	-	-	6.0.0	-	-	Poll Tax on	400.0.0
Masengill, Henry Jr	-	-	-	8	700	8	80	0.1.0	-	-	-	780.1.0
Matlock, John	1	100	100	-	-	-	-	-	-	-	-	100.0.0
Maxey, Jesse	1	200	200	2	290	15	150	49.14.10	-	-	-	689.14.10
	(The Manor Plantation)											
McNabb, Baptist	1	600	1500	6	675	15	150	53.14.0	-	-	-	2378.14.0
	(Includes the manor plantation & mill)											

McNabb, John	3	1240	1300	12	2150	7	70	55.0.0	-	-	-	3575.0.0
	1	100	(Unimproved)									
McNabb, Wm, Esqr	2	707	1000	9	752	11	110	4.12.0	-	-	-	1866.12.0
	(Including the Manor Plantation)											
McPicke, William	1	200	50	1	165	-	-	7.8.0	-	-	-	222.8.0
				(mair & colt)								
Millieken, James	(Single		-	1	150	-	-	101.18.0	-	-	-	400.0.0
				(breeding mair)								
Moor, John	1	230	250	3	175	6	60	-	-	-	-	485.0.0
	(The Manor Plantation)											
	(For Matthew Arthur)				-	8	80	-	-	-	-	80.0.0
Moore, Robert	(Single man)		-	1	146	-	-	-	-	-	Poll Tax -	400.0.0
Morrell, John	1	400	300	4	525	7	70	31.9.4	-	-	-	926.9.4
	(Land unimproved)											
Morrell, Jonathan	-	-	-	2	200	3	30	6.0.0	-	-	-	236.0.0
Morriss, Gideon	1	200	375	14	1435	16	160	0.4.0	1	Negro man	£700	2670.4.0
	1	100										
Morris, Shadrack	4	1314	1700	8	1125	18	180	140.0.0	-	-	-	3019.0.0
Mulkey, James	No property - The same with Haislip, therefore a fourfold tax on (Failed to give in his Tax. for 1779)											400.0.0
Nave, Teter	1	300	800	6	825	15	150	24.16.0	-	-	-	1799.16.0
	(The Manor Plantation)											
Oadle, Caleb Senr	1	87	40	3	250	5	50	10.3.0	-	-	-	400.3.0
Oadle, Caleb Junr	1	57	40	2	115	3	30	2.9.0	-	-	-	187.9.0
Oadle, Isaac	1	50	40	5	275	4	40	3.4.6	-	-	-	358.4.6
Oadle, John	1	350	450	3	310	7	70	9.6.0	-	-	-	989.6.0
	(The Manor Plantation)											
	1	280	150	(Nichls Fain's land)								
Oadle, Tompkins	(Single man)		-	2	50	1	10	1.12.0	Taxed on £ 400 or equal			61.12.0
Oadle, William	1	640	400	2	200	1	10	4.0.0	-	-	-	614.0.0
	(Single man)											
Parker, William	1	300	225	4	700	16	160	40.0.0	3	10-40	£2100	4780.0.0
	(On Nob Creek)											
	1	350	85	(On Little River Indian Lands)								
	2	940	230	(On Richland Creek, no. side Holsten)								
	2	640	640	(On big creek)								
	1	350	500	(Near the big Island Holsten, including Fort Henry)								
	1	100	100	(Head of Indian Creek)								
Parkerson, George	-	-	-	-	-	-	-	-	-	-	-	100.0.0
Philipps, Charles	-	-	-	5	450	1	10	0.9.8	-	-	-	460.9.8

Reaves, George	1	640	600	4	275	10	100	17.5.10	-	-	-	992.5.10
	(Including the Manor Plantation)											
Reaves, Jordan	(Dunkard to profeshon)		-	8	700	4	40	0.4.0	-	-	-	749.4.0
									(Threefold Tax)			
Reaves, William	(Single)		-	5	500	3	30	2.3.8	-	-	-	532.3.8
Roach, Jordan	-	-	-	3	450	4	40	44.0.0 (Incl.1int)	-	-	-	534.0.0
Roberson, Julis	1	640	1000	6	700	5	50	12.0.0	-	-	-	1762.0.0
Robertson, Charles Bflo.	1	275	450	3	250	10	100	5.0.0	-	-	-	405.0.0
	(The Manor Plantation)											
Robertson, James	1	250	250	-	-	-	-	-	-	-	-	550.0.0
Esqr	1	300	300	(On Beach Creek)								
Robertson, John	1	500	500	-	-	-	-	-	-	-	-	500.0.0
Royley, John	1	200	400	2	240	9	90	11.0.0	-	-	-	741.0.0
	(The Manor Plantation)											
Sevier, Valentine Junr	1	500	1300	2	450	35	350	157.4.0	-	-	-	2282.4.0
	(The Manor Plantation land)											
	1	25	25									
Sevier, Valentine Senr	1	360	800	1	175	6	60	0.1.8	-	-	-	1035.1.8
	(The Manor Plantation)											
Shelby, John Esqr	1	640	1750	6	1725	12	120	300.0.0	1	9 yrs @ £400		4495.0.0
	(On Wataugah)											
	1	200	200	(On Nolechuckey)								
Shells, Arnold	1	200	200	5	650	14	140	30.0.0	-	-	-	920.0.0
	(Incl. the Manor Plantation)											
Shules, Christian (Shultz) D. ½	1	400	500	4	440	7	70	1.16.0	-	-	-	1011.16.0
	(Manor Plantation)											
Shules, Martin	1	200	150	6	650	6	60	60.6.0	-	-	-	920.6.0
Smith, Samuel	2	900	1000	12	1400	20	200	12.19.0	-	-	-	2612.19.0
Smith, Solomon	1	420	800	6	700	13	130	35.1.10	-	-	-	1666.1.10
	(Manor Plantation)											
Smith, William (living at Col Carrs)	1	350	350	11	1575	-	-	4.0.0	-	-	-	2519.0.0
	(No. side Holsten River)											
	1	290	290	(On Big Creek)								
	1	300	300	(On No. side Holsten for Calton James)								
Smithpeters, Michael	1	300	20	18	1525	1	10	36.12.0	-	-	-	1591.12.0
Sowell, Lewis	1	200	300	1	150	-	-	-	-	-	-	450.0.0
Stuart, James Esqr & Robert	2	600	1500	42	6139	36	360	113.12.0				17337.12.0
	(Manor Plantation)							235.0 (bond at int.)				
	4	400	280									
	1	640	1300	(J.J. old place)								

Stuart, James	1	500	375	-	-	-	-	-	2	10-40 @	£1400	
& Robert (Cont'd)	7	2100	2300						1	6 yrs	400	
	4	1600	1200									
	6	1200	950									
Stuart, John (Buffilow)		-	-	2	200	1	10	-	-	-	-	210.0.0
Talbott, Matthew Sr	2	1140	3500	12	2570	57	570	8.4.0				14373.19.4
	(On Wataugah, incl. the M.Pn.)							(Paper currency)				
	1	640	800					14.16.8				
	2	975	800					(Hard money)				
	1	640	1000	(from Shelby)				10.18.8				
	2	800	400					(Bond on interest)				
	(The Negros given in, in Virginia and rect.								4	10-40 @	£2800	
	from that state and Bedford county to be								1	under 60	150	
	taken as money in discharge of the Tax								1	under 50	400	
	hereon, for what sum may be there pd for								2	7 yrs	800	
	this present year.)								1	6 yrs	400	
									1	2 yrs	150	
Talbott, Matthew Jr	1	640	600	1	100	-	-	92.4.0	-	-	-	792.8.0
Taylor, Andrew	2	700	1750	8	2100	8	80	108.17.0	-	-	-	4038.17.0
Taylor, George (Single)	1	200	150	1	175	-	-	8.0.0	-	-	Pole Tax on	400.0.0
Taylor, Isaac	(Single)		-	2	250	5	50	10.8.0	-	-	Pole Tax on	400.0.0
Taylor, Isaac Junr	-	-	-	1	290	1	10	103.2.8	-	-	-	403.2.8
				(Mare)								
Thurmond, John	(Single)		-	1	200	-	-	-	-	-	Pole Tax on	400.0.0
Tipton, Joseph	1	530	1000	12	1607	12	120	24.18.4	-	-	-	2751.18.4
	(Ye Manor Plantation)											
Topp, Roger	1	200	200	-	-	-	-	-	-	-	-	200.0.0
Turbut, John	1	200	200	1	150	2	20	-	-	-	-	370.0.0
	(The manor plantation)											
Turbut, Samuel	(Single)		-	1	120	-	-	9.13.0	-	-	Pole Tax on	400.0.0
Vandepole, Abraham (dec.) Estate of	1	100	100	1	100	5	50	-	-	-	-	250.0.0
Ward, William	1	250	250	3	350	7	70	21.2.8	-	-	-	691.2.8
	(The manor plantation)											
Watson, William	1	400	300	3	550	1	10	0.2.8	-	-	-	860.2.8
				(Mairs)								
Weaver, Christian	1	400	500	4	530	5	50	-	-	-	-	1080.0.0
Weaver, Michael	1	540	1000	10	1325	17	170	40.0.0	-	-	-	2535.0.0
	(Manor Plantation)											
Webb, Benjamin	1	240	150	4	600	-	-	-	-	-	-	750.0.0
	(The manor Plantation)											

Webb, Forriett	-	-	-	2	175	9	90	9.8.8	1 ab 40 @ £ 400	674.8.8
Webb, Jonathan	1	500	500	-	-	1	-	18.11.0	- - -	518.11.0
Wells, William	5	800	275	2	250	7	70	28.16.0	- - -	623.13.0
								(Incl Bond on Int & 23-on usur)		
Whitson, William	-	-	-	3	500	2	20	-	- - -	520.0.0
Williams, Edmund	-	-	-	4	675	5	50	1400.0.0	1 man 42 @ £400	3475.0.0
									1 girl 6 400	
									1 girl 5 400	
									1 boy 2 150	
Williams, William	-	300	200	1	200	-	-	3.8.0	- - -	403.8.0
Willoughby, Matthew	1 - Acres assessed by Court @ 20 sh per acre (sum not entered)									
Young, Charles	2	400	400	1	150	-	-	44.0.0	- - -	594.0.0
Young, John	-	-	-	-	-	9	90	-	- - -	90.0.0
Young, Robert, Jr	1	640	1000	9	1075	8	80	50.9.0	- - -	2205.9.0
	(The manor plantation)									
Young, Robert, Sr	1	640	1000	20	2140	31	310	92.18.0	1 19 yrs @ £700	5642.18.0
	(The manor plantation)									
	1	640	600 (On Holsten)							
	1	640	800 (Beaverdams of Brush Creek)							
Young, Thomas	1	550	500	-	-	-	-	118.1.4	- - -	618.11.4

In testimony of the truth and justice of the foregoing list and value of Taxable Property of the inhabitants of the First & Fifth Districts of Washington County, we have hereunto set our hands this 23rd day of August, 1779.

Andrew Taylor
Matthew Talbot
Cleavers Barksdill

Thos. Houghton, J.P.
And Receiver of Inventories, etc.

Thomas Houghton, answerable for -

James Guinn's Tax for ye year 1778	£2.10.0
John Crawthers " " " " "	1.0.6
William Brown " " " " "	1.0.6
John Guinn " " " " "	1.0.6
	£5.11.0

The clerk is directed to issue the order accordingly.

Taxable Property Worth....................	£ 242104.6.1¼
Aded......................	18425.9.8
2nd Addition..................	1014.0.0
3rd Addition..................	21732.16.4
	£ 283276.12.1¼
4th- Patience Cooper's Property.........	1105.0.0

The above sum appears to be the Total Valuation of the Taxable Property of the 1st and 5th Districts of Washington County for the year 1779.

Also to be added.....John Matlock....... 100.0.0

£ 3682.11.9 The Publick & 1/s County Tax for the year 1779, exclusive of some three & four fold tax.

LIST OF TAXABLE PROPERTY IN CAPT JOSEPH WILLSON'S DISTRICT FOR THE YEAR 1779

KEY TO COLUMNS: (1) List of Names; (2) Land; (3) Houses; (4) Cleared Land; Slaves as follows- (5) Under 5 & Above 50 yrs, (6) 5-10 & 40-50 yrs, (7) 10-40 yrs; (8) Money; (9) Stock in Trade; (10) Horses; (11) Old Horses; (12) Cattle; (13) Total Sums

(1)	(2)	(3)	(4)	(5)	(6)	(7)	(8)	(9)	(10)	(11)	(12)	(13)
Adams, John	200	2	10	-	-	-	1.12.0	-	-	1	3	216.12.0
Allison, Robert	300	1	14	-	-	-	18.4.0	-	6	1	12	723.14.0
Anderson, Barnabas	-	-	-	-	-	-	27.5.4	-	3	-	4	217.5.4
Armstrong, Lanty	300	1	6	-	-	-	47.17.0	-	16	-	28	2185.7.0
Arnett, Jacob (single)	-	-	-	-	-	-	19.5.0	-	6	-	6	289.5.0
Bleakley, Robert	500	-	5	-	-	-	0.9.0	-	2	-	-	437.19.0
Borders, Michael	250	2	6	-	-	-	12.12.0	-	16	1	33	1098.11.0
Box, Edward	65	1	5	-	-	-	6.8.0	-	2	-	10	295.18.0
Brown, Michael	100	2	10	-	-	-	10.0.0	-	4	-	10	396.7.8
Burlitton(Burleson),Aaron	100	-	-	-	-	-	3.12.0	-	5	-	2	326.2.0
Cambel, Robert	550	2	6	-	-	-	6.7.8	-	3	1	4	591.1.0
Davie, John (single)	-	-	-	-	-	-	15.0.0	-	1	-	-	50.0.0
Davies, James	-	-	-	-	-	3	11.4.0	-	5	3	26	2636.4.0
Delaney, James	200	1	5	-	-	-	-	-	5	-	3	420.0.0
Denton, Jonathan	100	2	14	-	-	-	4.8.0	-	6	-	10	606.18.0
Diarment, James	150	1	3	-	-	-	-	-	-	4	4	363.15.0
Dougherty, George	300	23	4	-	-	-	70.0.0	-	3	-	9	497.10.0
Dunham, Henry	-	-	-	-	-	-	-	-	10	6	9	1020.0.0
Dunham, Joseph	-	-	-	-	-	1	14.18.0	-	24	4	22	2374.18.0
Eakens, Edward	200	1	1	-	-	-	8.0.0	-	2	-	4	243.0.0
Edmonds, John	-	-	-	-	-	-	-	-	2	-	3	100.0.0
Edwards, Evan	200	2	15	-	-	-	20.2.0	-	17	-	3	930.2.0
Elder, James	-	-	-	-	-	-	39.12.0	-	1	-	-	79.12.0
English, Joseph Jr	462	5	22	-	-	-	87.1.4	-	10	-	19	1114.11.4
English, Andrew	250	1	10	-	-	-	43.4.0	-	3	-	5	534.9.0
Ferrill, Smythe (single)	-	-	-	-	-	-	-	-	1	-	-	40.0.0
Galoger, John	-	-	-	-	-	-	-	-	2	-	-	60.0.0
Gillan, John	350	1	4½	-	-	-	187.4.0	-	4	-	10	654.19.0
Gillaspy, George	1812	4	55	-	1	2	690.0.0	-	11	-	23	4782.15.0
Gillaspie, Thomas, Sr	100	1	4	-	-	-	16.0.0	-	5	-	14	438.10.0
Gillaspie, Thomas	490	-	-	-	-	-	240.0.0	-	1	-	-	547.5.0
Hamilton, John	500	2	20	-	-	-	-	-	2	-	9	592.10.0
Handley, Samuel (single)	200	-	-	-	-	-	13.14.0	-	2	-	4	358.14.0
Hays, Nathaniel	-	-	-	-	-	-	3.4.0	-	3	2	-	203.4.0
Hays, Charls	600	2	12	1	2	2	-	-	7	2	15	3456.0.0

Henderson, James	-	-	-	-	-	-	-	-	4	-	2	170.0.0
Helms, John	-	-	-	-	-	1	-	-	3	-	4	840.0.0
Holly, John	540	2	26	-	-	-	-	-	3	-	25	912.8.8
Holly, Jonathan	250	2	6	-	-	-	-	-	1	1	6	385.0.0
Hopton, John	150	1	4	-	-	-	14.9.4	-	2	-	12	343.9.4
Howard, John Sr	200	2	10	-	-	-	10.6.8	-	4	-	11	520.6.8
Hughs, Francis	200	2	20	-	-	-	55.4.0	-	16	2	22	1645.9.0
Hughs, John (L. Creek)	450	1	8	-	-	-	4.0.0	-	7	1	11	755.5.0
Hughs, John	-	-	-	-	-	-	-	-	2	-	-	125.0.0
Inman, Abednego	800	1	3	-	-	-	-	-	-	-	-	445.0.0
Jack, Jeremiah	620	2	15	-	-	-	80.0.0	-	6	-	6	983.10.0
Keeney, John	650	2	6	-	-	-	10.13.0	-	5	2	14	956.18.0
Keeney, Joseph	450	-	-	-	-	-	3.4.0	-	1	-	-	319.9.0
Kennedy, Daniel	514	3	10	-	-	-	5.4.2	-	5	3	14	860.1.2
Kennedy, John (dec) Estate of	400	2	5	-	-	-	-	-	-	-	-	255.0.0
Linvil, Moses	200	2	8	-	-	-	4.16.0	-	1	-	5	294.16.0
Maney, Martin (single)	-	-	-	-	-	-	6.0.0	-	1	-	-	36.0.0
Martin, Joseph	350	1	6	-	-	-	175.12.0	-	9	1	3	1004.7.0
Martin, Josiah	200	1	17	1	1	2	146.1.0	-	5	4	12	2430.1.0
Martin, Richard (single)	-	-	-	-	-	-	17.0.0	-	2	1	-	169.0.0
Michael, Thos	-	-	-	-	-	-	5.6.0	-	3	-	3	135.6.0
Mires, Adam	100	1	3	-	-	-	0.17.0	-	3	-	3	264.10.0
Mires, Jacob	300	-	6	-	-	-	24.18.8	-	2	-	5	382.8.8
Mitchell, James	-	-	-	-	-	-	1.2.6	-	5	-	6	311.26.0
Moor, Moses	444	1	10	-	-	-	10.4.8	-	4	4	6	658.6.8
Moore, Moses Jr	200	1	2	-	-	-	28.12.0	-	4	1	2	423.12.0
Moor, Samuel	300	1	7	-	-		116.0.0	-	5	2	5	708.10.0
Morgan, Lewis	200	1	5	-	-	-	15.4.0	-	4	-	9	445.4.0
Morrow, Alexander	300	1	10	-	-	-	-	-	6	-	7	1227.10.0
McBee, William	400	1	6	-	-	-	20.8.6	-	4	1	21	1560.8.6
McBride, Francis	-	-	-	-	-	-	-	-	3	3	12	245.0.0
McBride, William	200	-	-	-	-	-	107.14.0	-	6	-	21	572.14.0
McCartney, James	100	-	-	-	-	-	27.16.0	-	8	-	7	440.10.0
McCord, David	450	1	10	-	-	-	-	-	10	-	8	876.0.0
McCord, James	650	1	7½	-	-	-	38.0.0	-	3	3	4	681.15.0
McLoughlan, John	200	1	5	-	-	-	-	-	1	-	3	200.0.0
McNamee, Peter	1340	1	8	-	-	-	64.3.0	-	1	1	6	265.0.0
McNeas, Robert	300	1	5	-	-	-	12.0.0	-	2	-	4	342.10.0
Nelson, William	450	2	8	-	-	-	32.16.0	-	2	3	6	614.1.0
Owens, Owen	150	1	2½	-	-	-	-	-	4	-	5	274.5.0
Pate, Matthew	-	-	-	-	-	-	6.14.6	-	7	-	35	704.6.0
Paterson, John	-	-	-	-	-	-	9.6.8	-	5	6	10	289.6.8

Peblet, John	300	2	10	-	-	-	-	-	3	-	6	407.10.0
Perkins, John	250	1	3½	-	-	-	97.9.4	-	1	-	4	347.4.9
Perrymore, Ezekiel	-	-	-	-	-	-	25.0.0	-	2	-	1	115.0.0
Pruits, William	-	-	-	-	-	-	24.0.0	-	14	-	3	759.14.0
Pyburn, Benjamin	250	-	-	-	-	-	14.0.1	-	1	3	10	345.5.0
Randolph, James	300	1	9	-	-	-	-	-	2	-	4	352.10.0
Randolph, Thomas	200	1	4	-	-	-	2.4.0	-	2	-	3	267.4.0
Ray, Joseph	-	-	-	-	-	-	40.0.0	-	4	-	3	315.0.0
Richey, John	500	1	18	-	-	-	3.8.0	-	2	1	6	546.8.0
Richey, William	1500	3	12	-	-	-	212.4.0	-	4	7	16	1969.14.0
Robertson, James	-	-	-	-	-	-	46.10.6	-	9	-	11	441.10.6
Robinson, John	200	3	25	-	-	-	35.11.0	-	11	-	7	914.11.0
Robinson, David	400	1	7	-	-	-	4.1.0	-	3	-	4	494.1.0
Rodgers, Thomas	300	1	13	-	-	-	37.17.0	-	6	-	12	692.9.0
Ronnels, William	200	-	4	-	-	-	-	-	1	1	6	265.0.0
Sample, Saml	150	1	-	-	-	-	18.7.0	-	4	-	-	227.2.0
Shanks, James	160	1	5	-	-	-	18.8.0	-	6	-	6	437.8.0
Sherill, Philip	100	2	4	-	-	-	39.18.0	-	2	3	8	436.10.0
Shorrill, Samuel	400	4	32	1	1	1	36.3.4	-	-	3	33	1546.3.4
Sloans, Archd.	640	1	5	-	-	-	-	-	2	-	1	491.0.0
Smaser, Jacob	100	1	3½	-	-	-	2.0.0	-	6	-	6	382.0.0
Studard, David	-	-	-	-	-	-	2.0.0	-	4	-	5	202.0.0
Tedlock, John	140	2	7	-	-	-	3.4.0	-	4	2	7	446.14.0
Thomson, Andrew	-	-	-	-	-	-	334.3.4	-	7	2	9	914.3.4
Trimble, John	-	-	-	-	-	-	19.4.0	-	5	1	4	384.4.0
Vaunce, Jacob	600	3	8	-	-	-	39.14.6	-	4	-	4	621.14.6
Waddel, John	500	2	16	-	-	-	-	-	6	-	6	837.10.0
Williams, Benjamin	175	2	7	-	-	-	11.1.8	-	4	-	13	957.9.2
Williams, Courtice	100	-	-	-	-	-	-	-	2	-	2	172.10.0
Williams, John (Lick Creek)	-	-	-	-	-	-	4.8.0	-	4	-	4	139.8.0
Wilson, James	350	2	8½	-	-	-	13.15.3	-	6	1	10	675.0.3
Wilson, Joseph	850	3	5½	-	-	-	65.16.4	-	13	2	23	1372.11.4
Wilson, Robert	240	-	-	-	-	-	23.8.4	-	7	1	3	509.8.4
Wood, Bartholomow	640	2	15	-	-	-	-	-	2	2	9	631.0.0

Scrap "Belonging to Joseph Willson's Return"
Washington County, North Carolina

Amount of the Taxable Property of Assessr Henry Earnest - the Whole Amount is .... Ł 1641.18.8

Amount of the Taxable Property of Saml Lyle, Assessr of the Lower District .... Ł 906.5.0

Amount of the Taxable Property of Asal Rawlings, Assessr of the Lower District .... Ł 1481.4.0

Valued by Jesse Walton, Benjm Gist, Joseph Willson

(See Abstract of Washington County Minutes of 1779)

The North State-
Washington County
For 1780 & 81
Taken 1781

An Inventory of the Taxable Property of the Fifth District in the Present Circulating Currancy

KEY TO COLUMNS: (1) List of Names, (2) Acres of Land, (3) Value, (4) Horskind, (5) Value, (6) Neat Cattle, (7) Value, (8) Cash, (9) Negros, (10) Value, (11) Total Sum

Acars, Uriah	100	129.10.0	6	305.0.0	8	80	5.8.0	-	-	529.18.0
Adams, John	-	-	2	205.0.0	5	50	3.0.0	-	-	158.4.0
Adams, John	-	267.15.0	3	157.10.0	4	40	4.0.0	-	-	469.5.0
Aldridge, Thomas	-	-	5	262.10.0	6	60	-	-	-	322.10.0
Alexander, John	350	451.0.0	3	157.10.0	2	20	144.0.0	-	-	772.10.0
Allison, Charles	400	405.0.0	7	367.10.0	8	80	-	-	-	852.10.0
Allison, James	100	164.10.00	6	315.0.0	5	50	25.14.0	-	-	555.4.0
Allison, John	200	280.0.0	4	210.0.0	4	40	158.0.0	-	-	688.0.0
Allison, Robert	300	285.0.0	8	420.0.0	9	90	72.5.0	-	-	967.5.0
Allison, William	200	252.0.0	2	157.10.0	7	70	-	-	-	479.10.0
Anderson, Barnas.	200	210.0.0	3	157.10.0	1	10	1.1.0	-	-	378.11.0
Anderson, James	520	622.10.0	3	157.10.0	5	50	240.0.0	1 @ Ⱡ700		1760.0.0
Armstrong, Lanty	300	378.0.0	24	945.0.0	21	210	83.4.0	-	-	1615.4.0
Arnet, Jacob	-	-	6	315.0.0	2	20	-	-	-	335.0.0
Ashore, James	100	105.0.0	2	70.0.0	8	80	16.0.0	-	-	271.0.0
Aylot, James	-	-	2	105.0.0	-	-	42.0.0	-	-	147.0.0
Baker, William	-	-	1	52.10.0	5	50	-	-	-	102.10.0
Ballard, Joseph	1570	1648.10.0	26	1365.0.0	25	250	24.16.0	1 @ Ⱡ700		4002.6.0
							14.0.0 (bond)			
Barrimore, Amos	-	-	1	52.10.0	-	-	100.0.0	-	-	152.10.0
Bennet, John	-	21.0.0	6	315.0.0	2	20	-	-	-	356.0.0
Barry, William	725	759.10.0	5	263.0.0	6	60	532.16.0	-	-	1615.6.0
Biddle, Thomas	200	290.10.0	4	210.0.0	5	50	-	-	-	550.10.0
Blackburn, Robert	220	290.10.0	2	105.0.0	5	50	14.0.0	-	-	459.10.0
Blackley, Robert	600	682.10.0	3	157.10.0	8	80	20.0.6	-	-	885.0.6
							25.0.0 (bond)			
Blackwell, David	100	140.0.0	1	52.10.0	2	20	-	-	-	212.10.0
Blackwell, John	100	126.10.0	4	210.0.0	5	50	28.0.0	-	-	414.10.0
Blair, Hugh	150	192.10.0	3	157.10.0	4	40	-	-	-	390.0.0
Blair, John	250	314.10.0	3	157.10.0	9	90	44.16.0	-	-	606.16.0
Boyd, John	100	175.0.0	4	210.0.0	4	40	600.0.0	-	-	1025.0.0
Boyle, Thomas	-	-	2	105.0.0	5	50	0.15.0	(bond)	-	155.15.0
Bradsha, John	100	110.0.0	6	315.0.0	15	150	3.4.0	-	-	578.14.0
Brandon, Thomas	1000	1092.0.0	4	210.0.0	2	20	4.0.0	-	-	1726.0.0
Brumley, Thomas	200	210.0.0	6	315.0.0	7	70	36.16.0	-	-	631.16.0

Brunk, Christian, Dunkard	800	882.0.0	5	262.0.0	6	60	-	-	-	1202.0.0
Brunk, John Dunkard	200	273.0.0	3	157.0.0	1	10	-	-	-	440.10.0
Brown, David	100	126.0.0	3	126.0.0	3	30	22.0.0	-	-	304.0.0
Brown, Thos.	-	-	7	367.10.0	13	130	-	3 @	£1500	1997.10.0
Brown, William	-	-	4	210.0.0	1	10	64.8.0	-	-	284.8.0
Browning, Francis	-	-	2	105.0.0	4	40	18.0.0	-	-	163.0.0
Bryan, William	100	138.10.0	3	112.0.0	4	40	400.0.0	(bond)	-	690.10.0
Brunk, Chrisn. Dunkard	-	119.0.0	1	52.10.0	-	-	-	-	-	171.10.0
Bullock, Ritchard	100	150.0.0	2	105.0.0	3	30	-	-	-	291.0.0
Bard or Byrd, William	-	-	7	367.10.0	4	40	51.4.0	-	-	458.14.0
Byrd, Thomas	250	472.10.0	22	1155.0.0	25	150	22.16.0	2 @	£1400	3290.6.0
Campbell, Alexdr.	550	801.0.0	8	315.0.0	24	240	120.0.0	-	-	1476.0.0
Campbell, James	-	-	2	105.0.0	-	-	40.0.0	-	-	145.0.0
Campbell, John	300	437.10.0	2	157.10.0	3	30	120.0.0	-	-	745.0.0
Campbell, Robert	400	717.10.0	3	157.10.0	12	120	28.0.0	1 @	£100	1723.0.0
Campbell, William	300	392.0.0	5	262.10.0	11	110	12.0.0	-	-	176.10.0
Campbell, James	-	450.0.0	4	210.0.0	8	80	-	-	-	740.0.0
Carpenter, Wm	100	126.0.0	3	175.10.0	7	70	-	-	-	353.10.0
Carpender, Boston	-	-	3	157.10.0	1	10	-	-	-	167.10.0
Carrier, John	100	140.0.0	16	1067.0.0	7	70	a heap of cash	1 @	£700	1977.10.0
Carriger, Jonathan	100	105.0.0	1	52.10.0	2	20	40.16.0	-	-	218.6.0
Carter, Abrn.	200	221.15.0	4	210.0.0	6	60	-	-	-	491.15.0
Carter, Caleb	-	-	5	262.10.0	5	50	-	-	-	312.10.0
Carter, John	200	210.0.0	3	155.10.0	-	-	19.8.0	-	-	386.18.0
Carter, Joseph	1300	1458.0.0	7	367.10.0	12	120	703.10.0	-	-	2649.0.0
Carter, Levi	-	-	3	105.0.0	-	-	-	-	-	105.0.0
Casey, Moses	-	-	4	210.0.0	4	40	-	-	-	250.0.0
Cason, Robert	150	163.15.0	3	105.0.0	7	70	6.0.0	-	-	344.15.0
Chamberlen, Ninian	800	962.10.0	3	157.10.0	13	130	396.0.0	-	-	1646.0.0
Colbreth, Alexdr.	230	242.10.0	1	52.10.0	2	20	-	-	-	315.0.0
Combs, Joseph	-	-	3	157.10.0	3	30	-	-	-	187.10.0
Cook, James	-	-	2	105.0.0	-	-	-	-	-	105.0.0
Coward, Zacariah	300	315.0.0	1	52.10.0	1	10	400.0.0	-	-	777.10.0
Cox, Ephraim	300	467.0.0	5	262.10.0	5	50	6.4.0	-	-	885.14.0
Creadick, David	-	140.0.0	2	150.0.0	2	20	-	-	-	265.0.0
Crow, John	250	195.0.0	6	315.0.0	10	100	-	-	-	610.0.0
Cumins, Joseph, Dunkard	-	-	2	105.0.0	-	-	2.16.0	-	-	107.16.0
Cunningham, Wm.	150	210.0.0	4	210.0.0	10	100	3.8.0	-	-	523.8.0
Davis, Isaac	200	210.0.0	1	52.10.0	2	20	-	-	-	282.10.0
Davis, James	-	-	6	315.0.0	18	180	96.13.0	3 @	£2100	2691.13.0
Davis, Robert	600	630.0.0	3	157.10.0	1	10	-	-	-	797.10.0

Deal, Martha	-	-	8	420.0.0	8	80	-	-	-	500.0.0
Deall, James	200	262.10.0	7	367.10.0	9	90	-	-	-	720.0.0
Deall, William	100	157.10.0	6	315.0.0	7	70	-	-	-	522.10.0
Delany, Francis	200	234.0.0	4	210.0.0	5	50	160.0.0	-	-	654.0.0
Delany, John	700	819.0.0	8	420.0.0	4	40	162.0.0	-	-	1441.0.0
Denton, John	-	-	2	105.0.0	-	-	-	-	-	105.0.0
Denton, Jonathan	100	185.10.0	7	367.10.0	10	100	72.0.0	-	-	725.0.0
Denton, Samuel	-	-	5	262.10.0	9	90	-	-	-	325.10.0
Dickson, Hugh	-	-	4	210.0.0	2	20	8.0.0	-	-	238.0.0
Dodan, Charles	300	357.0.0	3	157.10.0	6	60	-	-	-	574.0.0
Dotty, Eazra	-	-	7	367.10.0	4	40	71.16.0	-	-	480.6.0
Duggard, Miller	-	-	4	210.0.0	14	140	-	-	-	350.0.0
Doak, Samuel	180	259.0.0	3	157.10.0	6	60	200.0.0	1 @	£700	1376.10.0
Dulaney, James	640	679.10.0	4	210.0.0	2	20	-	-	-	909.10.0
Duncan, John	100	105.0.0	3	157.10.0	-	-	834.5.0	-	-	1096.15.0
Dunham, Ruben	-	-	8	420.0.0	15	150	-	-	-	570.0.0
Dunn, William	400	432.10.0	5	262.10.0	3	30	16.0.0	-	-	885.0.0
Dunwoody, Adam	200	224.0.0	-	-	-	-	-	-	-	224.0.0
Durnham, Henry	-	-	19	997.10.0	7	70	-	-	-	1067.10.0
Durnum, Daniel	-	-	11	577.10.0	4	40	-	-	-	617.10.0
Eaton, Joseph	200	231.0.0	2	105.0.0	2	20	6.0.0	-	-	362.0.0
Edwards, Evan	140	236.0.0	17	892.10.0	13	130	163.12.0	-	-	1522.2.0
Ellis, Ephm	-	-	1	52.10.0	2	20	-	-	-	72.10.0
Fain, Niclos	600	714.0.0	4	168.0.0	15	150	193.4.0	-	-	1225.4.0
Fain, William	-	-	6	315.0.0	-	-	180.4.0	-	-	495.4.0
Fargison, John	-	665.0.0	2	105.0.0	10	100	40.0.0	-	-	900.0.0
Farris, Thomas	-	-	3	231.0.0	-	-	38.16.0	-	-	269.16.0
Ferrel, Smith	-	-	2	105.0.0	-	-	-	-	-	105.0.0
Flipping, Thos.	100	157.0.0	4	210.0.0	9	90	11.10.0	-	-	468.10.0
Fowler, Thomas	-	133.0.0	2	52.10.0	2	20	-	-	-	205.10.0
Francisco, John	-	-	4	262.10.0	3	30	32.0.0	-	-	534.10.0
Gammel, Robert	400	507.10.0	-	-	7	-	-	-	-	507.10.0
Gann, Adam	150	262.0.0	2	105.0.0	7	70	-	-	-	427.0.0
Gentery, Robert	-	525.0.0	-	-	16	160	91.4.0	-	-	1248.14.0
Gibbson, James	400	472.10.0	2	105.0.0	6	60	6.0.0	-	-	643.10.0
Gibson, Humphry	-	-	3	157.10.0	13	130	-	1 @	£700	887.10.0
Gilleham, John	600	651.0.0	7	367.10.0	5	50	14.16.0	-	-	1088.6.0
Gillespy, George	2500	7157.10.0	14	735.0.0	30	300	24.0.0	4 @	£2800	11016.10.0
Glass, Wm.	450	504.0.0	4	210.0.0	6	60	-	-	-	774.0.0
Gooden, James	-	-	2	105.0.0	-	-	-	-	-	105.0.0
Gooden, Thomas	200	221.10.0	2	105.0.0	4	40	-	-	-	366.10.0

Goodin, Ben.	-	-	3	157.10.0	1	10	2.0.0	-	-	169.10.0
Goodin, Ben, Jr	-	-	2	105.0.0	2	20	-	-	-	125.0.0
Green, Jesse	-	-	1	52.10.0	-	-	600.0.0	-	-	2007.10.0
							1300.0.0 (bond)			
Green, John	-	-	4	210.0.0	8	80	350.16.0	-	-	640.16.0
Griems, James	400	452.10.0	4	210.0.0	9	90	2275.0.0	-	-	5177.10.0
							1250.0.0 (bond)			
Grimes, Thomas	250	294.0.0	3	157.10.0	4	40	-	-	-	491.10.0
Hadden, Elisha	200	220.10.0	2	105.0.0	2	20	4.0.0	-	-	349.10.0
Hamilton, Francis	200	220.10.0	5	262.10.0	5	50	-	-	-	533.0.0
Hamilton, Isaac	-	-	3	175.10.0	4	40	-	-	-	215.10.0
Hamelton, John	100	124.10.0	3	184.0.0	3	30	-	-	-	339.10.0
Hamelton, John	500	542.10.0	2	105.0.0	4	40	-	-	-	687.10.0
Hammon, John	-	-	2	105.0.0	2	20	-	-	-	125.0.0
Handley, Samuel	-	154.10.0	1	52.10.0	2	20	-	-	-	227.10.0
Harden, Ben	-	-	5	262.10.0	19	190	286.14.0	-	-	739.4.0
Harden, Joseph	150	203.0.0	16	839.10.0	12	120	7800.0.0	2 @ £1100		10060.10.0
Harrison, Danl.	465	488.5.0	9	552.0.0	8	80	-	-	-	1120.5.0
Harsha, John	150	163.0.0	3	157.10.0	6	60	-	-	-	385.10.0
Hatcher, Jamston	140	184.9.0	4	210.0.0	2	20	-	-	-	414.9.0
Hatcher, William	-	-	2	105.0.0	1	10	0.2.0	-	-	115.2.0
							a heap of cash			
Hays, Charles	640	741.0.0	9	427.10.0	11	110	288.0.0	2 @ £1400		4766.10.0
								2 @ £1400		
								1 @ £ 400		
Hays, James	-	-	7	367.10.0	11	110	122.12.0	1 @ £ 700		1302.0.0
Hemphill, Andrew	-	-	3	157.10.0	3	30	400.0.0	4 @ £2200		2787.10.0
Henderson, Daniel	250	262.10.0	2	105.0.0	2	20	0.15.0	-	-	402.10.0
Henderson, Joseph	250	290.0.0	1	52.10.0	2	20	0.16.0	-	-	363.16.0
Henderson, William	400	448.0.0	6	315.0.0	10	100	10.0.0	-	-	873.0.0
Hill, Samuel	490	647.0.0	9	472.10.0	12	120	-	-	-	1035.10.0
Holly, Jno.	400	1470.0.0	8	410.0.0	9	90	42.8.0	-	-	2012.8.0
Howard, George	200	210.0.0	2	105.0.0	5	50	-	-	-	365.0.0
Howard, John	350	367.10.0	4	210.0.0	12	120	-	-	-	697.10.0
Howard, John, Jr.	100	126.0.0	5	262.10.0	8	80	-	-	-	468.10.0
Hubbard, James	980	1081.10.0	2	84.0.0	4	40	3.4.0	-	-	1208.14.0
Hughs, John	450	532.0.0	11	577.10.0	13	130	16.4.0	-	-	1265.14.0
Hutton, William	200	252.0.0	5	262.0.0	9	90	-	-	-	604.10.0
Inglish, Andw.	550	650.10.0	2	105.0.0	10	100	-	-	-	855.10.0
Inglish, James	1175	2537.5.0	7	367.10.0	14	140	296.0.0	-	-	3326.15.0
Inglish, John	300	340.0.0	1	52.10.0	8	80	28.0.0	-	-	490.10.0

Inman, (Abednego) Ebedo	450	556.10.0	7	343.0.0	8	80	38.0.0	2 @ £1400	2418.10.0
Irvine, Robert	400	433.10.0	6	315.0.0	12	120	349.9.0	4 @ £2100	3322.19.0
Jack, Jeremiah	840	1480.10.0	6	315.0.0	9	90	8.8.0	1 @ £ 700	2593.18.0
James, Isaac	-	-	2	105.0.0	5	50	-	- -	155.0.0
Joans, John	-	-	2	105.0.0	2	40	0.12.0	- -	145.12.0
Johnson, Jacob	-	115.10.0	3	157.10.0	5	50	-	- -	323.0.0
Jonson, Francis	150	178.10.0	3	157.0.0	9	90	0.1.0	- -	426.1.0
							to pay taxes		
Jonston, Thos.	600	668.10.0	6	315.0.0	5	50	-	- -	1033.10.0
Keel, James	-	-	5	262.10.0	2	20	129.12.6	- -	411.2.6
Kenedy, Danl.	720	983.0.0	8	420.0.0	11	110	222.10.6	- -	1735.10.6
Kenedy, Moses	120	120.10.0	2	105.0.0	2	20	-	- -	245.10.0
Kercheval, John	-	-	2	105.0.0	-	-	84.0.0	- -	189.0.0
Kerr, Robert	-	-	4	210.0.0	5	50	268.0.0	- -	568.0.0
Kerr, Robert, Jr.	-	-	1	52.10.0	-	-	1.12.0	- -	54.2.0
Keyth, Daniel	-	385.0.0	10	525.0.0	7	70	32.0.0	- -	1012.0.0
Kuykendol, Abram	390	322.15.5	24	1487.0.0	21	210	1106.8.0	7 @ £2350	5476.3.5
Kuykendol, Adam	150	185.10.0	6	315.0.0	2	20	78.0.0	- -	598.10.0
Kuykendol, James	130	111.0.0	5	237.10.0	-	-	20.0.0	- -	358.10.0
Kuykendol, Peter	900	1196.0.0	9	472.10.0	19	190	26.0.0	3 @ £2100	3984.10.0
Kuykendol, Saml.	150	192.10.0	8	420.0.0	3	30	-	- -	642.10.0
Lady, Howel	-	-	4	84.0.0	5	50	-	- -	134.0.0
Lain, Corbin	-	140.0.0	3	157.10.0	5	50	11.12.0	- -	359.2.0
Lane, Dutton	-	-	4	210.0.0	2	20	-	- -	230.0.0
Lemons, Wm	200	224.0.0	1	14.0.0	4	40	46.0.0	- -	324.0.0
Lee, Thomas	200	234.0.0	-	-	-	-	-	- -	234.0.0
Lee, Nicoles	340	357.0.0	1	52.10.0	-	-	12.0.0	1 @ £ 700	1121.10.0
Lewis, Aaron	1150	1155.0.0	-	-	-	-	-	- -	1155.0.0
Lialer, Wymor	300	315.0.0	1	52.10.0	-	-	32.0.0	- -	399.10.0
Lovelaty, John	200	329.0.0	3	84.0.0	9	90	3.7.0	- -	506.7.0
Lowry, Rebecca	-	137.0.0	3	157.10.0	5	50	-	- -	344.10.0
Lyle, Samuel	130	205.4.0	4	210.0.0	14	140	133.4.0	- -	688.8.0
McAdoo, David	-	-	7	339.0.0	10	100	66.16.0	- -	501.16.0
McAdoo, John	350	388.10.0	10	525.0.0	8	80	1629.0.0	- -	2622.10.0
McAdoo, William	100	133.0.0	8	420.0.0	6	60	-	1 @ £ 700	1313.2.0
McAnear, Robert	300	365.15.0	5	210.0.0	6	60	34.5.0	- -	670.0.0
McCartney, Charles	-	-	6	315.10.0	6	60	-	- -	375.10.0
McCartney, James	-	-	6	315.10.0	14	140	46.0.0	- -	510.10.0
McCollum, Thos.	500	630.0.0	3	157.10.0	6	60	241.12.0	- -	1089.2.0
McCord, David	550	653.10.0	10	525.0.0	8	70	450.0.0	- -	1708.10.0
McCord, James	500	581.0.0	5	175.0.0	5	50	46.10.6	- -	852.10.6

McClure, Andw.	164	114.12.0	5	262.10.0	7	70	4.6.0	-	-	451.8.0
McClure, Thos.	-	-	1	52.10.0	3	30	-	-	-	82.10.0
McFarland, Alexr.	900	962.10.0	7	367.10.0	3	30	4.0.0	-	-	1364.0.0
McGlaughlen, Alexdr.	200	260.15.0	4	210.0.0	6	60	21.4.0	-	-	551.19.0
Mcglaughlen, Alexdr.	100	112.0.0	1	52.10.0	2	20	-	-	-	184.10.0
McMin, Robert	300	378.0.0	10	525.0.0	10	100	48.0.0	-	-	1051.0.0
McNamee, Peter	1200	1315.0.0	11	577.10.0	9	90	16.0.0	-	-	1998.10.0
McVay, John	-	122.15.0	2	75.0.0	1	10	-	-	-	207.15.0
McLen, Robert	-	186.0.0	3	157.10.0	4	40	4.0.0	-	-	387.10.0
Maghon, James	-	-	5	262.10.0	2	20	-	-	-	282.10.0
Martain, James	100	157.10.0	7	367.10.0	5	50	43.12.0	-	-	565.10.0
Martain, Joseph	350	462.0.0	6	315.0.0	7	70	69.2.0	-	-	916.2.0
Martin, Andrew	100	133.0.0	4	163.0.0	3	30	8.0.0	-	-	394.16.0
							55.16.0	(bond)		
Matain, Joshua	300	402.10.0	8	420.0.0	11	110	1.0.0	3 @	£1550	2483.10.0
Matain, Richard	-	472.10.0	3	157.10.0	-	-	21.4.0	-	-	651.4.0
Mathess, Wm	-	-	5	262.10.0	19	190	12.0.0	-	-	464.10.0
Miller, David, Dunkard	-	151.0.0	1	52.10	2	20	-	-	-	223.10.0
Miller, James	60	63.0.0	5	262.10.0	4	40	-	-	-	365.10.0
Mitchell, James	100	136.0.0	4	221.0.0	4	40	260.5.6	-	-	646.5.6
Mitchell, Thos.	-	-	3	157.10.0	3	30	373.6.0	-	-	560.16.0
Mitchell, Thos, Jr.	100	119.0.0	3	175.10.0	2	20	-	-	-	304.10.0
Montgomery, James	350	394.10.0	2	103.10.0	7	70	80.0.0	-	-	647.0.0
Moor, Anthony	700	750.0.0	3	118.0.0	9	90	122.14.4	-	-	1071.14.4
Moor, Moses, Jr.	200	234.10.0	4	210.0.0	2	20	76.0.0	-	-	540.10.0
Moor, Samuel	300	350.0.0	5	672.10.0	3	30	2.0.0	-	-	644.10.0
Moor, William	200	247.10.0	2	105.0.0	4	40	-	-	-	372.10.0
Moore, James	200	224.0.0	2	105.0.0	7	70	-	-	-	399.0.0
Moore, James	-	-	4	168.0.0	5	50	-	-	-	218.0.0
Moore, Moses	200	280.0.0	3	84.0.0	4	40	4.0.0	-	-	408.16.0
Morris, Drury	600	630.0.0	6	315.0.0	9	90	-	-	-	1035.1.0
Morris, Gideon	700	899.0.0	18	845.0.0	15	150	3.11.0	1 @	£ 700	2617.11.0
Morris, Shed	700	791.0.0	8	420.0.0	8	80	-	-	-	1291.0.0
Morrow, Alexander	300	367.10.0	5	262.10.0	7	70	81.4.0	1 @	£ 700	1481.4.0
Morrow, James	-	-	2	105.0.0	1	10	12.6.0	-	-	127.16.0
Myers, Adam	100	138.0.0	3	157.10.0	5	50	30.0.0	-	-	375.10.0
Myrs, Christephor	-	-	2	105.0.0	6	60	0.1.6	-	-	161.1.6
Newman, John	400	468.0.0	4	210.0.0	7	70	0.10.0	-	-	748.10.0
Noland, John	-	-	4	210.0.0	5	50	101.4.0	-	-	461.4.0
Owens, Owen	150	199.10.0	3	105.0.0	7	70	-	-	-	374.10.0
Parker, Wm	100	105.0.0	-	-	1	10	20.0.0	-	-	135.0.0

Parris, Robert	200	252.0.0	7	367.10.0	11	110	48.8.0	-	-	777.18.0
Parrimore, Amos	-	-	1	52.10.0	-	-	100.0.0	-	-	152.10.0
Parrimore, Azecial	400	427.0.0	2	105.0.0	2	20	-	-	-	552.0.0
Parrimore, Matthew	800	945.0.0	3	157.10.0	12	120	100.0.0	-	-	1322.10.0
Parrimore, William	-	-	3	157.10.0	4	40	212.0.0	-	-	411.10.0
Parry, David	-	-	4	210.0.0	8	80	40.0.0	3 @	£2100	2430.0.0
Pate, Matthew	-	-	10	525.0.0	21	210	-	1 @	£ 700	1435.0.0
Patterson, John	200	250.0.0	6	242.0.0	8	80	160.0.0	-	-	734.0.0
Peblet, John	500	588.0.0	2	105.0.0	8	80	16.0.0	-	-	789.0.0
Pickens, James	400	458.10.0	6	315.0.0	5	50	104.4.0	-	-	927.14.0
Poore, Moses	200	210.0.0	7	367.10.0	9	90	-	-	-	667.10.0
Pope, John	-	-	1	52.10.0	-	-	80.0.0	-	-	132.10.0
Powers, John	-	-	1	52.10.0	1	10	-	-	-	62.10.0
Price, John	200	122.10.0	5	262.10.0	3	30	60.5.0	-	-	475.5.0
Pruet, Martain	100	147.0.0	6	215.0.0	4	40	-	-	-	505.0.0
Pruet, William	-	-	10	472.10.0	4	40	-	-	-	512.10.0
Pruet, William	250	260.10.0	7	367.10.0	13	130	-	1 @	£ 700	1458.0.0
Pursley, William	160	203.10.0	3	84.0.0	3	30	3.12.0	-	-	321.2.0
Pursley, William, Jr.	-	-	2	205.0.0	-	-	674.16.0	-	-	879.16.0
Ranols, William	-	-	3	157.10.0	5	50	43.12.0	-	-	251.2.0
Randolph, James	-	134.15.0	1	52.10.0	5	50	58.8.0	1 @	£ 700	995.15.0
Randolph, Ridlegarin	-	-	1	52.10.0	-	-	8.0.0	-	-	60.10.0
Randolph, Thomas	222	255.10.0	2	84.0.0	5	50	90.16.0	-	-	480.6.0
Ray, Joseph	400	420.0.0	4	210.0.0	5	50	102.0.0	-	-	782.0.0
Ray, Thomas	100	132.0.0	5	262.10.0	22	220	402.0.0	1 @	£ 700	1717.10.0
Reed, Solomon	-	-	3	157.10.0	3	30	-	-	-	187.10.0
Reid, Daniel	300	337.0.0	2	105.0.0	6	60	1.5.0	-	-	505.5.0
Read, John	50	54.5.0	2	240.0.0	4	40	11.4.0	-	-	145.9.0
Renken, David	150	196.0.0	2	105.0.0	10	100	49.14.0	-	-	466.5.9
							15.11.9	(bond)		
Richeson, John	-	-	3	157.10.0	10	100	-	-	-	257.10.0
Riddle, Mary	25	43.15.0	2	105.0.0	1	10	-	-	-	158.15.0
Riggs, Edw.	-	-	6	315.0.0	9	90	-	-	-	405.0.0
Riggs, Ruben	200	238.0.0	2	105.0.0	7	70	10.0.0	-	-	423.0.0
Ritchey, John	250	332.10.0	5	262.10.0	8	80	23.4.0	-	-	698.4.0
Ritchey, William	1000	1119.0.0	9	378.0.0	13	130	679.4.0	-	-	2306.4.0
Roberts, Edmd.	300	364.0.0	3	157.10.0	8	80	20.0.0	-	-	621.10.0
Robinson, John	300	300.0.0	11	563.10.0	7	70	6.0.0	-	-	939.10.0
Robison, David	400	472.10.0	5	262.10.0	6	60	2.4.0	-	-	797.4.0
Robison, David	200	283.0.0	3	175.10.0	2	20	-	-	-	478.10.0
Robison, James	500	560.0.0	3	157.10.0	8	80	8.0.0	-	-	805.10.0

Robison, James	-	-	3	157.0.0	-	-	30.0.0	-	-	187.8.0
Robison, Mathew	-	109.0.0	3	157.10.0	3	30	-	-	-	296.10.0
Rodgers, James	600	729.10.0	6	318.10.0	15	150	32.8.0	-	-	1210.8.0
							40.0.0	(bond)		
Rodgers, Thos.	500	630.0.0	9	472.10.0	13	130	24.1.6	-	-	1256.11.0
Rolengs, Ashel	3300	3471.10.0	9	472.10.0	6	60	1437.8.0	-	-	5440.8.0
Sample, Moses	-	295.0.0	4	220.0.0	9	90	0.8.0	-	-	605.8.0
Sample, William	250	281.0.0	4	210.0.0	10	100	8.0.0	-	-	608.0.0
Sanders, John	-	-	5	262.10.0	5	50	3.4.0	-	-	315.14.0
Sarrett, Joseph	-	-	6	325.0.0	5	50	-	-	-	365.0.0
Scott, Thos.	200	280.0.0	4	210.0.0	9	90	-	-	-	580.0.0
Semple, Saml.	200	105.0.0	5	262.10.0	-	-	4.16.0	-	-	1067.10.0
Sims, Job	-	228.0.0	3	126.0.0	5	50	-	-	-	404.0.0
Simson, Saml.	-	-	4	210.0.0	3	30	-	-	-	240.0.0
Shanks, James	150	244.0.0	9	472.0.0	12	120	188.0.0	-	-	1024.0.0
Sholey, Luke	100	106.15.0	2	105.0.0	3	30	5.6.0	-	-	247.1.0
Sloan, Archbd	-	333.10.0	1	52.10.0	4	40	28.0.0	-	-	1174.0.0
Smelser, Jacob	400	462.0.0	2	105.0.0	5	50	5.11.0	-	-	622.11.0
Smith, Thos	200	290.10.0	8	420.0.0	11	110	93.0.0	-	-	913.10.0
Starns, Adam	-	-	5	262.10.0	2	20	2.0.0	-	-	284.10.0
Steel, Robert	300	369.5.0	3	157.10.0	7	70	20.0.0	(bond)	-	616.15.0
Stevenson, Robert	100	140.0.0	6	315.0.0	4	40	-	-	-	495.0.0
Stockton, Wm	300	374.10.0	3	157.10.0	16	160	8.0.0	-	-	700.0.0
Story, William	200	262.10.0	6	252.0.0	11	110	36.5.0	-	-	660.15.0
Strain, John	-	-	1	52.10.0	-	-	4.0.0	-	-	56.10.0
Stuard, David	-	490.0.0	4	140.0.0	5	50	80.0.0	-	-	760.0.0
Stuart, Benn.	-	-	4	210.0.0	4	40	110.0.0	-	-	560.0.0
Stuart, Joseph	-	-	2	105.0.0	7	70	4.16.0	-	-	179.16.0
Swerins, John	-	162.10.0	2	105.0.0	4	40	12.0.0	-	-	325.10.0
Tarbot, James	-	-	3	157.10.0	4	40	-	-	-	197.10.0
Taylor, Christr	208	277.0.0	4	160.0.0	9	90	440.0.0	1 @ Ь	700	1667.0.0
Taylor, Leroy	-	246.0.0	6	315.0.0	8	80	-	-	-	1194.0.0
		553.0.0	Land in Burke Co.							
Tedlock, Thomas	-	-	1	52.10.0	4	40	-	-	-	92.10.0
Temple, Majer	-	-	7	367.10.0	7	70	16.0.0	2 @ Ь	1400	2003.10.0
								1 @ Ь	150	
Thomson, Andrew	-	-	7	367.10.0	7	70	28.16.0	-	-	466.6.0
Tooley, John	250	262.10.0	4	210.0.0	4	40	-	-	-	512.10.0
Trimble, Walter	-	-	3	157.10.0	6	60	20.0.0	-	-	237.10.0
Trimble, William	400	441.0.0	4	210.0.0	6	60	474.0.0	-	-	1185.0.0
Tye, John	20	21.0.0	5	262.10.0	2	20	-	-	-	303.10.0

Vanhouser, John	200	213.10.0	6	315.0.0	4	40	-	1 @ Ŀ	700	1238.12.0
Vermillion, Jesse	-	-	1	52.10.0	-	-	10.0.0	-	-	62.10.0
Watson, John	-	-	1	52.10.0	1	10	-	-	-	62.10.0
Watson, Jonathan	100	115.10.0	3	157.10.0	2	20	12.0.0	-	-	315.0.0
Watson, Saml	-	-	2	105.0.0	1	10	-	-	-	115.0.0
Wear, Robert	-	-	3	157.10.0	3	30	-	-	-	187.10.0
Weer, John	-	452.0.0	4	140.0.0	6	60	-	-	-	652.0.0
Weer, Saml	240	311.10.0	2	52.0.0	4	40	64.2.0	-	-	467.12.0
West, Thos.	750	820.5.0	3	157.10.0	3	30	80.16.6	-	-	1088.11.6
White, Isaac	-	-	5	262.10.0	3	30	18.0.0	1 @ Ŀ	700	1010.10.0
White, James	-	-	7	367.10.0	8	80	-	-	-	447.10.0
White, John	-	-	3	157.10.0	5	50	-	-	-	107.10.0
Whittenberger, Jos.	200	262.10.0	4	210.0.0	22	220	11.4.0	-	-	728.14.0
							25.0.0	(bond)		
Wilson, Adam, Sr.	340	1039.10.0	5	262.10.0	12	120	950.2.0	2 @ Ŀ	1400	3772.2.0
Wilson, Capt. Jas.	650	692.0.0	8	416.10.0	13	130	188.16.0	-	-	1428.6.0
Wilson, John	-	-	5	262.10.0	6	60	-	-	-	322.10.0
Wilson, John	300	357.0.0	3	140.0.0	10	100	116.0.0	-	-	713.0.0
Wilson, Joseph	-	-	3	157.10.0	4	40	32.8.0	-	-	229.18.0
Wilson, Joseph	800	840.0.0	16	710.10.0	20	200	249.12.0	-	-	2012.0.0
Wilson, Joseph	-	234.10.0	5	210.0.0	4	40	6.0.0	-	-	480.10.0
Wilson, Robert	340	123.0.0	11	577.10.0	4	40	4.15.0	-	-	745.5.0
Wilson, William	799	919.9.0	7	367.10.0	6	60	227.10.0	-	-	1554.11.0
Wood, Bartw.	640	1008.0.0	3	52.10.0	6	60	-	-	-	1120.10.0
Wood, Barthow, Jr.	-	-	2	105.0.0	-	-	50.0.0	-	-	155.0.0
Woodard, Thomas	-	-	2	105.0.0	-	-	120.4.0	-	-	225.4.0
Woods, Ritchard	400	486.0.0	8	420.0.0	7	70	320.0.0	1 @ Ŀ	700	1936.0.0
Woods, William	100	175.0.0	4	210.0.0	4	40	28.0.0	-	-	425.0.0

Assessd & Signed by Robert Irvine, Anthony Moore & Robt. Wear

The Taxes of the above Assessors were assessed & signed by Danl Kenedy, John Newman & Charles Allison.

This Scrap belongs to Capt Joseph Willson's Return for 1780.

"......... Samuel Moore's ....

John Alexander	Land 350 acres	....	350 Ŀ
	Horses 3	....	150 Ŀ
	Cattle 3	....	30 Ŀ
	Cash	....	28 Ŀ
			558 Ŀ

Adam Willson	Land 840 acres	....	1290 £
	Horses 8	....	480 £
	Cattle 13	....	130 £
	Cash	....	160 £
	Negroes 2	....	1400 £
			3460 £

William McNabb
Joseph Willson
Benjamin Gist

Belonging to Joseph Willson's Return.

A True Inventory of Saml Sherrill's Taxable Estate, North Carolina, Washington County. Land 220 acres, 1 caben, 7 acres cleared.

Horses 4 head	....	800 £
Cattle 6 "	....	60 £
Cash	....	218 £
Land	....	250 £
		1328 £

Note: Samuel Sherrill Senr's Will on file in Washington Co., dated June 4, 1800, proven Aug. sessions, 1800.

Lincoln Co.
Oct. 9th 1782. This is to certify that JAMES McAFEE hath given in his Taxable Property that he has at his brother Robt. McAfees in Washington County, Consisting of Negros & Stock here before us, for the year 1780 & 1781, and has paid Tax for the same.

Certified by us.

John Barber Assesr.
Thomas Espey.

(Note: The above scrap of paper is attached to 1780 & 1781 List. MHMc)

NOTE: This Undated List of eighteen pages resembles the same form as those of the 1780s- except that it omits the number of acres of land, number of horses, and number of cattle, yet it gives the assessed value of them. It must be dated before 1783 when Greene County was cut off, as it contains those names which were in Greene County after 1783. Several years ago Capt John Wear's List for 1785 in Greene County was published, which contains many of these same names. MHMc.

Name	Land	Horses	Cattle	Cash	Total Value
Adams, John	300	160	30	-	490.0.0
Adcok, Daniel	200	350	10	11.0.0	571.0.0
				1 negro	
Adkin, Charls	-	240	-	0.8.0	240.8.0
Akers, Uria	-	350	70	175.0.0	595.0.0
Alison, Charls	720	460	70	300.4.0	1550.4.0
Alison, James	200	560	20	22.8.0	800.2.8
Alison, John	540	350	100	2.8.0	992.8.0
Allison, James	900	880	90	80.0.0	3350.0.0
				2 negors @ Ł1400	
Allison, Robert	540	640	100	37.12.0	1317.12.0
Allison, William	270	370	50	-	660.0.0
Anderson, Barnabas	200	320	20	0.4.0	540.4.0
Anderson, Isaac	350	160	-	130.0.0	540.0.0
Anderson, James	900	250	-	3.0.0	1153.0.0
Armstrong, Lanty	720	1900	260	33.0.0	2913.0.0
Arnit, Jacob	-	400	30	61.4.0	491.4.0
Bakers, William	-	160	40	4.2.0	204.2.0
Barkly, Gorge	-	180	70	31.0.0	281.0.0
Baskin, John	200	90 (1)	30	-	320.0.0
Bayles, Samuel	300 & 200	440	30	0.2.8	970.2.8
Beavvor, Thomas	-	170	20	-	190.0.0
Bennitt, John	-	600	10	35.7.0	645.7.0
Betty, William	400	-	-	-	400.0.0
Biddle, Thomas	300	140	30	4.6.0	474.6.0
Biram, Ebnezer	150	320	200	9.8.0	679.8.0
Bird, Amos	-	2290	290	193.5.8	4073.5.8
				2 slaves Ł 1400	
Blackburn, Robert	360	400	60	85.0.0	1105.0.0
land on Richland (creek)	200				
Blackly, Robert	500	270	60	64.8.6	894.8.6

Blackwell, John	100	400	30	-	530.0.0
Blackwill, David	100	-	-	-	100.0.0
Blare, John	400	380	100	5.0.0	885.0.0
Boyd, William	200	100 (1)	30	-	330.0.0
Breed, Mary	300	1100	-	-	1300.0.0
Brelor, Joseph	4500 & 390 & 540	1800	250	74.0.0 negors £1400	8954.0.0
Brown, Joseph	2020	1100	negors £2600	-	5720.0.0
Brunk, Christophier	1800	300	50	20.0.0	2170.0.0
Brunk, Christin, Menonist	-	100	-	-	100.0.0
Brunk, Jno., Menonist	-	100	-	-	100.0.0
Bulard, John	-	1430	280	64.18.0	2774.18.0
Bullah, Isaac	-	1400 460	140	60.0.0	2060.0.0
Bulock, Richard	200	240	30	-	470.0.0
Campbel, Alexander littel limestone	200	440	50	0.16.0	690.16.0
Campble, Alxander	960	540	170	-	1670.0.0
Cambell, James	720	320	100	8.8.0	1148.8.0
Cambell, James Jr. unmaried	-	160	-	8.8.0 in hand	168.8.0
Campbel, John	300	-	-	-	300.0.0
Campble, Robert	960	400	80	82.8.0	1522.8.0
Campble, William	540	420	90	16.8.0	1066.8.0
Campble, William	-	360	120	226.16.0 Virginia Corency	706.16.0
Carik, John	100	1900	90	26.0.7	2816.0.7
			1 negor £ 700		
Carpendar, Owla	-	900	130	-	103.0.0
Carter, Joseph	2340	560	100	140.10.0	3140.10.0
Campbel, John	300	-	-	-	300.0.0
Chambers, Alexander	200	160	30	-	390.0.0
Chambers, David	-	640	100	-	740.0.0
Chambers, John	100	420	80	-	600.0.0
Coningham, William	200	300	90	96.10.7	686.10.7
Coopper, Phillip	200	80	-	-	280.0.0
Coward, Zachirah	300	100 (1)	-	4.0.0	404.0.0
Cradik, David	200	200	30	-	430.0.0
Crafford, Isiah	600	240	30	-	870.0.0
Crafford, Moses	-	400	110	-	510.0.0
Crow, John	540	120 (1)	90	50.13.4	800.13.4

Davis, Isaac	200	240	30	1.0.0	471.0.0
Davis, Joseph	-	640	100	-	740.0.0
Davis, Nathen	200	400	80	216.6.0	682.16.6
Davis, Nathaniel	750	310	-	-	1060.0.0
Delaney, Francis	200	360	70	176.6.0	806.6.0
Delaney, James	600	630	20	0.10.0	1250.10.0
Deal, James	250	400	80	170.10.0	910.0.0
Denton, Jonathan	240	500	100	0.8.0	840.8.0
Denton, Samuel	-	310	-	0.12.0	310.12.0
Dicks, Jaccob	-	100	40	12.8.0	212.8.0
Dickings, James	720	100	-	10.16.0	830.16.0
Dillon, Daniel, Quaker	360	120	-	12.10.0	672.10.0
				Bond at Interest 150 £	
Dilson, Elisha	150	400	40	-	590.0.0
Doddy, Howell	100	20	-	-	120.0.0
Dodson, Charls	300	300	80	17.12.0	597.12.0
Dogat, Miler	-	590	110	205.0.0	905.0.0
Duncan, Crauen	-	100	10 (1)	-	110.0.0
Dunham, Joseph	-	2610	270	6.3.0	3486.3.0
			1 negor @	700.0.0	
Dunkan, John	-	320	-	16.3.0	336.3.0
Edwards, Evan	240	1080	110	56.4.0	1486.4.0
Edmons, Jno.	-	160	50	-	210.0.0
Elexander, David	-	350	100	24.0.0	474.0.0
English, John	300	160	60	14.16.0	534.16.0
Errenton, Charles	-	1600	330	16.18.0	4046.18.0
			Negros @	2100.0.0	
Evans, Nathaniel	-	160	20	112.20.0	292.2.0
Ferel, Smith	-	100	-	-	100.0.0
Flemming, Peter	400	400	40	64.8.0	504.8.0
Fowler, Thomas	100	80	50	-	230.0.0
		1 mare			
Gans, Adam	180	200	90	-	470.0.0
Gans, Clement	-	160	20	-	180.0.0
Gans, Nathan	-	140	1 cow 10	-	150.0.0
Gaskins, Frances	-	280	80	-	360.0.0
Gentrey, Charles	300	350	70	-	1420.0.0
			1 negor @ £ 700		
Gentrey, Robert	1185 & 200	600	100	55.17.11	2140.17.11
Gess, Benjamin	1800	800	80	3.0.0	2683.0.0
Gess, Joseph	250	300	160	-	710.0.0

Gibson, James	720	320	20	3.4.0	1063.4.0
Gillaspy, George	3000	1220	300	1000.0.0	8570.0.0
			3 negors @	2700	
			1 Negor @	150	
Gillaspy, Thomas on Midle Creek	360	280	100	8.0.0	848.0.0
Gillaspy, Thomas	690	300	-	-	990.0.0
Gillbreath, Alaxander	360	230	10	-	600.0.0
Glass, William	600	160	30	-	790.0.0
Graham, Hiram	300	400	150	-	850.0.0
Graham, Thomas	250	210	30	-	490.0.0
Greer, William	550	300	10	-	850.0.0
Hadan, Elisha	300	120	40	11.4.0	471.4.0
Hail, William	180	160	20	0.4.0	360.4.0
Hamilton, Francis, Senr.	100	480	70	4.0.0	654.0.0
Hambelton, John	1500	100	-	1.12.0	1601.12.0
				in hand	
Handley, Samuel	450	120	50	351.12.0	871.12.0
Hareson, Danial	900	690	70	-	1660.0.0
Hays, Charls	720	560	120	60.2.8	3310.2.8
			2 old negors @	300	
			2 negors @	1400	
			1 Negor @	150	
Hayworth, Absalam, Quaker	-	370	10	19.7.10	399.7.10
Hendrson, Joseph	250	280	20	2.5.0	552.5.0
Hill, Saml.	490	700	100	36.10.0	1326.10.0
Hill, Shedrick	100	160	50	18.13.4	318.13.4
Hogden, William	750	360	140	1.8.0	1251.8.0
Holey, John	1500	200	130	-	1830.0.0
Hood, Robert	180	120	40	-	340.0.0
Howard, John	350	400	110	84.16.0	944.16.0
Howerd, John	180	350	70	-	600.0.0
Howland, John	-	160	50	6.0.0	216.0.0
Hubbard, James	800	160	-	-	960.0.0
Hughs, David	900	-	50	2.0.0	952.0.0
Huses, Frances	820	950 (11)	-	0.6.0	-
Huse, John Lick Creek	450	600	120	6.16.0	676.16.0
Huse, John	100	160	30	-	290.0.0
Hutton, William	360	560	60	-	980.0.0
Inman, Abednego	450	460	50	140.0.0	2350.0.0
			1 negor @	150	
			1 negor @	700	

Jack, Jaremy	960	600	120	48.4.0	1788.4.0
Johnston, James	200	240	50	60.0.0	550.0.0
Johnston, Thomas	200	400	50	5.6.0	655.6.0
Jons, Evan, Quaker	540	-	-	-	540.0.0
Jonston, Jacob	-	180	40	-	220.0.0
Jonston, Moses, s man	-	10	-	40.0.0	50.0.0
Keeny, John	700	490	100	14.8.0	1304.8.0
Keeth, Daniel	540	500	20	0.18.0	1130.18.0
Keley, Moses	-	300	20	0.16.0	320.16.0
Kelley, Richard	-	160	-	-	160.0.0
Kelly, James	-	480	50	44.16.0	574.16.0
Kelly, Jno.	180	180	50	-	410.0.0
Kennedy, Daniel	540	640	110	123.4.0	2713.4.0
			1 negro man @	700	
Kirkindal, Abram	1100	4316	220	142.0.0	9078.0.0
		2 negros	betw40-50	@ 800	
		2 Negors		@1400	
		2 Negors		@ 800	
		2 Negors	under 5	@ 300	
Kirkindal, Adam	-	400	40	100.0.0	500.0.0
Kirkindal, John	270	400	40	-	710.0.0
Kuykendal, Petter	900	500	60	2138.0.6	4798.16.0
			Negors @	1200.0.0	
Lemons, Bitlom (?)	240	50	30	4.0.0	324.0.0
		1 small old horse			
Lile, Capt John	550	700	20	-	2670.0.0
			Negors @	1400	
Loe, Acquilla	1100	400	110	5.15.8	1615.15.8
Lovelady, John	300	420	90	10.0.0	820.0.0
Lovelady, Marshal	-	540	110	-	650.0.0
Lowry, John	200	240	40	16.8.0	496.8.0
Lowrrey, David	150	300	20	82.18.0	552.18.0
Lyle, Saml.	250	240	120	-	610.0.0
McAdoo, John	340	800	110	307.19.6	1567.19.6
McAdou, John Juner	-	200	-	12.16.0	212.16.0
McCartney, James	360	610	140	44.0.0	1154.0.0
McColam, Thomas	300	-	-	892.12.0	1192.12.0
McCool, Gaberal, Quaker	100	120	50	-	270.0.0
McCord, David	930	660	70	6.0.0	1666.0.0
McCord, James	1050	360	60	45.6.0	1515.6.0
McCray, Daniel	560	160	-	268.0.0	988.0.0

McFarlin, Exander	-	260	-	28.0.0	288.0.0
McGhe, Feral	-	60	-	2.3.4	62.3.4
McGlaughlain, Alexander	200	100	50	-	350.0.0
McGloughlain, John	-	50	-	57.17.0	-
McMeen, Robert	330	630	110	36.2.0	1106.2.0
McNamee, Petter	1400	870	10	640.2.0	2920.2.0
Maglan, Robert	350	200	70	0.16.0	620.16.0
Martain, James	180	280	40	0.9.0	500.9.0
Martain, Joseph	630	480	40	20.0.0	1170.0.0
Martain, Richard	-	260	-	91.12.0	351.12.0
Martin, Andrew	100	220	40	0.8.0	360.8.0
Martin, Joseph (marked out)					
Martin, Josia	360	570	130	2.2.0	2762.2.0
			Negors	@ 1700.0.0	
Mcadow, William	100	300	-	63.4.0	463.4.0
Mathes, Samuel	100	120	20	40.0.0	320.0.0
Mier, Christopher	150	-	30	60.0.0	240.0.0
Miller, David	150	120	20	2.2.0	292.2.0
Miller, James	200	220	30	15.2.0	285.2.0
Mitchal, James	360	360	40	19.6.0	779.6.6
Mitchell, Thomas	100	320	60	447.9.0	1327.9.4
			1 Copper Still-	400.0.0	
Mitchell, Thomas	100	180	10	13.4.0	303.4.0
More, Moses	240	320	60	-	620.0.0
More, James - on sinking creek	200	120	80	6.0.0	406.0.0
Moore, Anthony	720	160	80	164.12.0	1124.12.0
Moore, James	200	160	30	4.0.0	394.0.0
Moore, William	360	160	40	1.4.0	561.4.0
Morrow, Alexander	300	250	70	64.0.0	1384.0.0
			1 Negor	@ 700	
Morrow, James	100	80	10 (1)	-	190.0.0
		1 small mare			
Moris, Drury	600	480	130	-	1210.0.0
Nelson, Southey	100	350	10	2.0.0	462.0.0
Nodding, William	1440	420	10 (1)		3270.0.0
			2 negors	@ 1400.0.0	
Norton, David	-	390	80	-	470.0.0
Owens, Owen	250	160	60	0.12.0	370.12.0
Paremor, Matthew	1920	360	100	4.16.0	2384.16.0
Paremor, William	-	180	20	4.0.0	104.0.0
Pate, Matthew	-	480	390	9.12.0	1579.12.0
			1 Negor	@ 700.0.0	

Peree, James	180	420	30	4.8.0	1334.8.0
			1 negor @	700.0.0	
Perey, David	900	320	90		2010.0.0
			1 negor @	700.0.0	
Perrymore, Ezekel	500	80	10	-	590.0.0
Person, Joseph	200	210	40	-	450.0.0
Phain, Nicholas	1530	460	150	56.1.0	2196.1.0
Phain, William	-	400	-	-	400.0.0
Philipint, Thomas	100	790	69	16.16.0	1066.16.0
Pikins, John	200	230	1 cow 10	452.12.0	892.12.0
Poor, Moses	200	480	90	9.5.8	729.5.8
Price, John	200	400	30	85.15.4	715.4.0
Pruit, Martin	-	320	Bull 10	0.10.0	330.10.0
Pruit, William	-	790	50	7.2.8	847.2.8
Pruit, William	280	560	140		1680.0.0
			1 Negor @	700.0.0	
Pursley, William	-	200 (1)	-	8.10.0	208.10.0
Pyburn, Banjamin	290	400	170	3.4.0	863.4.0
Randolph, James	-	160	40	0.18.0	900.18.0
			1 Negor @	700.0.0	
Rankin, David	150	160	-	60 in hand	385.11.0
				15.11.0 at interest	
Ray, Joseph	-	320	80	20.8.0	420.8.0
Reed, George	100	320	70	2.0.0	492.0.0
Ritchey, William	1680	820	90	45.6.0	2635.6.0
Riggs, Edward	-	460	90	1.13.0	551.13.0
Riggs, Rubin	200	160	50	-	410.0.0
Robberts, Edmon	300	300	70	1.6.8	671.8.0
Robertson, Col.	-	800	-	4000.0.0	7050.0.0
			2 neagors	1400	
in another place			1 Neagor	150	
			1 neagor	700	
Robertson, Charls	600	-	150		750.0.0
				Grand Total -	8080.0.0
Robens, John	-	160	20	2.8.0	182.8.0
Robertson, David	300	350	50	16.0.0	716.0.0
Robertson, David	200	240	20	-	460.0.0
Robeson, James	500	400	50	11.4.0	961.4.0
Roggan, Thomas	720	630	150	0.18.0	1500.18.0
Roggers, James	1400	480	180	61.14.6	2146.14.6
Rolling, Mihel	-	840	70	239.13.4	124[illegible].13.4

Runland, William	-	160	90	4.0.0	254.0.0
Scott, Thomas	360	430	80	-	870.0.0
Semple, Samuel	-	400	-	0.8.0	400.8.0
Sheral, Jno.	-	150	-	282.4.0	432.4.0
		1 mare			
Sheral, Saml. Jr.	720	333	30	0.16.0	1083.16.0
Sheral, Saml. Senr.	1200	680	250	39.7.0	3019.7.0
			Negors @	850.0.0	
Sims, Joab	200	210	90	2.16.0	502.16.0
Simsons, Saml.	-	630	30	-	660.0.0
Sisks, John	200	490	130	-	820.0.0
Slone, Archebald	540	100 (1)	20	12.0.0	672.0.0
Smelser, Jacob	360	230	50	5.11.3	645.11.3
Smith, John	100	160	20	40.0.0	320.0.0
Smith, Thomas	200	640	90	21.0.0 in hand	951.0.0
Starns, Adam	-	400	30	-	430.0.0
Steel, William & Robert	550	-	-	-	550.0.0
Stephenson, Robert	150	500	40	-	690.0.0
Storry, William	300	640	70	12.8.0	982.8.0
Stuart, David	540	280	40	14.0.0	874.0.0
Stuart, Joseph	-	120	60	-	180.0.0
Studard, David	-	240	30	-	270.0.0
Sullavan, Saml.	-	260	20	0.5.4	280.5.4
Swerence, Jno.	150	100 1 cow	10	10.0.0	265.0.0
Taylor, Christepher	400	300	100	213.9.0	1013.9.0
Taylor, Leroy	300	620	80	47.4.0	1047.4.0
Temple, Major	-	500	60	-	2260.0.0
			2 negors & 1 child	1700.0.0	
Tettlock, John	2500	480	50	-	3030.0.0
Tolbet, James	-	-	-	12.17.8	12.17.8
Tompson, Andrew	-	560	80	68.5.6	708.5.6
Trimble, John	-	320	60	20.16.0	400.16.0
Trimble, Walter	-	100	40	24.5.0	164.5.0
Trimble, William	1080	400	50	24.4.0	1554.4.0
Umphery, Richard	300	680	60	4.0.0	1044.0.0
VanHouser, John	-	400	30	-	430.0.0
Vermillion, Jessey, single man		100 (1)	-	140.0.0	240.0.0
Vinsent, John	300	-	-	-	300.0.0
Walker, Daniel	-	160	30	10.0.0	200.0.0
Walker, Richard	450	160	50	-	660.0.0
Wadel, Jno.	1500	470	140	-	2110.0.0

Watson, Samuel			Pole Tax		
Weer, John	200	300	20	-	720.0.0
Land out of the line	200				
Whitanberger, Joseph	360	560	320	401.40.0	1641.40.0
Wiet, Samuel	200	240	50	-	490.0.0
Williams, John	200	240	80	52.0.0	572.0.0
Willson, James	630	520	120	200.0.0	1470.0.0
Willson, William not maryed	-	1 horse 130	-	-	130.0.0
Wilson, Joseph, Esqr.	400 & 300	840	200	132.8.0	1872.8.0
Wilson, Joseph	-	320	60	0.8.0	380.8.0
Wilson, Robert	300	580	30	10.18.4	920.18.4
Wilson, William	650	400	60	32.16.0	1142.16.0
Wood, Absolam, single man	-	-	-	39.10.8	39.10.8
Wood, Batholemy	1900	160	50	-	2110.0.0
Wood, John	-	350	60	-	410.0.0
Woodard, Thomas	150	70	-	100.0.0	320.0.0
		1 small mare			
Wright, James, a Quaker	100	120	40	-	260.0.0
Wyet, William	200	400	-	-	600.0.0
Yerby, Isam	-	80 (1)	20	0.2.8	100.2.8

UNDATED LIST - Likely after 1780-81, but before 1783- Same form & statistics as those 1780s Lists - Begins with "Mathew Huston" -

KEY TO COLUMNS: (1) List of Names, (2) Land, (3) Value, (4) Horses, (5) Value, (6) Cattle, (7) Value, (8) Cash, (9) Negros, (10) Value, (11) Total

Armstrong, Robert	300	378	5	262.10	7	70	28.16.0	-	-	732.6.0
Atkins, Charles	900	930.10	1	52.10	1	10	0.12.0	-	-	983.12.0
Bealey, Samuel	460	588	6	315	5	50	100.0.0	-	-	1053.0.0
Biram, Ebenezer	100	126	6	315	16	160	-	-	-	601.0.0
Breed, Avery	200	210	10	525	-	-	1.18.0	-	-	421.0.0
Calwell, Sarah	450	472.10	5	262.10	4	40	-	-	-	775.0.0
Chambers, ----n	200	273	7	368	10	100	4.0.0	-	-	795.0.0
Chambers, Alexander	200	265	1	52.10	4	40	-	-	-	357.10.0
Chambers, David	-	-	5	262.10	8	80	-	-	-	342.10.0
Craford, Isaac	-	-	3	157.10	11	110	-	1 @ £	700	967.10.0
Crump, Adam	200	245	4	140	8	80	34.8.0	-	-	499.8.0
Dunham, Joseph	-	-	26	1365	22	220	6.0.0	1 @ £	700	2291.0.0
Dunkin, Craven	-	-	2	105	2	20	-	-	-	125.0.0
Gann, -----	200	210	4	168	-	-	3.9.0	-	-	381.9.0
Gentrey, Charles	250	262.10	4	210	3	30	-	1 @ £	700	1202.10.0
Gist, Benjamin	1000	1022	5	262.10	6	60	-	-	-	1314.10.0
Gist, John	-	-	3	157.10	-	-	-	-	-	157.10.0
Gist, Joseph (Exempted of duty)	200	245	5	262.10	19	190	-	-	-	------
Hay, Charles	200	232.15	4	210	4	40	1.12.0	-	-	484.7.0
Hightour, John	POLE TAX									-
Howard, Absolom	-	-	4	119	2	20	13.9.0 30 (Bond, South Currancy)	-	-	152.9.0
Huston, Mathew	400	420	8	420	-	80	123.2.0	1 @ £	150	1193.2.0
Keeney, Joseph	-	-	3	157.10	-	-	141.4.0	-	-	298.14.0
Kuykendall, Benjamin	200	210	7	367.10	9	90	36.0.0	-	-	703.10.0
Low, Acquilla	600	680	7	367.10	11	110	7.8.6	-	-	1160.18.6
Lyle, -----	840	1022	10	525	6	60	157.19.0	1 @ £ 1 @ £ young @ £	1900 150 600	3914.19.6
Lyle, David	300	315	1	52.10	-	-	720.0.0	-	-	1087.10.0
McSpadden, John	-	-	2	105	2	20	78.8.0	-	-	203.8.0
Moore, Samuel, Jr.	200 200	210 220.10	3	157.10	2	20	-	-	-	610.0.0
Neal, Nicloss	200	210	2	105	12	120	-	-	-	335.0.0

Pearce, James	200	238	3	157.10	3	30	68.0.0	2 @ £1400	1883.10.0
Pyburn, Benjamin	400	420	5	262.10	8	80	8.9.0	- -	762.19.0
Randolph, Isom	-	-	1	52.10	-	-	-	- -	52.10.0
Reed, Jacob	-	-	8	920	5	50	19.16.0	- -	989.16.0
Reed, William	-	-	2	42	2	20	-	- -	62.0.0
Robinson, Luke	-	1126	-	-	3	30	-	- -	1156.0.0
Rutherford, Benjamin	-	-	2	105	4	40	-	- -	145.0.0
Sherral, Samuel, Sr	700	733	3	157.10	22	220	9.9.0	4 @ £2800 2 @ £ 500	3321.19.0
Tadlock, John	590	672	12	630	5	50	1426.1.0	- -	2778.1.0
Tadlock, Josuah	-	-	1	52.10	-	-	-	- -	52.10.0
Trimble, John	640	672	4	210	6	60	10.16.0	- -	952.16.0
Umphreys, Robart	100	355	8	336	3	30	9.0.0	- -	615.0.0
Weathers, Zebulon	-	-	2	105	5	50	-	- -	155.0.0
Wood, John	250	272	2	105	3	30	14.0.0	- -	421.0.0
Wright, James	100	171.10	2	105	7	70	20.0.0	- -	366.10.0
Wyatt, William	100	122.10	1	52.10	3	30	-	- -	205.0.0

....

NOTE: The size and quality of the paper, the enumerations, and other similarities strongly indicate the date of this List to be after the 1780-81 Lists, and before the 1787 List, which were found. It could be one District of the 1781 Lists, as only the Fifth District was found. MHMcC.

A Return of the Taxables of Capt Fain's Company - Returned by John Hammer, Esqr. 1787

KEY TO COLUMNS: (1) No Acres Land, (2) Poles, (3) Black Poles, (4) Males above 60, (5) Widows, (6) Feme Coverts, (7) Feme Soles, (8) Male Minors, (9) Male Infants, (10) Female Infants, (11) Black Male Infants, (12) Black Female Infants, (13) Casualities

Names	(1)	(2)	(3)	(4)	(5)	(6)	(7)	(8)	(9)	(10)	(11)	(12)	(13)	
Alison, John	75	1	-	-	-	-	-	-	-	-	-	-	-	Capt Greggs Co.
Bogart, Henry	-	1	-	-	-	1	-	-	2	2	-	-	-	
Bogart, Samuel	640	1	-	2	-	1	2	1	2	3	-	-	-	
Carr, John	250	1	2	-	-	1	2	1	3	3	1	-	-	
Collins, Joseph	100	1	-	-	-	1	-	-	6	1	-	-	-	Capt Greggs Co.
Daniel, William	200	1	-	-	-	1	2	-	1	2	-	-	-	
Denton, Samuel	250	1	-	-	-	1	-	-	3	-	-	-	-	
Duncan, Charles	432	1	-	-	-	1	1	2	2	3	-	-	-	
Fain, John	240	1	-	-	-	1	-	-	2	1	-	-	-	
Fain, Samuel	400	1	1	-	-	1	-	-	3	2	-	-	-	
Gibson, Thomas	100	1	-	-	-	1	-	-	1	1	-	-	-	
Great, David	100	1	-	-	-	-	-	-	-	-	-	-	-	
Grissom, William	300	1	1	-	-	1	-	-	2	4	-	-	-	
Hammer, Jacob	100	1	-	-	-	1	-	-	-	-	-	-	-	
Hodge, Frances	348	2	-	-	-	1	3	1	-	-	-	-	-	Capt Greggs Co.
Humphreys, John	100	-	-	1	-	1	-	2	1	-	-	-	-	
Kelley, Kinchin*	-	1	-	-	-	1	-	-	-	1	-	-	-	
McBee, William	150	1	-	-	-	1	-	-	1	3	-	-	-	
McMahon, John Blair	348	1	1	-	-	1	-	-	4	-	-	1	-	
Miller, Andrew	-	1	-	-	-	1	-	-	2	3	-	-	-	
Mitchel, Adam	300	1	-	-	-	1	1	2	3	3	-	-	-	
Morrison, Joseph	200	1	-	-	-	1	-	-	2	-	-	-	-	
Nelson, William	500	1	1	-	-	1	1	-	3	3	1	1	-	
Oldham, Henry	100	1	-	-	-	1	-	-	1	5	-	-	-	
Range, Peter	200	1	-	-	-	1	-	-	1	5	-	-	-	
Thomas, John	250	1	-	-	-	1	-	1	2	1	-	-	-	NOTE:
Tullis, Jonathan	400	1	-	-	-	1	-	-	2	2	-	-	-	Capt Greggs Co was
Tullis, Michael	280	1	-	-	-	1	-	-	3	2	-	-	-	in Sullivan Co.
Underwood, Samuel	-	1	-	-	-	-	-	-	-	-	-	-	-	MHMcC.
White, John	640	1	-	-	-	1	-	-	2	1	-	-	-	

*...Discharged.

There are no Black Males above 60 yrs on this List.

Justices appointed to take in the Inventories of Taxable Property for the years 1790-1791 in the bounds of Captain Greer & Maxfield companies for the years 1790-1791.

Ord- that Edmd Williams Esq. take in the Inventories of the Taxable property within the bounds of Capt Williams' Company for the year 1790-1791.

Ord- That John Strain, Esquire, take in the Inventories of the Taxable property within the bounds of Capt Murrays & Campbells Companies for the years 1790-1791.

Ord- That John Chism Esquire take in the Inventories of the Taxable property within the Bounds of Captain Browns Company for the year 1790-1791.

....

A List of the Company in Captain (Thomas) Biddle's Company for the years 1790-1791

Names	Land	Wh Pole	Bl Poles
Alexander, Francis		1	
Alexander, John	250	1	
Bell, James	100	1	
Biddle, Thomas	400	1	
Blair, Major John	249	1	
Blair, Richard	170	1	
Blair, Robert	175	1	
Brown, David	200	1	
Campbell, John, Esqr.	300	1	
Cason, John	850	1	
Carson, Andrew	------	1	
Carson, Moses	450	1	
Davis, George	100	1	
Harrison, Michael	360	1	
Houston, William		1	
Keevill, Richard		1	
King, Henry	170	1	
Martin, Joseph		1	
Rodgers, Moses		1	
Rodgers, Thomas	500	1	
Sands, Benjamin	220	1	
Shanks, James	352		
Shanks, William		1	
Shields, David	250	1	
Shields, George	197	1	
Shields, Joseph	150	1	
Smith, Richard		1	
Stewart, Charles		1	
Thompson, Andrew	150	1	
Trotter, John	150	1	1
Vickery, Francis		1	
Williams, John	200	1	

....

A List of the Taxable Property in Capt Biddle's Company for the years 1790-1791 & 1792. Made out by Jas. Sevier, Clk.

1790

An Undated List of Taxable Property in Captain Blair's Company
Note: Likely belongs to 1790 as it is of that form
(On same sheet with Captain Depue)

Names	Land	White Poles	Black Poles	Studs
Alexander, Frances		1		
Alexander, John	210	1		
Alexander, Jonathan		1		
Babb, George	300	1		
Biddle, Thomas	500	1		
Bell, James	100	2		
Blair, Hugh	520	1		
Blair, John		1		
Blair, John	50	1		
Blair, John	277	1	2	
Blair, Joseph		1		
Blair, Robert	175	1	2	
Blakely, Daniel		1		
Blakely, Robert	506	1		
Boid, George	200	1		
Brown, David	300			
Brown, David M. ?		1		
Burk, John	175	1		
Campbell, Hugh	100	1		
Campbell, John		1	1	
John Campbell, guardian for orphans of Robt Fowler	185			
Campbell, Robert	100	1		
Campbell, William		1		
Carmichael, John	200		1	
Carson, Andrew	100	1		
Carson, John	700			
Carson, Moses	85			
Davis, George		1		
Davis, Samuel	124	1		
Fowler, Robert, dec'd (see John Campbell above)				
Hail, Abednego	100	1		
Humphreys, William	590	1	1	
Kendall, Richard		1		
King, Henery	170	1		
Loid, Abel in Gr	103	1		
MacLin, Alexander	200	1		1
McC-----, John	300	1		
McCollom, John	50	1		
McWhorter, John	150	1		
Martin, Joseph	100			
Miser, Peter		1		
Patterson, James	143	1		
Richards, David		1		
Robertson, James		1		
Rodgers, James		1		
Rodgers, Moses		1		
Rodgers, Thomas	500			
Sands, Benjamin	220	1		
Sands, Edmond	57	1		

Captain Blair's Company (cont'd)

Names	Land	White Poles	Black Poles	Studs
Seahorn, James		1		
Shanks, James	200	1		
Shanks, William	150	1		
Shields, David	250	1		
Shields, George	250	1		
Shields, Joseph	220	1		
Smith, Richard		1		
Stanton, Richard	28	1		
Thomson, Andrew	157		2	
Thomson, Andrew		1		
Williams, John	200	1		
(?) Iffin, Henry J.	250	1	2	

Recorded J. Sevier

....

A List of Taxables for the year 1790 taken by John Chisolm, Esq.

Persons Name	No. Acres	Situation	Free White Poles	Black Poles
Bailey, Reudin	170	Nolachucky	1	
Bare, Alex	640	do	1	9
Barnet, William in trust for				
Bounds, Jesse	400	do river	1	2
Bounds, Obediah			1	
Boye, Henry			1	
Brown, Benjamin	220	do	1	
Brown, Jacob	220	do	1	
Brown, John G.	220	do	1	
Brown, Ruth	427	do		3
Brown, Thomas	220	do	1	1
Carsoner, Jacob	70	Cherokee	1	
Chism, John			1	5
Collett, Isaac			1	1
Colyer, William	130	Nolachucky	1	2
Dobkins, Evan	76	Up Little Limestone	1	
Embree, Isaac			1	
Embree, Moses	100	Nolachucky		
Foose, Nicholas	150	Head of Clark Branch	1	
French, Peter	200	Cherokee Creek		
Green, William	200	Nolachucky		
Hammon, Christopher			1	
Hampton, Robert	200	do	1	
Handley, George, Sr.			1	
Keel, John	178	Cherokee	1	
Murphy, Dennis			1	4
Robertson, Chas., Jr.			1	
Robinson, Col. Chas.	334	do		4
Rodgers, Joseph	50	N Chuckey	1	
Thomas, Isaac, Senr.			1	7
Weir, John	100	Cherokee		

Taken the 28th day of Jany 1792 - John Chism Esq.

1790

A List of the Taxable property in Captain Depews company
Undated - Belongs likely to 1790 as of same form

Names	Land	White Poles	Black Poles	Stud Horses	Town Lots
Adair, James	100				
Allison, Robert	675	1	2		
Allison, Ann	145				
Allison, Robert	400	1	4		
Anderson, John	200	1			
Anderson, Margaret			1		
Archer, Benjamin	100	1			
Archer, John	200				
Bailes, Isaac	130				
Beals, Jacob	250	1			
Bell, Elesebeth	140				
Bell, George	145	1			
Blair, James	300	1			
Blair, John	125	1			
Blair, Samuel	175	1	3		
Boman, Elias	100	2			
Boman, Elias, Grn Co.	200				
Burk, William		1			
Campbell, Abraham	153	1			
Campbell, James	250	1			
Campbell, John	200	1			
Carmichael, James	850		2		
Carson, David	58	1			
Carson, David	253	1			
Carson, Robert		1		1	
Carson, William	150	1			
Carsoner, David	100				
Cowan, John	240	1			
Craig, Thomas		1			
Currey, John		1			
Depue, Capt. Isaac	118	1			
Duncan, Andrew	229	1			
Duncan, Joseph	310	1		1	
Farguson, Alexander		1			
Farguson, Henry		1			
Farguson, John	293	1			
Farguson, Thomas		1			
Gann, Nathaniel	300	1			
Glass, William	434				
Graham, William		1			
Hunt, Uriah	240	1	1		
Hunter, James		1			
Kelsey, William	300	1	1		
McOrd, James	318				
McCorkle, Joseph	200	1			
McCord, David	100	1			
McNitt, Alexander	150			1	
McNitt, John		1			
Machlin, Robert	200				
Montgomery, William	105½	1			
Neel, Samuel	113	1			

Capt Depew's Company- likely 1790, as same form (cont'd)

Names	Land	White Poles	Black Poles	Stud Horses	Town Lots
Netherland, Isaac		1			
Newel, Joseph		1			
Odeneal, Bartholomew	100				
Reed, James	106½	1			1
Reed, James	200				
Robertson, James		1			
Robertson, David	51	1			
Robertson, Mary	240				
Russell, David	282	1			
Russelley (?) David	242				
Shaw, Francis	100		1		
Shaw, Samuel	200	1	1		
Shipley, Thomas	200	1			
Simmons, (?) Samuel		1			
Smith, Abraham in Gr Co	265				
Smith, Abraham	400	1			
Stewart, David, Sr.	329				
Stewart, David, Jr.	50	1			
Stewart, John	42				
Stuart, Alexander		1			
Stuart, Charles	300	1			
Strain, John	100	1			
Tadlock, Lewis	300	1	1		
Taylor, Leeroy	250	1	2		
Thomson, David	100				
Trotter, Alexander	176	2			
Tucker, Joseph	345	1			
Walker, William	180	1			
Witt, Jesse		1			
Woods, William	155				

....

Return of the Taxable Property of the Inhabitants within the District of Captain Greers Company for the year 1790

Names	Acres	Free Poles	Black Poles
Arendell, John	100	1	
Bass, Jeremiah		1	8
Bowers, Leonard	50	1	
Carriger, Godfrey, Sr.	2167	1	
Carriger, Michael		1	
Carriger, Nicholas	550	1	
Cox, Abraham		1	
Cox, Richd		1	
Duggard, William	200	1	
Duncan, Thomas		1	
Gillam, John		1	
Grears, John		1	
Greer, Captain Alexd		1	1
Greer, Alexander, Senr.	216	1	2
Greer, Joseph	400	1	1

Captain Greers Company (Cont'd)

Names	Acres	Free Poles	Black Poles
Heatherick, Jacob	300	1	
Heatherick, Jacob Jr		1	
Heatherick, Joseph		1	
Hollitt, Solomon	283	1	
Humphreys, Elisha		1	
Ivy, Jas.	50	1	
Kerr, John		1	
Kite, Richard	150	1	
Lacy, John		1	
Lincoln, Isaac	500	1	
Miller, Thos	200	1	
Moore, John Parker		1	
Murrey, William		1	
Nave, Teter	350	1	
Sevier, Abraham			
Sevier, Joseph		1	
Sevier, Valentine, Senr	360		
Smithpeters, John Michael	375	1	
Tate, Samuel			
Tipton, Isaac	200	1	
Tipton, Samuel	744	1	

NOTE: Copied on back of Total Schedule for 1791-

....

The Taxables of Captain Henley's Company for 1790
Taken by John Were, J P

Names	White Pole	Land	Black Poles
Allison, John	1		
Bitner, John	1		
Blackburn, Archibald	1	200	2
Brown, William	1	150	1
Brown, Wm	1		
Broyles, Adam	1		
Broyles, Adam	1	300	
Broyles, Cyrus	1	100	2
Broyles, Reuben	1		
Broyles, Samuel	1	250	
Clark, John	1	200	
Clark, William	1	300	3
Cowan, Susannah		150	
Galliher, James	2	400	1
Gann, Adam		150	
Gann, Adam	1	100	
Gann, Clem	1	100	
Gann, Isaac	1		
Gann, John	1		
Gann, Nace	1		
Gann, Thomas	1		
Gordon, John	1		

Captain Henley's Company (cont'd)

Names	White Pole	Land	Black Poles
Haines, Andrew	1		
Hanley, Samuel	1	200	
Hanna, John	1		
Harbison, William	1		
Humphrey, Richard	1	307	
Huston, Absolum	1		
Kennedy, David	1	200	
Leeman, John	1		
Logan, Charles	1	17-	
McKee, Alexr	1	400	
McKee, John	1	100	
Moore, Alex	1		
Moore, Wm		357	3
Nelson, Southey	1	1	
Nelson, Wm	1		
Painter, Adam	1	200	
Reed, Andrew	1	284	2
Robertson, George	1		
Seaver, John	1		8
Shields, Henry	1		
Waddle, John	1	189	
Waddell, John	1		
Weer, John	1	514	
Wilhoit, Conrad	1	205	
Wilhoit, Samuel	1		
Woods, Michl	1	640	2

....

Capt Thomas Maxfields Company for the year 1790

NOTE: This Tax List was not found, but two Scraps were found to be added to Maxfields List.

#1-

Carter, Landon 3000 Acres- 1 wh pole- 4 black poles
Cobb, Pharoh 500 " 7 Poles
Hendrake, John 440 " 1 Pole
" " for 1791 500 " 1 Pole
Robertson, John-for 1790 & 1791
50 " 1 Pole

The Return of Taxable Property of Capt Maxfields Company, except myself & that in Captain Greers Company.

L Carter.

....

#2-

Captain Thomas Maxfields-for the year 1790-
194 acres- 1 Pole.
& for 1791-- the same.
Tate, Samuel- for 1790 & 1792-
779 acres- 1 Black Pole.

....

1790

A List of Taxable Property in the bounds of my Company for the year 1790------ John Millikin.

Names	Poles	Land
Adams, Wm	1	200
Bowman, John	1	
Breedin, William	1	100
Broyles, Abraham	2	100
Campbell, John	2	300
Cleeck, Martin	1	
Cleeck, Suens (?)		200
Click, Peter	1	
Crookshanks, George	1	133
Denton, Jonathan	1	100
Doak, Rev. Sam.	2	180
Gann, Adam Jun.	1	100
Gann, Adam Senr		100
Gann, John	1	320
Gann, Nathan	1	
Gann, Thos.	1	
Gillespie, Thos	3	1090
Grahams, John	1	
Hall, Wm	1	245
Hannah, Andrew	1	
Holt, Alex	1	
Holt, Jas.	1	
Jordan, Quens (?)	1	375
Leman, John	1	
Lott, Casper	1	
Lyle, John	1	470
McEwen, Alex	1	312
Millikin, John	1	216
Montgomery, Alex	1	150
Montgomery, Hugh	1	
Montgomery, James	1	200
Montgomery, Wm	1	
Nelson, John	2	200
Roberts, John	1	
Scot, Thos.	1	200
Scroggs, Ebenezer	1	203
Stevenson, William	1	300
Taylor, David	1	150
Thompson, Andrew	1	
Trimble, Wm	1	400
Vickery, Francis	1	
Yeager, Solomon	2	100

....

Captain Henry Nelson's Company- Undated-but of same form as 1790- so included in that year.

Names	Land	Wh Pole	Bl Pole	Town Lot	Stud
Adair, James	100				
Alexander, John	166	1			
Allison, Robert	1000	1	4	1	

Captain Henry Nelson's Company (cont'd)

Names	Land	Wh Pole	Bl Pole	Town Lot	Stud
Bails, David	56	1			
Bails, Isaac	74				
Bails, Jacob	190				
Barcroft, Jonathan		1		9	
Barkley, John	137	1	1	0	1
Bell, George	178	1	1		
Blair, Samuel	200	1	1		
Blair, Thomas		1			
Bowman, Elias	124				3½
Bowman, George	150	1			
Carson, David	125	1			
Carson, Robert	134	1			
Carson, William	49				
Charlton, John		1			
Charlton, Pointan, Jr.	700	1	2		
Clawson, Jacob	147			2	
Cunningham, James	125	1			
Davis, John		1			
Davis, Nathaniel	400		3		
Depue, Isaac	225	1			
Duncan, Andrew	229				
Duncan, Joseph	418		1		
Farguson, Alexander	78	1			
Farguson, John	59	1			
Farguson, Thomas	138	1			
Ford, John		1			
Glass, Joseph		1		3	0
Glass, William Junior		1			
Glass, William, Senior	384				
Gray, William			1		
Guin, William	150	1			
Hartman, Joseph	100				
Haslet, Kinster (?)	50				
Hunt, Uriah	1280	1	3		
Jones, Nathaniel	100	1			
Kees, Philip	160	1			
Kufhover, Nicholas	186	1			
Korts, John		1		1½	0
Langley, Thomas		1			
McAdams, Hugh	100	1			
McAdams, Robert	100	1			
McCaleb, Ann					1
McCary, Joseph		1		1½	0
McClure, James		1		1	
McLin, Robert	200				
McLin, William		1			
McNutt, Anthony	138	0	1		
Marsh, Henry	239	1			
Mathes, William					
Miller, William		1	1	8½	0
Million, John	106	1			
Nelson, Nathan	100	1			

1790

Captain Henry Nelson's Company (cont'd)

Names	Land	Wh Pole	Bl Pole	Town Lot	Stud
Nelson, Thomas		1			
Orre, Robert	70	1			
Palmer, Joshua		1			
Powel, Henry	161	1			
Purselley, William	154				
Raston, John	155	1			
Rector, Benjamin		1			
Richards, David		1			
Rodgers, William	166	1			
Rusell, David	300				
Russell, George			1	2	0
Seay, Christian	285				
Shields, John		1			
Shields, William		1		1	0
Simmons, John		1			
Slaughter, William	57	1			
Smith, Abraham	350				
Smith, Richard		1			
Smith, William	850	1			
Snyder, Daniel		1			
Squib, John	211	1	1		
Stelle, Andrew		1	2	4	0
Stewart, Alexander		0	1		
Stewart, David	643	2	2	1	0
Sueman (?), Jacob	122	1			
Taylor, Leeroy	222				
Tucker, Jonathan	50	1			
Tucker, John	331	1	0	1½	0
Tucker, Nicholas	156	1			
Van Seyou (?), Moses		1			
Walker, William	184	1			
White, John		1			
Woods, Isaac		1			
Woods, William	155				

....

Return of the Taxable Property in Capt. Shipley's Company for the years 1790 & 1791.

Names	1790			1791		
	wp	blp	acres	wpl	blp	acres
Austin, John	1	0	350	1	0	350
Britten, Joseph	1	0	172	1	0	372
Bull, Jacob	1	1	225	1	1	225
Bullington, William	1	0	150	1	0	
Burch, Richard	0			1		100
Chamberlain	1	1	110	1	1	110
Chapman, John	1			1	0	100
Collins, Joshua	1			1	0	
Cotrel, John				1		
Crouch, John Senr			100	0	0	100
Demott, Robert	1	0	200	1	0	200

		1790			1791	1790
Names	wp	blp	acres	wpl	blp	acres
Dunham, Charles	1			1		
Ellis, John	1	0	100	1	0	100
Epheson, Anthony	1	1	250	1	1	250
Epheson, Samuel	1	1	250	1		250
Farley, Odbediah	1			1		
Finn, Peter	1	0	100	1		
Finley, Thomas	1	0	118	1		
Foord, Mordecai	1	0	100	1	0	100
Giddings, Clark				1		
Gott, Anthony			550			550
Gott, John	1	0	125	1	0	125
Gray, George	0	1	338	0	1	138
Gray, Robert	1			1	1	
Gristham, Thomas	1	1	184	1	1	184
Haile, Abedenego	1	2	1136	1	2	1036
Haile, Joshua	1	0	270	0	0	270
Haile, George, Junr				1	2	250
Hall, Nathaniel	1	0	291	1	0	291
Holland, Benjamin	1	2	420	1	2	420
Hunt, Jesse	1	0	306	1	0	386
Hunt, Uriah	1	0	230	1		
Lane, Elezebeth	0	0	230	0	0	230
McCubbins, Zachariah	1	1	200	1	1	200
McDonald, John	1	0	225	1	0	225
Maden, Andrew	1	0	150	1		
Martin, James				1	0	99
Moore, Samuel	1	0	240	1	0	240
Moseley, John	1	0	49-2/4	1	0	49-2/4
Mulkey, Jonathan	1	0	100	1	0	100
Noban, George	1	4	300	1	4	300
Oen, James	1	0	100	1	0	100
Paine, Reubin	1	0	200	1	0	200
Shaw, Benjamin	1	1	186	1	1	186
Shaw, Samuel	0	0	100	1	0	100
Shipley, Benjamin	2	0	170	0	0	170
Shipley, Edward	1	0	490	2	0	490
Shipley, Peter	1	0		1		150
Shipley, Thomas	1	0	200	1	0	200
Standback, Michael	0			1		
White, Archible	1	0	200	1	0	200

Returned by me- Joseph Britten, Aug 10, 1791.

Casualties - The under mentioned names are persons who are returned to me as being warned to meet on the day I appointed to take the Taxable property of Capt. Shipleys District, have failed to give in to me.

- George Haile, son of George, Jr.
- Elesebeth Duncan
- Peter Holland.

Joseph Britten.

....

1790

Return of the Taxable Property in Capt Stones Company for the years 1790 & 1791. Returned by me- Joseph Britten, Aug 10, 1791

Names	1790 Poles wh	1790 Poles bl	1790 acres land	1791 Poles wh	1791 Poles bl	1791 acres land
Baker, Isaac	0	0	110	0	0	110
Bean, Edmund	1	0		1	0	
Bean, George	1			1		
Bean, Russell	1		400	1	0	400
Beard, Robert	1		142	1-	0	241
Brown, John	1		450	1	0	450
Car, Thomas	1		120	1	0	120
Carney, Thomas Senr	0	2	520	0	2	520
Cowin, John	1	0	97	1	0	97
Cox, James	1	1	50	1	1	50
Crabtree, John	1	0	100	1	0	100
Crouch, Joseph	1	0	355	1	0	155
Crabtree, William	1	0		1	0	
Dungworth, Charles	1	0	110	1	0	110
Dyer, David	1	0		1	0	100
Dyer, John	1	0	100	1	0	100
Ellis, Shable	0			1		
Ellis, William	1	1	325	1	2	325
Engle, George	1	0	200	1	0	200
Engle, Michael	1	0	225	1	0	225
Ensor, Thomas	1	0	45	1	0	45
Everett, James	1	1	100	1	1	100
Gates, Jacob	2	0	200	2	0	200
Gates, Richard	1	0	120	1	0	120
Hagan, Arthur	1			1		
Hall, Samuel	1			1		
Hammer, Baltis, Sr	0			1		75
Hammer, Baltis, Jr	0			1		
Hickey, David			100	0		100
Hodges, John Senr	2	2	330	2	2	330
Hoss, Jacob	1		700	1		700
Hunt, Thomas	1		270	1	0	270
Jinkins, George	2	0	500	2	0	500
Long, Henry	1		115	1		115
McCloud, James	1			1		
McCloud, William Jr	1			1		
McCord, William Senr	0		132	0	0	132
Matlock, Zachariah	1	0	150	1	0	150
Melvan, John	1	1	140	1	1	140
Melvan, Samuel	1	0		1		
Melvan, Thomas	0	0	150	0	0	150
Milborn, Samuel				1		
Miller, Peter	1		200	1	0	200
Mitchell, James	0			1		
Moser, Anthony	1			1		40
Nelson, John	0			1	0	100
Oldham, Henry	1	0	100	1	2	100
Pearce, Philip Godfred	1	0	150	1	0	150
Pritchard, Charles	1		150	1	0	150

Captain Stones Company (cont'd)

Names	1790 Poles wh	bl	acres land	1791 Poles wh	bl	acres land
Starnes, Peter	1	0	150	1	0	150
Stone, Robert	1	1	243	1	1	243
Stone, William	1	1	243	1	1	243
Ward, William				1		
Whethers, William	1	0	137	1	0	137
Whiley, William				1		
York, William				1		

Casuelties----

The undermentioned names are persons who are returned to me as being warned to meet on the day I appointed to take the Taxable property of Captain Stones District and have failed to give in to me.

David Dunham
Isaac Mange
Peter Brown

....

Captain Tullis's Company for 1790.

NOTE: 1 Scrap- There is no List of Captain Tullis' Company.

An Inventory of Wiliam Cobb's Taxable Property-

Land.................. 720 acres
White Pole........... 1
Black Poles.......... 10

The Same for the year 1791

Land.................. 720 acres
White Pole........... 1
Black Poles.......... 7

The above to be added to Captain Tullis Company.
Returned by Landon Carter.

....

List of Taxable Property Taken by Richard White for 1790.

Names	Free Poles	Slave poles	acres
Ashurst, John	1	0	100
Baker, William	1		
Beckman, Michael	1		
Bowman, Cornelius	over age		100
Bullinger, Peter	1	0	150
Campbell, Zachariah	over age	0	200
Chambers, John	1		
Coffee, Charley	1		100
Cook, William	1		

List of Taxable Property Taken by Richard White (cont'd)

Names	Free Poles	Slave poles	acres
Duggard, Julius	1		50
Farguson, John	1		100
Flannery, William	1		
Ford, Joseph	1		175
Gentry, Joseph	1		100
Griffin, William	1		304
Grindstaff, Catherine	0		100
Guinn, Champ	1		
Heatherley, Ewins	over age		95
Hoskins, Ninean	1		
Jenkins, Roland	1		248
Jones, James	1		
Jones, Lewis Senr	over age		100
Jones, Lewis, Jr	1		
Kane, John	1		
Kane, Peter	1		
Miller, Daniel	2		300
Miller, George	1		60
Miller, John	1		100
Perkins, George	1		200
Perkins, Joshua	1		
Potter, Hannah			100
Rainboldt, Adam	1		
Runnals, Henry	1		
Runnolds, Moses	1		
Smith, Jacob	1		100
Smith, Edward			600
Smith, John	1		200
Snyder, Adam	1		115
Swiney, William	1		
Tate, John	1		100
Vandergriff, Jacob	1		
Vantreece, John	1		325
Waggoner, David	1	2	500
Wallace, Aaron	1		
Whitson, Thomas	over age	1	350
Wilder, Joab	over age		50
Wilson, John Senr	over age	1	83
Wilson, John Junr	1		70
Wilson, Samuel	1		
Wilson, William	1		

....

List of Taxable Property Return'd by E. Williams for the year 1790-1791.

Persons Named	Acres of Land	White Polls	Black Polls
Ash, Thos Lewis	0	1	
Ball, Amos	206	1	
Bayley, Cottrell	500	1	
Boring, Nicholas		1	

List of Taxable Property Return'd by E. Williams (cont'd)

Persons Named	Acres of Land	White Polls	Black Polls	
Boring, William	100	1		
Cooper, Job	150	1		
Cooper, Joel Senr	177	1		
Cooper, Joel		1		
Cunningham, Mary	590			
Davis, Nathan	362½	1		...100 deducted for 1790
Davis, William	478	1		
Denton, Isaac	75	1		
Denton, Joseph	185	1		
Eagin, Barny	189	1		
English, Robert	300			
Gourley, Thos	50	1		...Land only for 1790
Hains, George	300	1		...1 year
Hampson, James		1		...for 1 year
Haun, Adam	200	1		...1 year
Haun, Bauston		2		...1 year
Hendrix, Solomon	113	1		
Henry, Abraham		1		
Widow Elizabeth Hider	200			
Hider, John	200	1		
Hider, Michael	142¼	1		...1 year
Humphris, Jesse	296	1		
Ivey, Howel		1		
Job, David	280	1	2	
Lusk, Robert	264	1		
McFall, Francis	235	1		
Macinturf, Christopher	482	1		
Macinturf, Gasper	100	1		
Macinturf, John	200	1		
Macinturf, John Jr	218	1		
McNabb, David	755	1		
McNabb, William	446 3/4s	2		
Nelson, Henry	103	1	2	
Nelson, Jane	103	0	2	
Peoples, John	166	1		
Odle, Caleb	100			
Price, Mordecai	400	1		
Widow Susanna Pugh	471			
Reasoner, Garret	280	1	2	
Reno, Charles		1		
Smalling, Saml	29 3/4s	1		
Stuart, James Esqr.	4422	1	6	
Taylor, Andrew	225	1		
Taylor, Isaac	700	1		
Taylor, Matthew		1		
Taylor, Nathaniel	255	1		
Tipton, Colo John	2013	2		
Watson, William	600	1		
Whitson, Jesse	280	1	3	
Williams, Edmund	1440	1	4	
Wood, William	177			

....

1790

List of Taxable Property Taken by Order of the Court.

NOTE: Undated- but form resembles the Lists of 1790-1791.
No Captain Listed.

Names	Land	WhPoles	Bl Poles
Allison, Robert	245	0	
Anderson, John	200	1	
Archer, William		1	
Barron, Joseph	180		
Bell, George	145		
Bell, John	100	1	
Bell, William	70	1	
Blair, Agnes	300		
Blair, James	260	1	
Blair, James	300	1	
Blair, Jane	300		
Blair, John	300	1	
Blair, John	200	1	
Blair, Mary	300		
Blair, Samuel		1	1
Bleackely, Robert	470	1	
Boman, Elias	100	1	
Campbell, John	271	1	
Campbell, John Senr	211	1	
Carmichael, James	350	1	1
Carr, Thomas	90	1	
Carson, David Senr	100	2	
Carson, David Junr	280	1	
Carson, Robert Junr		1	
Carson, Robert	160	1	
Carson, William	150	1	
Carson, William	200	1	
Chinchlow, Charles	100	1	1
Chinchlow, George	150	1	
Chinchlow, John	125	1	5
Depew, Isaac	10	1	
Dotson, William		1	
Dun, James	200	1	
Duncan, Andrew	329	1	
Duncan, Anthony	200	1	
Duncan, Joseph	100	1	
Emberton, Richard	150	1	
Farguson, John	300	1	
Ford, John	170	1	
Glass, William	434	1	
Glasscock, Archibald	240	1	1
Hail, Abednego	100	1	
Jones, Nathaniel	100	1	
Law, James		1	
McBee, Samuel	100	1	
McCall, John	250	1	
McClain, Robert	200	1	
McCord, James	300	2	
McCorkle, Joseph	200	1	
McFerson, Bartin		1	

List of Taxable Property Taken by Order of the Court (cont'd)

Names	Land	WhPoles	Bl Poles
McFerson, Daniel	150	1	
McFerson, Henery	250	1	
McKnitt, Anthony	85	1	
Montgomery, William	116	1	
Murrey, Morgan	200	1	
Odnell, Bartholomew	100	1	
Purselley, William	250		
Richards, David		1	
Rion, James	110	1	
Robertson, David	245	1	
Russell, David	282	1	
Smith, Abraham	495	1	
Smith, Anderson	250	1	
Stewart, David	370	1	
Taylor, Leeroy	254	1	1
Thompson, David	100	1	
Trotter, Alexander	99	1	
Tucker, Nicholass	305	1	
Whealock, John	350	1	

....

1791

Justices appointed in 1790 for 1790 & 1791 (see 1790 List).

....

Capt. Biddle's Co. (see 1790 List).

....

A list of Taxables for the year 1791 Taken by John Chisom.

Names	number acres	Situation	white poles	black poles
Bailey, Reubin	170	Nolachucky river	1	
Barnit, William, for Alexander Bane	640	do	1	9
Bounds, Jesse				2
Bounds, Obediah			1	
Boye, Henry			1	
Brown, Benjamine	220	Nolachucky river	1	
Brown, Jacob	220	do	1	
Brown, John Gordon	220	do	1	
Brown, Ruth	427	do		3
Brown, Thomas	220	do	1	1
Carsoner, Jacob	70	do	1	
Chisom, John			1	5
Collett, Isaac			1	1
Colyer, William	430	do	1	2
Dobkinds, Evan	761½	Little Limestone	1	
Embree, Isaac	64	Nolachucky river	1	
Embree, Moses	100	do		
Foose, Nicholas	150	head of Clarks Creek		
French, Peter	200	Cherokee		
Green, William	200	Nolachucky river		
Hammens, Christopher			1	
Hampton, Robert	200	do	1	
Handley, George			1	
Keel, John	170	Cherokee	1	
Messer, Joseph			1	
Murphy, Dennis			1	4
Robertson, Charles, junr			1	
Robertson, Colo Charles	334	do	0	4
Rodgers, Joseph	50	Nolachucky River	1	
Thomas, Isaac, senr	0		1	7
Weir, John	100			

Taken in the 28th day of Jany 1792 by John Chisolm.

....

A list of Taxable Property in Captain Hanley's Company for 1791 taken by John Weer, J.P.

Names	white poles	land	black poles
Allison, John	1		
Bitner, John	1		
Blackburn, Archibald	1	400	2
Brown, Wm.	1	150	1

Captain Hanley's Company (cont'd)

Names	white poles	land	black poles
Brown, Wm.	1		
Broyles, Adam	1	300	
Broyles, Adam	1		
Broyles, Cyrus		100	2
Broyles, Reuben	1		
Broyles, Samuel	1	250	
Clark, John	1	200	
Clark, William	0	300	2
Collam, Jonathan	1		
Conklin, David	1		
Cowan, Susannah	0	150	
Gallaher, James	2	400	1
Gann, Adam	1	215	
Gan, Adam	1	150	
Gann, Clem	1	100	
Gann, Isaac	1		
Gann, John	1	215	
Gann, Nace	1	220	
Gann, Thomas	1		
Gordon, John	1		
Hanna, John	1		
Hanley, Samuel	1	200	
Harbison, William	1		
Heines, Andrew	1		
Humphrey, Richard	1	307	
Huston, Absolem	1		
Keneday, David	1	200	
Leaman, John	1		
Logan, Charles	1	175	0
McKee, Alexr	1	400	
McKee, John	1	100	
Moor, Alex	1	0	1
Moore, Wm.	1	357	4
Nelson, Southey	1	1	
Nelson, Wm.	1		
Penter, Adam	1	200	
Reed, Andrew	1	281	2
Robertson, George	1		
Seaver, John	1	3	8
Waddell, John	1		
Waddell, John Sr.	1	189	
Were, John	1	514	
Willhoit, Conrad	1	205	
Willhoit, Samuel	1		
Woods, Michael	1	640	4

....

A List of Taxable Property in the bounds of John Millikins Company for the year 1791.

Names	poles	acres land
Adams, Wm.	1	100
Archer, Benjamin	1	

John Millikins Company (cont'd)

Names	poles	acres land
Bellemy, Elisha (?)	2	
Boothe, Joseph	1	200
Bottles, Henery	1	125
Breeden, Wm	1	100
Broyles, Abraham	2	
Broyles, Nicholas	3	130
Click, Lewis	2	200
Cox, William	10	220
Crookshanks, George	1	133
Dentin, Jonathan	1	100
Doak, Rev. Saml	2	100
Embree, John	1	200
Embree, Thos	1	413
Gillespie, Thos	1	1090
Gordon, Lewis	1	250
Green, Joshua	1	170
Guin, Hugh		200
Hall, Wm. Jr.	1	245
Hall, Wm. Sr.	1	
Hanna, And.	1	320
Hatcher, John	1	
Hatcher, Samson	0	225
Lyle, John	1	470
McAlister, John	1	225
McEwen, Alex.	1	300
McCrath, Andrew	0	250
Mathes, Alex	4	400
Montgomery, Alex.	1	100
Montgomery, James	1	200
Montgomery, Thos.	1	100
Nelson, John	2	200
Padfield, William	1	
Robertson, John	1	
Scott, Thos.	1½	200
Scroggs, Ebenezer	1	203
Smith, John	1	
Stephenson, William	1	300
Sunderland, Isaac	1	
Taylor, David	1	100
Willson, Isaac	1	350
Yeager, Solomon	2	200

....

Captain North's Company 1791

Name	acres land	white	black
Allison, James	1100	1	2
Andis, Fedrick	150	1	
Anthony, Abraham	400	1	
Bails, Daniel	200		
Balis, John	300	1	
Boring, Ablam		1	

Captain North's Company (cont'd)

Name	acres land		white	black
Boring, Chene			1	
Boring, Ezekiel	70		1	
Boring, James	750			
Brooks, Giles	300		1	
Comtain, Jeremiah Horn			1	
Coper, Joseph	69		2	
Dickson, Thos.	100		1	
Ervin, Jas	200		1	
Ervin, Robert	180		1	
Ervin, Sam	105		1	
Fine, John	250		1	
Fitzgerell, George	25		1	
Freintch, George	250		1	
Goodpasture, Isaack			1	
Goodpasture, Solomon	62		1	
Got, John	100		1	
Hartzel, Hanna	30			
Hedrick, Charles	140			
Heslin, Abraham junr			1	
Heeslin, Abram senr	223		1	
Hestain, Samuel			1	
Hufman, David	250		1	
Hunter, Jacob	138		1	
Huntter, John	850		1	
Leatch, William	100		1	
Leman, John junr			1	
Leman, John senr	450		1	
McCree, Danel	200	disputed	1	
McCree, Daniell	100		1	
Moor, James			1	
Nortth, George			1	
North, John	100			
Ozemes, Philip	200			
Rodgers, John			1	
Rodgers, Robert	200		1	
Rodgers, Thomas			1	
Roos, Hose	320		1	
Smith, Edward	218		1	2
Steelman, John Hance	0		0	
Tadlock, John	650		1	6
Tipton, Jonathan	150		1	
Watkins, Barbara	133			
Watson, Jonathan	115		0	
Young, Charles	320		1	1
Young, Thomas	320		1	2

....

Capt. Shipley's Co. (See 1790 List)

....

Capt. Stone's Co. (See 1790 List)

....

1791

A List of Capt. Tole's (Tullis) Company June the 30 day 1791

Names	land	white	black
Been, John	1000	1	
Bell, John	200	1	
Bleyth, Samuel		1	
Bogart, Henery	0	1	
Bogart, Samuel	640	0	
Bradley, Andrew	0	1	
Bradley, Jonathan		1	
Carr, John	232	2	2
Cobb, Benn	100		5
Crabtree, Barnet	0	1	
Deniall, Wm.	200	1	
Denton, Samuel	402	1	
Denton, Samuel	400	1	
Duncan, Charles	432	1	
Eleson, James		1	
Engle, John	400	1	
Fean, Agnes wd.	230	0	0
Fain, Samuel	400	1	1
Garland, Umphreys		1	
Gibson, Thomas	140		
Great, David	100	1	
Greney, William (?)	260	1	
Hamar, Jacob		1	
Hamer, John	200	1	
Humphrey, George		1	
Huston, John- a substitute		1	
Jones, Darling		1	
Kelley, Kinchon	200		
Lord, Levi			1
Little, Jonas	300	1	
McIntosh, Peter		1	
McMahan, John Blair	660	1	
Masangill, Henery	520	1	2
Masingell, Solaman	200	1	
Melvin, Joseph	250	1	
Miller, John	142		
Mitchell, Adam	300	2	
Moo, Abraham		1	
Morison, Joseph	200	1	
Nelson, Wm	500	1	1
Odell, Job	120	1	
Radar, Adam	540	1	
Renge, Peter	559	1	1
Stephens, Henry	700	1	1
Subel (?) Moses		1	
Toley, Jonathan	400	1	
Whit, John	450	1	
Young, John	637	1	
Young, Joseph	300	1	0
Young, Robert Jr.	640	1	
Young, Robert, Sr.	640	0	3

NOTE: See 1790 List for William Cobb.

A List of Taxable Property Taken by Richard White for the Year 1791

Names	free poles	slave poles	land
Anderson, Thomas	1		
Ashurst, David	1		100
Ashurst, John	1		100
Ashurst, Robertson	1		100
Baker, William	1		
Beckman, Michael	1		100
Bowman, Cornelius (over age)			100
Buck, Abraham	1		
Bucknal, William	1		
Bullinger, Peter	1		150
Campbell, Isaac	1		
Campbell, James	1		100
Campbell, Jeremiah	1		100
Campbell, Solomon	1		200
Campbell, Zachariah (over age)			200
Coffee, Chesley	1		100
Duggard, Julius	1		50
Duncan, Patrick	1		
Eastridge, Richard	1		
Eaststep, Moses	1		
Farguson, John	1		
Flannery, William	1		
Ford, Joseph	1	1	100
Garland, Samuel	1		250
Gentrey, Joseph	1		110
Griffin, William	1		304
Grimes, John over age	0		100
Grindstaff, Catherine	0		100
Guinn, Champness	1		
Guinn, James Jr.	1		
Guinn, James Sr. over age			277
Heatherley, Ewins over age			195
Hoskins, Ninean	1		
Hoskins, Thomas	1		
Jones, James	1		
Jones, Lewis Sr. over age	1		100
Jinkins, Rowland	1		248
Kane, John	1		
Kane, Peter	1		
Lindsey, Mathew over age			200
McGee, Thomas	1		
McQueen, Samuel over age			270
May, John	1		100
Moreland, William	1	1	200
Parkerson, Mary	0		200
Perkins, George	1		200
Perkins, Jacob	1		200
Perkins, Joshua	1		100
Pierce, Arthur	1		
Potter, Hannah	0		100
Rainbolt, Adam	1		
Rainbolt, Joseph over age			200
Roberts, Reubin	1		50

1791

List Taken by Richard White (cont'd)

Names	free poles	slave poles	land
Runnals, Moses	1		
Russell, James	1		
Smith, Edward	1		
Smith, Jacob	1		100
Smith, John			600
Smith, William	1		
Snider, Adam	1		115
Snider, Peter over age			133
Swiney, William	1		
Tate, John	1		100
Vantreece, John	1		375
Waggoner, David	1	3	540
Wallace, Aaron	1		
Walter, George	1		
Wilder, Joab over age			50
Willson, John Jr.	1		60
Willson, John Sr. over age		1	83
Willson, Samuel	1		
Wilson, William	1		

Territory of the United States of America South of the River Ohio

....

A List of Captain Willey's Company for the year 1791

Name	Acres	white poles	black poles
Allison, Frances	324		1
Allison, John Virginia	150		
Baker, Frances	102	1	2
Barger, George	130	1	
Baxtor, Francess	70	1	
Belis, Samuel	1400	1	
Bromit, Samuel		1	
Brown, Abraham	150	1	
Brown, Jacob	100	1	
Buchanan, Zecal	290	1	
Calvert, Wm.	127	1	
Cartor, John		1	1
Cash, Ingo		1	
Cash, James	328	2	1
Charlton, James	128	1	
Cowen, Nath.		1	
Cowen, Samuel		1	
Deaderick, David		1	
Disney, Thomas		1	
Eskerson, Rob.		1	
Fain, Wm.	900	1	
Fintch, Calvin	150	1	
Frentch, Henery	50	1	
Harmon, Adam	100	1	
Harmon, Joseph	0	1	
Harrell, John (?)	0	1	

Captain Willey's Company (cont'd)

Name	Acres	white poles	black poles
Hay, Charles	173	1	
Heris, Jushea		1	
Humbord, John	172	1	
Kindell, George	100	1	
King, James for the year 1791		1	2
McEname, Peter	450	1	
McCree, Charles	100	1	0
Megines, John		1	
Miler, Henery	240	1	
Milim, Edward	160	1	
Morison, John	90	1	
Noding, Wm. Jr.	100	1	1
Noding, Wm. Sr.	300	0	6
Persifeld, Samuel	200	1	
Pring, Nicholas		1	
Rimal, John	142	1	
Scott, James	200	1	
Sevier, John		1	
Shanan, John		1	
Shanan, William	150	1	
Slager, John	350	1	
Smith, James		1	
Stover, Christopher		1	
Telon, Christefor (?)	305	1	2
Tiler, Adam (?)	120	1	
Walton, (?)sellar	100	1	
Willey, Capt. James	180	1	2
Wood, Samuel	268	1	

....

List of Taxables in Capt Edmund Williams Company for 1791.
Taken with the 1790 list.

Scrap to be added to Edmund Williams List.

Dear Sir-- As there was some omission in the return I made, I hope you'll receive them now, and believe me to be yr friend and humble servt.

Edmund Williams.

James Sevier Esquire
November 19, 1791

Taxable Property.

Cooper, Abraham	150 acres of land	1 pole
Edwards, Solomon		1 pole
Kind, William		1 pole
Hudiburg, Thomas	150 acres of land	1 pole
Peoples, William	100 acres of land	0 poles
Williams, George	100 acres of land	1 pole

They were given in since Nov. Court.

....

A Schedule of the Whole Number of Persons within the County of Washington in the Territory of the United States of America South of the River Ohio on the last Saturday in July, 1791.

Districts	White free males of 21 yrs. & upwards including heads of families	Free white males under 21 yrs. age	Free white females including heads of families	All other persons	Slaves	The Whole Amount
Capt. Jonathan Tullis	69	130	190	-	66	455
Capt. James Wiley	69	118	140	-	23	340
Capt. John Campbell	84	102	167	4	14	371
Capt. Morgan Murry	48	79	147	-	24	298
Capt. Geo. Williams	70	128	67	130	43	438
Capt. Thos. Maxfield	54	119	168	-	7	348
Capt. Geo. North	52	119	148	1	15	335
Capt. James Love	40	90	113	-	26	269
Capt. Jacob Brown	55	112	155	3	81	406
Capt. John Millikin	73	117	163	1	61	415
Capt. Saml. McQuean	38	72	104	-	7	221
Capt. Edward Shipley	60	116	163	-	33	372
Capt. Saml. Handley	69	123	172	1	48	413
Capt. Alexd. Greer	77	110	142	-	35	364
Capt. William Stone	84	139	188	-	34	445
Capt. Solemon Campbell	47	118	167	2	18	372
	1009				535	5862

(Note: This is the Census of Washington County, which was ordered by Governor William Blount, after his appointment as Territorial Governor in 1790. MHMcC.)

A Schedule of the Whole Number of Persons within the County of Washington in the Territory of the United States of America South of the River Ohio in the last Return in [illegible] 1791

District

	[illegible]	[illegible]	[illegible]	[illegible]	[illegible]	[illegible]
Capt Jonathan Tullis	69	130	190		22	455
Capt James Ellis	69	113	140		23	340
Capt John Campbell	84	102	167		[illegible]	371
Do Morgan Murry	43	79	147		24	298
Do Jno Williams	70	123	67	130	43	438
Do Thos Maxfield	54	119	163	0	7	343
Do Geo North	[illegible]2	[illegible]	[illegible]		15	335
Do James [illegible]	[illegible]	[illegible]	[illegible]		[illegible]	269
Do [illegible]	53	112	135	3	81	406
~~[illegible] Aitken~~	[illegible]	[illegible]			[illegible]	[illegible]
[illegible]	3[illegible]	11[illegible]	60			215
[illegible]	103	[illegible]				221
[illegible]	[illegible]	[illegible]			[illegible]	[illegible]
[illegible]	[illegible]	23				[illegible]
[illegible]	27	[illegible]			[illegible]	[illegible]
[illegible]	[illegible]	29			[illegible]	[illegible]
[illegible]	6					[illegible]2

Facsimile of
Census of Washington County
Terr. S. of River Ohio - 1791

Capt. Biddle's Company (See 1790 List)

....

A List of the Taxable Property in Capt. Brown's Company, taken by Charles Robinson 1792

Names	land	white poles	black poles
Archer, ---man	128	1	
Bales, Rueben	170	1	
Boyd, Henry	90	1	
Brown, ---am	420	1	
Brown, ---ob	220	1	
Brown, John	220	1	
Brown, Ruth	723	0	4
Brown, Thomas	220	1	1
Casner, Jacob	150	1	
Cash, Ingodasher		1	1
Collet, ---		1	1
Colyer, William	300	1	2
Conklin, David		1	
Disney, Thomas		1	
Dobbins, --vin	96½	1	
Embree, ----	62	1	
Embree, Jacob		1	
Embree, Moses	350		
Fips, Iziah		2	
Hampton, Robert	200	1	
Hendley, George		1	
Jones, Richard	130	1	
Keel, James	120	1	
Leman, --vid	200	1	
Murphey, Dinnis		1	4
Rodgers, John	100	1	
Rogers, Joseph	50	1	
Tedlock, John	650	1	6
Terry, ----		1	
Weer, John	100		

....

A List of Taxable Property belonging to Capt. Carrigers Company Undated-----List seems to belong to 1792

Names	Land	Poles
Arnold, John	200	1
Bass, Jeremiah		10
Bowers, Leonard	50	1
Burden, Charles		1
Burper (?), Jaret	100	1
Carriger, Godfrey, Sr.	2912	2
Carriger, Michael	156	1
Carriger, Nicholas	450	1
Carter, John		3
Carter, Col. Landon	3340	6
Cobb, Pharoah	1000	10
Cox, Richard		1

Capt. Carrigers Company (cont'd)

Names	Land	Poles
Drake, Abraham	500	1
Duncan, Thos.		1
Gillam, John		1
Garland, Humphrey		1
Garland, John	200	1
Greer, Alexr		4
Greer, Andrew, Jr		4
Greer, Andrew, Sr	1650	4
Greer, David		1
Greer, Thos		1
Hedrick, Jacob, Jr.		1
Hedrick, Jacob, Senr		1
Hedrick, Peter		1
Helton, Abraham		1
Helton, Arnold	50	1
Helton, John		1
Hendrick, John	500	1
Humphrey, Elisha not returned	300	1
Johnson, Robert		1
Kite, Richard	150	2
Lacy, Filemon		1
Lacy, John		1
Lincoln, Isaac	600	1
Maiden, William		1
Maxwell, Thomas	180	1
Millard, Thos		1
Millsaps, Thomas	100	1
Musgraves, John		1
Nave, John		1
Nave, Teter	350	2
Nowlan, John		1
Price, James	225	1
Price, John		1
Robinson, John	50	1
Sevier, Abraham	142	1
Sevier, Joseph		2
Sevier, Valentine	410	
Shoults, Christian Sr		1
Shoults, Christian Jr		1
Smithpeters, John Michael	755	1
Stover, Christain		1
Tipton, Isaac	200	1
Tipton, Samuel	742	1
Tipton, Thos.		1
Wright, James		1

....

List of Taxable Property in Captain Depew's Company for the Year of 1792 - Made out by Jas. Sevier, Clk.
(This list is bound with Capt. Biddle's Co. for 1790, 91 & 92)

Names	Land	White poles	Black poles
Allen, Robert	640	1	1

Captain Depew's Company (cont'd)

Names	Land	White poles	Black poles
Allison, Ann widow	145	0	0
Anderson, John	200	1	1
Bails, Isaac	130	1	
Ballis, Samuel	1400	1	
Bell, Elizabeth	150	0	
Bell, George	145	1	
Bell, John	100	1	
Bell, William	70	1	
Blackley, Robert	570	2	0
Blair, John	300	1	
Boman, Elias	100	1	
Campbell, Abraham	150	1	
Campbel, James	250	1	
Campbell, John	211	1	
Carson, David	50	1	
Carson, David Jr.	0	1	0
Carson, David Sr.	0	1	
Carson, Little David	250	1	
Carson, Robert Jr.	0	1	
Carson, Robert Sr.	160	1	
Carmichael, James	350	1	1
Depew, Capt. Isaac	10	1	
Duncan, Andrew	311	1	0
Duncan, Joseph	428	1	
Fargason, John	300	1	
Glass, William	235	1	
Jones, Nathaniel	100	1	0
Kinchloe, Charles	100	1	1
McCall, John	250	1	
McCord, David	0	1	0
McCorkle, Joseph	200	1	
McFerson, Bartin	180	1	
McFerson, Henry	250	1	
McNitt, Anthony	85	1	
Machlin, Robert	200	1	
Montgomery, William	116	1	
Nail, George	0	1	
Neal, William	0	1	
Parr, Thomas	90	1	0
Purselly, William	250	0	
Reed, James	116	1	0
Reed, James	100	1	
Richards, David	0	1	0
Rion, James	110	1	
Robertson, David	245	1	0
Russell, David	284	1	
Shaw, Francis	0	1	
Shaw, Samuel	300	1	
Smith, Abraham	395	1	
Smith, Anderson	250	2	
Stewart, David Jr.	0	1	
Stewart, David Sr.	270	1	

1792

Captain Depew's Company (cont'd)

Names	Land	White poles	Black poles
Taylor, Leroy	250	1	1
Thomson, David	100	1	0
Tucker, Joseph	300	1	
Tucker, Nicolas	70	1	
Wards, William	150	1	

Note: Location Leesburg and Bowmantown vicinity.

....

A List of Taxable for the year 1792 Taken by Robert Love J.P.
Greasy Cove District

Names	quantity land	White poles	Black poles
Anderson, William	250	1	
Armstrong, Mathaniel	200	1	
Bevins, Andrew		1	
Bevins, Morgan			1
Biddlecum, William	1 white pole		
Blevins, William		1	
Burass, Elijah		1	
Colyer, Charles		1	
Culbertson, Joseph	300	1	
Culbertson, Samuel	1250	1	
Dickins, James		1	
Dickins, Richard	175	1	
Dillard, Martha	200	0	8
Dillard, Thomas	200	1	1
Doyl, Patrick	100	1	
Duncan, Thomas		1	
Ecton, James Jr.		1	
Ecton, James Sr.	100	1	
Edmunds, Dixon	1 white pole		
Evans, John	105	1	
Evans, Thomas	45	1	
Finker, William	1 white pole		
Hale, John		1	
Harrald, John		1	
Haynes, George	300	1	
Hilton, John	50	1	
Holloway, John	1 white pole		
Holloway, William		1	
Jarvis, Alexander	100	1	
Lewis, William		1	
Little, John	50	1	
Longmire, Charles	600	1	
Love, Thoamas	100	1	1
Lynch, Jesse	50	1	
McCoy, Enoch		1	
Murphey, Patrick	100	1	1
Newhouse, Lewis	2130	1	
Roberts, Jesse		1	
Samms, John	261	1	

List Taken by Robert Love J.P. (cont'd)

Names	quantity land	white pole	black pole
Samms, John in trust for James Samms -- 100 acres			
Simmons, Joseph		1	
Webb, John	275½	1	1
Webb, John in trust for Willm Young - 100 acres			
Young, John	30	1	

The 26th day of May 1792 this list of taxables by me exhibited is a just list to the best of my knowledge, given under my hand and seal this day and year above written.

Robert Love J.P.

....

The Taxable Property in Capt. Thomas Maxwells Company, Undated, likely 1792 as seems to belong there. See lists of Taxes returned.

Names	land	white poles	black poles
Ash, Thomas Lewis		1	
Bailey, Cotrel	500	1	
Boyler, Abraham		1 marked out	
Clark, Josiah	200	1	
Cooper, Abraham	100	1	
Cooper, Job	150	1	
Cooper, Joel, Jr		1	
Cooper, Joel, Sr.	177	1	
Cooper, widow Patience	640		
Cunningham, Mary widow	590		
Daniel, William	200	1	
Davis, Nathan	362	1	
Davis, William	478	1	
Denton, Isaac, jr		1	
Denton, Isaac	75	1	
Denton, Jos	185	1	
Edwards, Solomon		1	
English, Robert	300		
Garland, John			
Garland, Joseph	255	1	
Gourley, Thomas	150	1	
Hagan (Eagan) (?), Barnebas	200	1	
Hale, John		1	
Hampton, James		1	
Hampson, William		1	
Haun, Adam	200	1	
Haun, Sebastian	400	1	
Hendrix, Solomon	113	1 marked out	
Henley, Abraham		1	
Hider, widow Elizabeth	200	1	
Hider, John	200	1	
Hider, Michael	182 3/4	1	
Hudeburg, Thomas	294	1	
Huffman, Daniel		1	
Humphreys, Jesse			

1792

Capt. Thomas Maxwell's Company (cont'd)

Names	land	white poles	black poles
Ivy, Howel		1	
King, William		1	
Lacy, Philemon	630	1	
Lackey, Thos	280	1	
Lusk, Robert	294	1	
McInturff, Christopher	232	1	
McInturff, Gasper	100	1	
McInturff, John jr	200	1	
McInturff, John	200	1	
McNabb, David	258 & 500 in Cumberland	1	
McNabb, William			
Maracle, Frederick		1	
Maxwell, Capt. Thos.		1	
Moore, Absolam		1	
Nichols, Daniel		1	
Peoples, John		1	
Peoples, William	100	1	
Poland, John	200	1	
Pugh, widow Susannah	450		
Range, James	270	1	
Reno, Charles	150	1	
Reno, John		2	
Rockhold, Dowson	50	1	
Smalling, Samuel	29	1	
Smith, Brooks		1	
Simerly, Adam		1	
Taylor, Andrew	233	1	
Taylor, Isaac	350	1	
Taylor, Mathew		1	
Taylor, Nathaniel	350	1	
Tipton, Col. John	1865	0	2
Tipton, John jr son of Joseph		1	
Tipton, Jonathan		1	
Tipton, Joseph	1300	1	
Whitson, Jesse	291	1	3
Whitson, John		1	
Williams, Frances		1	
Williams, George	200	1	
Wyatt, Thomas			

Copied on the other sheet of this is Capt. Tullis old company, also undated but likely 1792.

....

A List of the Taxable Property in the bounds of Capt. John Millikins Company for the year 1792

Names	poles	land
Adams, Wm	1	200
Baxter, Frances	1	

Capt. John Millikins Company (cont'd)

Names	poles	land
Bocedon (?)	1	100
Bottles, Henery	1	125
Bowman, Joseph	1	
Broyles, Abraham	2	100
Broyles, Nicholas	3	130
Cain, Hugh	1	200
Cleck, Lewis	1	200
Cleck, Peter	1	
Condrum, William	1	
Crookshanks, George	1	133
Cunningham, Hugh	1	300
Cunningham, John	1	
Denton, Jonathan	1	100
Denwaddie, James	1	
Doak, Rev. Samuel	2	180
Embree, John	1	200
Gillespie, Thos	3	1290
Gordan, Lewis	1	300
Green, Joshua	1	170
Hall, Alexander	1	
Hall, James	1	
Hall, John	1	
Hall, William Jr.	1	240
Hannah, Andrew	1	320
Larkins, Jesse	1	
Lech, John	1	
Lott, Gasper	1	
Lyle, John	1	370
McAlister, John	1	100
McCrath, Andr.	1	250
McEwen, Alexander	1	312
Mathews, Alex	4	500
Messer, Joseph	1	225
Millikin, John	1	200
Montgomery, Alex	1	100
Montgomery, Jas.	1	181
Montgomery, Thos	1	100
Nelson, Henery	2	300
Nelson, John	2	200
Padfield, William	1	
Ramsey, F. A.	3	--
Roberts, John	1	
Scot, Thomas	1	200
Shields, Patrick	1	278
Smith, John	1	
Stephenson, William	1	391
Sutherland, Isaac	1	
Taylor, David	1	150
Wallas, James	1	
Willson, Isaac		350
Yeager, Solomom	2	200

(Wm. Hall has made no return to me.)

Made out by Jas. Sevier clk.

1792

A List of the Taxable Property in Capt. Norths Company (1792) taken by Charles Robinson

Names	land	white	black
Andis, Frederick	150	1	
Bass, Barbara widow	100	0	
Bell, John	200	1	
Boring, Chenia	750	1	
Boring, Dansey	0	1	
Boring, Ezekiel	70	1	
Boring, James	0	1	
Bowens, Jesse	0	0	2
Cooper, Joseph	69	0	
Embree, Thomas	350	1	
Fine, John	250	1	
Gaut, John	0	1	
Goodpasture, Abraham	200	1	
Goddpasture, Isec	0	1	
Goodpasture, John	0	1	
Goodpasture, Solomon	62	0	
Gray, Willes	0	1	
Green, William	100	1	
Headerick, Charles	140	1	
Hofman, David	250	1	
Horncumton, Jeremiah	180	1	
Hunter, John	640	0	
Irwin, James disputed	200	0	
Irwin, Robert	180	0	
Leman, Abraham	0	1	
Leman, John Jr.	0	1	
Leman, John Sr.	450	0	
McCray, Daniel	0	1	
Moor, James	105	1	
North, George Cpt.	0	1	
North, John	100		
Ozmus, Petter	200		
Price, Mordekie	401	1	
Rader, Adam	840	1	
Rodgers, Robert	200	0	
Rodgers, Thomas	0	1	
Rose, Hosea	320	0	
Rubell, John	200	1	
Smith, Edward	218	1	2
Tipton, Jonathan	150	1	
Walker, Barbrah widow	274	0	0
Walker, Gabrell	100	1	
Watson, Jonathan	105	0	
Young, Charls	640	1	
Young, Thomas	0	1	3

....

A List of the Taxable Property of the People within the District of Captain Scott's company for 1792

Names	white	black	land
Allison, Frank	1	1	324

Captain Scott's company (cont'd)

Names	white	black	land
Baker, Frances	1	2	302
Bayles, Daniel			100
Bayles, John	1		300
Boutwell, Stephoun	1		
Brown, Abraham	1		150
Brown, Jacob	1		100
Brown, James	1		
Brummitt, Samuel	1		50
Buckhanan, Ezekiel	1		
Calvert, William	1		127
Cash, James	1	1	328
Charter, James	1		138
Cloyd, William	1		210
Cowen, Natheial	1	0	
Deadrick, David	1		
Evens, George	1		57
Fain, William	1		850
Fellows, Adam	1		120
Finch, Colvin	1		150
French, Henery	1		50
Greer, Charles	1		
Harie, Isaac	1		130
Harman, Adam	1		100
Harmon, Abraham	1		
Harmon, Joseph	1		
Hawthron, Noah	1		
Hays, Charles			173
Humbert, John	1		172
Knody, William Junr	1	1	200
Knody, William Senr		6	300
Leach, William	1		150
Lilburn, Andrew	1		
Lovly, William L.	1		
McCray, Charles	1		100
McGinnis, John	1		200
Miller, Henry	1		190
Million, Edward	1		162
Rymal, John	1		230
Scott, James	1		200
Sevier, Jack	1		
Sevier, James	1		109½
Shenan, William	1		1150
Smith, John	1		250
Slaiger, John Junr	1		
Slaiger, John Senr	1		350
Taylor, Christopher	1	2	300
Waggenor, Phillip	1		
Woods, Samuel	1		373

....

List of Taxables in Captain Tullis old Company - Undated but likely 1792 List - On other side of Capt. Thomas Maxwells company

Captain Tullis old Company (cont'd)

Names	land	white poles	black poles
Ball, Amos	205	1	
*Been, Edmund		1	
*Been, John	1000	1	
Blithe, Samuel		1	
*Bogart, Henry	200	1	
Boring, Absolam		1	
Boring, William	100	1	
Carr, John	232	4	
Carruthers, Jonathan		1	
Carson, John		1	
Cobb, Benjamin			
Cobb, Capt. William	1000	1	14
Collins, Joseph	100	1	
Cox, Abraham	152	1	
Crabtree, Barnabas		1	
*Crusen, Jacob	90	1	
Daniel, William			
*Dungan, Jeremiah	1140		3
Dunken, Charles	432	1	
Engle, John	400	1	
*Fain, Widow Agnes	240		1
Fain, Samuel	400	1	1
Great, David	100	1	
Greenway, William	280	1	
Gibson, Thomas			
Hammer, Jacob		1	
Hammer, John, Esq	200	1	
*Harper, Josiah		1	
*Hendrix, John	500	1	
Humphreys, George		1	
Huston, John		1	
Job, David	280	1	3
Little, George		1	
Little, Jonas	320	1	
*McCormack, Robert	55		
McFall, Francis	235	1	
Masingale, Solomon	200	1	
*Miller, John	142	1	
*Miller, Kinchen	200		
Mitchell, Adam	300	2	
Moore, Abraham		1	
Morrison, Capt. Joseph	200	1	
Melvin, Joseph	250	1	
Nelson, Widow Jean	103		2
Nelson, William	500	1	1
Odle, Caleb		1	
Odle, Job	270	1	
Range, Peter	559	1	1
*Reasoner, Garret	208	1	2
*Smith, James		1	
*Smith, Zebulon		1	
Stephens, Henry	400	2	

Captain Tullis old Company (cont'd)

Names	land	white poles	black poles
*Taylor, Margaret	169		
Tullis, Capt. Jonathan	400	1	
*Ward, William	250	1	
White, John	300	1	
*Wood, William	177		
Woods, William			
Wyatt, William	100	1	
*Wyatt, William	100	1	
Young, John	487	1	
Young, Robert	640	1	

*These are in Maxwells district.

....

A List of Taxable Property taken by Richard White for year 1792

Names	land	free poles	slaves
Anderson, Thomas	150	1	
Ashurst, John	100	1	
Baker, William		1	
Bowman, Cornelius	100	0	
Buck, Adam Abram	0	1	
Campbell, Isaac	150	1	
Campbell, James	250	1	
Campbell, Solomon	200	1	
Campbell, Zachriah over age	100	0	
Chambers, John	0	1	
Coffee, Chesley	100	1	
Cook, William	0	1	
Duggard, Julius	250	1	
Duggard, William	250	1	
Duncan, Lawrence	240	1	
Eastep, Moses	0	1	
Eastrige, Richard	0	1	
Farguson, John	0	1	
Ford, Joseph	375	1	1
Gentry, Joseph	110	1	
Graves, James	0	1	
Griffin, William	304	0	
Grindstaff, Catherine	100	0	0
Guinn, Champness	0	1	
Guinn, James over age	250	0	0
Heatherley, Ewins over age	95	0	
Jenkins, Rowland	248	1	
Jones, James	0	1	
Jones, Lewis Jr.	0	1	
Jones, Lewis Sr. over age	100	0	0
Jones, William	130	1	
Kane, John	0	1	
Kane, Peter	0	1	
Lindsey, Matthew over age	176	0	

1792

List taken by Richard White (cont'd)

Names	land	free poles	slaves
McQueen, Samuel over age	270	0	
Miller, Daniel Jr.	0	1	
Miller, Daniel Sr. over age	300	0	0
Miller, Henry	240	1	
Miller, John	200	1	
Millsaps, James	0	1	
Mulkey, James	0	1	
Perkins, George	200	1	
Perkins, Jacob	200	1	
Perkins, Joshua	100	1	
Pirce, Hardy	0	1	
Potter, Hanner	100	0	0
Primmer (?), John	100	1	
Rainbolt, Adam	100	1	
Rainbolt, Susannah	100	0	
Richardson, John	98	1	0
Roberts, Rhubin	50	1	
Runnalds, Henry	0	1	
Simerley, John	300	1	
Smith, Edward over age	600	0	
Smith, Jacob	100	1	
Smith, Samuel	0	1	
Smith, John	150	1	
Snider, Adam	115	1	
Snider, Peter	132	0	0
Stought, Daniel over age	300	0	0
Tate, John	100	1	
Tate, Samuel over age	170	0	0
do do	50	0	0
Thornton, Rhubin	600	1	
Vandergriff, Jacob	0	1	
Waggoner, David	572	1	3
Waggoner, Mathius	0	1	2
Wallace, Aaron	0	1	
Walters, George	0	1	
White, Richard	700	1	7
Whitson, Thomas over age	400	0	1
Wilder, Joab over age	50	0	
Willson, John Sr.	60	0	1
Willson, William	0	1	
Wilson, John Jr.	70	1	
Wilson, Samuel	225	1	
Yates, Samuel		1	

....

Scrap --- Individual returns on loose scrap for 1792

James Allison Taxables --- 800 acres & 3 poles for the year 1792

Charles Robertson senr --- 350 acres & 5 poles for the year 1792

A LIST OF TAXES FOR THE YEAR 1792

Captain McQueans old company	£ 10-	9-	3¼
Captain Depews Company	£ 8-	17-	5
Captain Milligans Company	£ 9-	12-	0 2/4
Captain Melvins Company	£ 8-	12-	10 3/4
Captain Murreys Company	£ 15-	6-	5 2/4
Captain Browns Company	£ 7-	13-	3 2/4
Captain Norths Company	£ 5-	10-	5
Captain Biddles Company	£ 5-	4-	0½
Captain Maxwells Company	£ 14-	13-	4
Captain Tullis Company	£ 11-	3-	1

	dol	cts
Captain Handley	59	7
" Scott	36	21
" Carriger	62	43
" Maxwell	59	42
" Milligan	55	67
" Brown	28	93
" North	36	-7 81
" Melvin	50	31
" Murrys	66	86
" Biddle	23	42
" Depew	47	79
" Thornton & Campbell	56	87
James Allison Esquire	2	87
Dollars	596	67

On back page---

Monies due from the County £ 524 - 17 - 0

County Credits- £ 431 - 4 - 8

(NOTE: Copied in a small booklet.)

1793

Captain Blair's Company, formerly Capt Biddle's Company, for the year 1793- Taken by John Strain

Names	Land	White Pole	Black Pole
Alexander, Francis		1	
Alexander, John	250		
Bell, Elezabeth	150		
Bell, James	100	1	
Biddle, Thomas	400	1	
Blackley, Robert	500	2	
Blair, Brice		1	
Blair, Hugh	520	1	
Blair, John	250	1	
Blair, C--- John	279	1	1
Blair, Richard	60	1	
Boid, George	200	1	
Brown, David	200	1	
Brown, William		1	
Burk, John	173	1	
Humphreys, William	790	1	1
King, Henry	170	1	
McCall, John	250	1	
McWhorter, James	143	1	
Richards, David		1	
Rodgers, James		1	
Rodgers, Moses		1	
Rodgers, Thomas	500	1	
Shields, David	250	1	
Shields, Joseph	246	1	
Tiffin, Henry	250	1	2
Williams, John	200	1	

This list on same sheet as Captain Depews Co- both returned by John Strain.

....

An Inventory of Captain Browns District 1793

Names	White Pole	Land	Black Pole
Allison, John	0	100 (?)	
Bayles, Rubin	1	170	
Boon, Joseph	1	100	
Boyd, Henry	1		
Bredin, James	1		
Brown, Benj.	1	300	
Brown, Jacob	1	0	1
Brown, Thomas	1	150	1 -2
Burkhart, George	1	250	
Carsoner, Jacob	0	249	
Collet, Isaac	1		
Colyer, William	1		
Conklin, David	1	0	
Dobbins, Evins	1		
Embree, Isaac	1	64	

Captain Browns District (cont'd)

Names	White Pole	Land	Black Pole
Embree, Moses	0	160	
French, Peter	1	200	
Green, John	1		
Green, William	1	100	
Hammon, Christopher	1	100	
Hampton, Robert	1	200	
Hendley, George	1		
Hendley, Samuel	1		
Hofman, David	1	250	
Ingle, William	1	150	
Jones, Richard	1	130	
Keele, James	1	121	
Keel-, John	1	178	0
Lemans, Jacob	1		
Nail, William	1	96½	
Roberson, Charles	1		
Rogers, John	1	100	
Rogers, Joseph	1	50	
Shannon, John	1	100	
Spring, Nicholas	1		
Tedlocke, John	1	650	6
Terry, John	1		
Whet (?), Jesse	1		

....

Scrap- "The Clerk will annex the above Return to the Duplicate for the year 1793."
The Taxable property of Colo Charles Roberson for the year 1793---- 300 acres of land and 1 black pole.
Charles Roberson.

....

A List of Taxable Property belonging to the companies of Captain Campbell & Thornton Taken by Richard White for the year 1793

Names Viz:	Poles	Land
Anderson, Thomas	1	150
Ashurst, David	1	100
Ashurst, John	1	100
Ashurst, Robinson	1	100
Baker, William	1	
Campble, Isaac	1	50
Campbell, James	1	200
Campbell, Jeremiah Captain	1	100
Campbell, Zachariah	0	100
(Coffee), Chesley	1	
Cook, William	1	
Cooper, Robert	1	
Duggard, William	1	275
Duggar, Julius	1	125
Duncan, Benjamin	1	

1793

Captains Campbell & Thornton (cont'd)

Names Viz:	Poles	Land
Duncan, Patrick	1	
Eastridge, Richard	1	
Fariss, William	1	100
Flannery, William	1	
Ford, Joseph	2	100
Garland, Samuel	0	229
Gentry, Joseph	1	112
Graves, James	1	
Grimer, John	0	98
Guinn, Champ	1	100
Guinn, James Jr.	1	
Guinn, James Sr.	0	438
Guin, James Senr (?)	1	
Heatherley, Euins	1	70
Heatherley, John	1	
Hoskin, Thomas	1	
Jinkins, Hugh	1	
Jinkins, Rowland	1	248
Jones, Lewis Senr.	0	100
Kane, John	1	
Lindsey, Matthew	0	78
McQueen, John	1	270
May, John	1	100
Miller, Daniel, Jr.	1	
Miller, Daniel	1	100
Miller, Henry	1	240
Miller, John	1	
Miller, John	1	
Morrison, Thomas	1	
Mullings, William Jr	1	
Mullings, John	1	
Paine, John	1	
Perkins, George	1	200
Perkins, James	1	200
Peters, Daniel	1	
Primmer, Mary	0	100
Rainboalt, Adam	1	100
Rainboalt, Susannah	0	100
Ray, William	1	0
Richardson, Amos	1	
Russell, James	1	
Sands, Joseph	1	
Shible (?), William	1	
Simerley, John	1	300
Smith, Jacob	1	100
Smith, John	1	200
Smith, Samuel	1	
Smith, William	1	100
Stought, Daniel	1	300
Swiney, William	1	
Tate, John	1	65
Thornton, Reubin Captain	1	600

Captains Campbell & Thornton (cont'd)

Names Viz:	Poles	Land
Waggoner, David	4	572
Waggoner, Matthias	3	765
Wallace, Aaron	1	
White, Richard	11	500
Whitson, Thomas	1	400
Whitson, John	1	
Wilder, Joab	0	50
Wilson, John Jr	1	60
Wilson, John Senr	1	83
Wilson, Joseph	1	
Yates, Samuel	1	
-------, Charles	1	

....

Captain Depews Company 1793 Taken by John Strain

Names	Land	white	black
Adair, John	100	1	
Allien, Robert	750	1	1
Allison, Robert	400	1	3
Anderson, John	200	1	
Archer, William		1	
Bell, George	145	1	
Blair, Joseph	300		
Blair, Samuel		1	
Blackburn, Gabriel		1	
Bowman, Elias	100	1	
Brookshire, Joseph		1	
Campbel, John	211	1	
Carmichael, James	350	1	1
Carson, David	58	1	
Carson, David senr	100	1	
Carson, Robert		1	
Carson, William	150	1	
Conelly, David		1	
Depue, Isaac	50	1	
Duncan, Andrew	313	1	
Duncan, Joseph	428	1	
Evens, George	57	1	
Farguson, John	300	1	
Farler, Obediah		1	
Gar (?), Thomas	301	1	
Glass, William	434	1	
Hunt, Uriah	940	1	
Irvine, John		1	
Jenderson, Joseph		1	
Johnson, Samuel	100	1	
Jones, Nathaniel	100	1	
McCord, David		1	
McCord, James	350	1	
McCorkle, Joseph	200	1	

1793

Captain Depews Company (cont'd)

Names	Land	white	black
McGinnis, John	430	1	
McNight, Antony	150	1	
Neel, Samuel	226	1	
Newell, Joseph		1	
Pursley, William	241		
Russell, David	282	1	
Shanks, Holden	222	1	
Shanks, James		1	
Shanks, William		1	
Shaw, Samuel	300		1
Shipley, Thomas	200	1	
Smith, Abraham	375	1	
Stewart, David jr	85	1	
Stewart, David senr	341	1	
Sutherlane, Isaac		1	
Taylor, Leroy	235	1	1
Thomson, David	100	1	
Trotter, Alexander	33	1	
Tucker, Joseph	305	1	
Tucker, Nicholas	70	1	
Walker, William	180	1	
Woods, William	50	1	

A true return of all that came to give in both companies (Biddle's and Depue's)

NOTE: Above is on the same sheet as Captain Biddle's, now Capt. Blair's Company.

....

A List of the Taxable Property in Capt. Alexander Greers Company for the year 1793

Names	Land	Poles
Arnold, John		1
Bass, Jerimiah		9
Bowers, Leonard	50	1
Brown, Joseph		1
Burden, Charles		1
Burden, Jaret	100	1
Carringer, Godfrey Jr.		1
Carringer, Godfrey Sr.	2727	1
Carringer, Micheal		1
Carringer, Nicholas	500	1
Carter, Landon	2930	6
Carter, John		3
Cobb, Pharo	1000	10
Cox, Richard		1
Dary, Micheal		1
Duggar, William	100	1
Duncan, Thomas		1

Capt. Alexander Greers Company (cont'd)

Names	Land	Poles
Garland, Gutridge	130	1
Garland, Humphrey	0	1
Garland, John	200	1
Gillam, John		1
Greer, Adam		1
Greer, Andrew Sr.	2150	4
Greer, Joseph	400	3
Greer, Thomas		1
Headrick, Jacob	300	1
Hedrick, Jacob, jr		1
Helton, Abraham		1
Holbertt, Solomon	233	1
Hooker, Robert		1
Humphreys, Elisha	125	1
Ivy, James	100	1
Johnson, Robt		1
Kerr, John		1
Kite, Isaac	200	2
Lacy, John		1
Large, Joseph		1
Lincoln, Isaac	350	1
Miller, Old	150	1
Millsaps, James	100	1
Moore, John Parker		1
Murry, Ephraim		1
Musgraves, John		1
Nave, Abraham		1
Nave, Teter	150	1
Nowland, John		1
Peters, Christopher		1
Price, James	275	1
Price, John		1
Redmon, Stephen		1
Robison, John	50	1
Severe, Abraham	100	1
Sevier, Joseph		2
Sevier, Valentine, Jr		1
Sevier, Valentine Senr	350	0
Shoultz, Christian junr		1
Shoultz, Christian Senr		1
Smithpeters, J Michael	750	1
Stover, Christian		1
Tipton, Isaac	200	1
Tipton, Samuel	550	1
Tipton, Thomas		1
Worley, John	100	1
Wright, James		1

....

1793

A List of the Taxable Property in Captain Hale's Company for 1793

Names	land	w poles	b poles
Acton, James		1	
Anderson, William	150	1	
Colyer, Charles	334	1	
Cuberson, Samuel	650		
Dickins, James		1	
Dickins, Richard	137	1	
Diel, Patrick	109		
Dillard, Marth	100	0	7
Evens, John	125	1	
Evins, Thomas	45		
Garland, Gutridge	150	1	
Hale, Capt.	56	1	
Henly, Samuel	100	1	
King, Henry	130	1	
Lewis, William		1	
Longmires, Charles	600	1	
McCray, Daniel	316	1	
McCrea, Charles Esquire	100	1	
McInturff, Casper	100	1	
Pohan, William (?)	67	1	
Roberts, Jesse	50	1	
Samms, James	100		
Samms, John	261	1	
Smith, Henry		1	

(The List for 1794 is on the other side of this list.)

....

A List of the Taxable Property in Captain Handleys District for the year 1793

Names	poles	land
Beird, Andrew	3	100
Bitner, John	1	100
Blackburn, Archid	3	400
Brown, William	2	150
Broyles, Adam	1	
Broyles, Adam B Smith	1	300
Broyles, Daniel	1	100
Broyles, Rueben	1	
Broyles, Samuel	1	250
Broyles, Syries	2	100
Clark, Isaac	2	
Clark, Jesse	1	
Clarke, John	1	200
Clark, William	3	300
Collam, Jonathan	1	100
Condren, William	1	100
Cowen, Susana	0	150
Gallaher, John	2	400
Gann, Adam Jr.	1	100

Captain Handleys District (cont'd)

Names	poles	land
Gann, Adam Sr.	0	150
Gann, Clem	1	100
Gann, Isaac	1	
Gann, John	1	100
Gann, Nathan	1	220
Gann, Thomas	1	
Handly, Samuel	1	220
Hannah, John	0	120
Hannah, Joseph	1	0
Hannah, Samuel	1	100
Harbison, William	1	
Hetter, Sebaston (Hadler) (?)	2	300
Humphreys, Richard	1	307
Jurden, John	1	
Kenidy, David	1	200
Kimmings, Joseph	1	
Lamon, John	1	
Loggan, Charles	1	175
McFarland, Robert	2	
McGee, John	1	
McKee, Alex	1	400
McKee, John	1	100
McKiny, Henry	1	
Miller, James	1	100
Miller, Peter	0	400
Moore, Alexander	3	0
Moore, William	1	360
Nelson, Suthey	1	
Penter, Adam	1	164
Sevier, Genl. John	13	550
Sharp, Joseph	1	300
Shields, Henry	1	400
Waddill, John	1	310
Wallis, John	1	
Ware, John Esquire	2	574
Willhite, Conrad	1	205
Willhite, Samuel	1	
Woods, Michael	7	640

James Stuart Esquire--------------

....

Taxable Property in Capt. Maxwell's old Company - Took in by Edmund Williams for the year 1793

Person's name	Land	white poles	black poles
Ash, Thos Lewis	200	1	
Bogart, Henry	160	1	
Clark, Josiah	200	1	
Cooper, Abraham	100	1	
Cooper, Edward	0	1	

1793

Capt. Maxwell's old Company (cont'd)

Person's name	Land	white poles	black poles
Cooper, Job	150	1	
Cooper, Joel senr	177	1	
Cooper, Joel Jr.		1	
Cooper, John		1	
Cooper, Nathan		1	
Cooper, Patience	300		
Crowson, Samuel		1	
Cunningham, Mary	590	0	
Davis, Nathan	362½	1	
Davis, William	478	1	
Denton, Isaac	75	1	
Denton, Isaac Jr.	0	1	
Dungan, Jeremiah	1140		3
English, Robert	300		
Evens, Archer	160	1	
Garland, Joseph	270	1	
Gourley, Capt. Thomas	50	1	
Hagin, Barney	195	2	
Hail, John	349	1	
Hampson, James		1	
Harper, Josiah		1	
Haun, Adam	200	1	
Haun, Sebastian	500	1	
Hendrix, Solomon	113	1	
Hider, widow Elizabeth	200		
Hider, John	200	1	
Hider, Michael	132 3/4	1	
Hudiburg, Thomas	280 3/4	1	
Hufman, Dannell		1	
Ivey, Howell		1	
Job, Moses		1	
King, William		1	
Lackley, Thomas	200	1	
Large, Robert		1	
Lusk, Robert	248	1	
McCoy, John		1	1
McFall, Francis	235	1	
McInturff, Christopher	232	1	
McInturff, Gasper	100	1	
McInturff, John	200	1	
McInturff, John Jr.	218	1	
McNabb, David	255	1	
McNabb, William	332	2	
Millsaps, Thos	100	1	
Moffat, Alexander		1	
Nichols, Daniel		1	
Peoples, John	100	1	
Peoples, Wm	100	1	
Poland, John	200	1	
Price, Thomas	100	2	
Reasoner, Garrett	208	1	2
Renno. Charles		1	

Capt. Maxwell's old Company (cont'd)

Person's name	Land	white poles	black poles
Reno, John Sr.			2
Rockwell, Dorson		1	
Simmerley, Edam		1	
Smith, Brooks		1	
Smith, Zebulon		1	
Taylor, Andrew	225	1	
Taylor, Mathew		1	
Taylor, Capt. Nathaniel	990	1	
Tipton, Colo John	999		2
Tipton, Jonathan		1	
Ward, William	150	1	
Whitson, Jeremiah		1	
Whitson, Jesse	290	1	3
Whitson, John		2	
Williams, Edmund	1290		5
Williams, Francis		1	
Williams, Samuel		1	
Worley, John	100	1	
Wyatt, Thomas		1	
Wyatt, William	100	1	

....

Return of Captain Melvane's Company for the year 1793

Names	w pole	bl pole	land
Bacon, Isaac			200
Barnes, Joseph			100
Bean, Edmon	1		
Beard, Robert	1	0	142
Braden, James	1		
Bradley, Andrew	1		
Brown, John	1		320
Brown, Peter	0		30
Car, Thomas	1		139
Carney, John	1		
Carney, Thomas Senr	1		520
Cowen, John	1		97
Cox, James	1	1	150
Crabtree, Barnet	1		
Crabtree, John	0		100
Crouch, James, son of David	0		220
Crouch, Joseph	1		350
Dungwith, Charles	1		100
Dunham, David	1		100
Dyer, John	1		100
Elkins, William	1		
Ellis, William	2	1	675
Engle, George	1	1	190
Engle, Michael	1		225
Fraley, Christian	1		
Gates, Jacob	2		200

1793

Captain Melvane's Company (cont'd)

Names	w pole	bl pole	land
Gates, Richard	1		111
Gray, Absolam	1		
Greenway, William	1		50
Hagins, Arthur	1		
Hall, Nathaniel	2		290
Hall, Samuel	1		
Hall, Thomas	1		100
Hammer, Baltis senr	1		75
Hammer, Richard	1		
Hodges, John senr	2	1	330
Hoss, Jacob	1		700
Hunt, Simon	1		
Hunt, Thomas	1		275
Jinkins, George	2		500
McCloud, James	1		
McCloud, John	1		115
McCloud, Thomas	1		
McCloud, William jr	1		
McCloud, William senr	0		132
Matlock, Zachariah	1		150
Melvan, Jon	1	1	150
Melvan, Joseph, son of John	1		
Melvin, Joseph, son of Thomas	1		
Melvin, Thomas	0		160
Milburn, Samuel	1		
Miller, Peter	1		200
Moser, Anthony	1		40
Oldham, Henry	1	1	280
Pearce, Philip Groford	1		150
Prechard, Charles	1	1	150
Shaw, Benjamin		1	186
Starnes, Peter	1		150
Stone, Robert			243
Stone, William	1		243
Thomson, Richard	1		100
Umphres, John	1		
Umphres, Moses	1	1	205
Wiley, Thomas	1		
Wrighte, Thomas	1		
Young, John	1		

Returned by me J. Brittain

This list is on the back of Capt. Murry's Co. for 1793.

....

Account of the Taxable property in the bounds of Jno. Millikins Company for the year 1793

Names	white	black	land
Adams, William	1		200
Baldridge, James	1		

Jno. Millikins Company (cont'd)

Names	white	black	land
Blair, Richard	1		40
Bottles, Henery			125
Breeden, William	1		100
Broyles, Abraham	2		100
Broyles, Micholas	3		130
Cleck, Lewis			200
Cleeck, Peter	1		
Crookshanks, George	1		133
Cunningham, Hugh	1		130
Cunningham, John Jr.	1		
Cunningham, John Sr.	0		300
Denton, Johanan	1		100
Doak, Samuel	2		180
Dunn, Thomas	1		
Embree, John	1		200
Embree, Thomas	1		400
Gillespie, George	10	7	2020
Gillespie, Thomas	3		1290
Gordan, Lewis	1		350
Green, Joshua	1		170
Hall, Alexander	1		
Hall, James	1		
Hall, John	1		
Hall, William Jr.	1		200
Hall, William Sr.	1		440
Hanna, Andrew	1		320
Hatcher, John	1		100
Lott, Gasper	1		
McAllister, John	1		225
McBeath, Andrew	0		203
McBeath, Robert	1		
McEwen, Alexander	1		312
Mathews, Alexander	4		460
Meser, Jos	1		225
Montgomery, Alexander	1		100
Montgomery, James	1		100
Montgomery, Thomas	1		100
Millikin, John	1		200
Nelson, Henry	2		392
Nelson, John	2		200
Padfield, William	1		
Ramsey, Francis A.	4		
Rasor, Charles (?)	1		320
Roberts, John	1		
Scot, Thomas	1		200
Shields, Patrick	1		270
Stephenson, William	1		392
Taylor, David	1		100
Willson, Isaac	0		350
Woods, Archibald	1		

....

1793

Return of the Taxable property in Captain Morrisons Company for the years 1793 & 1794

Owners name	1793 poles white	1793 poles bl	1793 land	1794 poles white	1794 poles bl	1794 land
Badley, Andrew	1	0		1		
Ball, Amos	1		205	1		205
Bean, John	1		900	1		900
Bligh, Samuel	1					
Bogart, Samuel	1			1		
Boren, William			74			74
Bradley, John				1		564
Burningham, John				1		
Carr, John junr	1			1		
Carr, John senr	1	2	232	1	2	232
Carter, John				1		
Chance, Ezekiel				1		
Cobb, William	1	15	1000	1	15	1000
Collins, Joseph	1		100	1		100
Compton, John				1		
Creson, John	1			1		
Crouch, James	1					
Carruthers, Jonathan	1		102	1		102
Dannell, John	1			1		
Dannell, William	1		200	1		200
Davice, Thomas	1			1		
Denton, Isaac junr	1		100	1		100
Denton, Isaac senr	1		70	1		70
Denton, Jerry	1			1		
Denton, Joseph	1		185	1		185
Denton, Samuel	1		402	1		202
Duncan, Charles	1		432	1		432
Engle, John	1		350	1		350
Engle, Michael	1			1		
Fain, Nancy	0	1	200	0	2	200
Fain, Samuel estate by Adam Mitchel			400			400
Gibson, Thomas			117			117
Great, David	1		100	1		100
Greer, Charles	1			1		
Hammer, Jacob	1		100	1		100
Hammer, John	2		200	1		200
Huston, John	1			1		
Ivey, Howell				1		
Job, David	1	4	280	1	4	280
Kelley, Kintchin			200			200
Little, John				1		
Little, Jonas			320			320
McMahan, John Blair	1	1	490	1	1	490
Masengill, Henry	1	2	220	1	2	220
Masengill, Solomon	1	0	200	1	0	200
Melvane, Joseph the elder	0		250	0		450
Miller, John	1	0	142	1	0	142
Mitchel, Adam	2		300	2		300
Moore, Abraham	1			1		
Morrison, Joseph	1	0	200	1	0	200

Captain Morrison's Company (cont'd)

Owners name	1793 poles white	1793 poles bl	1793 land	1794 poles white	1794 poles bl	1794 land
Nelson, George	0	0	0	1		
Nelson, Jane	0	2	100	0	2	100
Nelson, William	1	1	500	1	1	500
Odle, Job	1	0	150	1	0	150
Odle, Templin	0			1		
Percefull, Samuel				1		87
Range, Peter	1	1	559	1	1	559
Reno, Charles	0	0	0	1	0	211
Reno, John	0	0		1		
Rice, Charles	0	0	0	1		
Stephens, Henry	1	2	400	1	2	400
Tullis, Jonathan	1		400	1		400
Ward, Dr. William	1	0	0	1	0	0
Whitacar, Mark	1	0	0	1	0	0
White, John	1		350	1		350
Wood, William			178			170
Young, John	1			1		252
Young, Robert	1		1004	1	0	1004

(NOTE: This list was likely not taken until 1794 as the list for the two years is on the one sheet. MHMcC & NEJS)

....

Return of Captain Murry's Company for the year 1793

Owner's name	white poles	black poles	Acres land
Barron, Joseph	1		325
Bell, John	1	1	100
Britten, William	1		100
Britten, Joseph Esq.	1		218
Bull, Jacob	1	1	225
Burch, Richard	1		150
Carson, William	1		200
Chapman, John	1		100
Chamberlain, James	1	1	47
Christean, John	1		
Christean, Ezeral	1		200
Cox, Elijah	1		162
Crouch, John Sr.			50
Dodson, William	1		
Dunham, Charles	1		
Ellis, John	1		100
Ensor, Thomas	1		250
Eppeson, Anthony	1		250
Eppeson, Peter	1		200
Eppeson, Samuel	1		250
Foord, John	1	1	200
Foord, Loyd Jr.	1		120
Foord, Loyd Sr.		1	100
Foord, Mordecai	1	0	100

1793

Captain Murry's Company (cont'd)

Owner's name	white poles	black poles	Acres land
Foord, Thomas	1	0	200
Foord, William	1	0	100
Glascock, Archabale	1	1	240
Gott, Anthony	0	0	570
Gott, John	1	0	120
Gray, George	0	1	336
Gray, Robert	1	1	
Gristham, Thomas	1	1	184
Haile, Abednego	1	3	249 3/4s
Haile, George Jr.	1	2	225
Haile, John	1		92
Haile, John Sr	1	1	500
Haile, Joshua	1		
Haile, Joseph the elder	2	2	836
Haile, Meschack son of George	1	0	420
Haile, Nathan	1	0	200
Haile, Nicholas Jr.	1	2	700
Haile, Nicholas Sr.	0	1	272
Haile, Richard	1	0	320
Haile, Samuel	1	1	195
Haile, William	1	0	200
Holland, Benjamin	1	3	550
Hunt, Jesse	1		540
Kincheloe, George	1	2	150
Kincheloe, John	0	6	200
McCubbin, Zachariah	1	1	200
McFerson, Barten	1	0	100
McFerson, Daniel	1	1	250
Maden, Andrew	1		
Martin, James	1		
Miller, Adam	1		
Moore, Samuel	1	0	240
Mulkey, Jonathan	1	0	100
Murry, Morgan	1	0	200
Murry, Shadrack	1	0	150
Murry, Thomas Sr.	0	0	290
Nolan, George	1	4	300
Nolan, James	1		
Norwood, John	1		
Owen, James	1		100
Pain, Reubin	1	0	200
Rector, John	1	0	180
Shipley, Adam	1		
Shipley, Benjamin	0	0	170
Shipley, Edward	1	0	490
Shipley, James	1		
Shipley, Nathan	1		
Shipley, Peter	1	0	150
Smith, Anderson	1	0	250
Stanback, Michael	1		
Wheelock, John	1	1	350
White, Archebele	1	0	200

Returned by me- J. Britten

This List is on back of Capt. Melvane's Company for 1793.

Captain North's Company 1793 Taken by Self

Names	Wh Pole	Black Pole	Land
Andis, Frederick	1		140
Antony, Abrahm	1		30
Barron, Dossey	1		
Barron, Ezkl	0	0	70
Barron, James	1		
Bayless, Daniel			100
Baylis, John	1		300
Bell, John	1		200
Boring, Absolam	1		
Boring, Cheney	1		750
Brooks, Giles	1		300
Buley, Antony	0		370
Cooper, Joseph			69
Cumton, Jeremiah	1		180
Dotson, Jonathan	0	0	115
Fine, John	1	0	250
Fitchgerrel, George	1	0	23
Gautt, John	1		100
Goodpasture, Abram			200
Goodpasture, Isaac	1		
Goodpasture, Solom			62
Gray, Willis	1		
Headrick, Charles	1		140
Heslan, Abram	1		100
Hunter, John			340
Irvin, James			200
Irvin, Samuel	1		
Lamon, Alexr	1		
Lamon, John	1		
Lamon, John			450
Leech, William	0		100
Moore, James	1		105
Murey, Ephrm	1		180
Myers, Fredk	1		
North, George Captain	1		
North, John	0	0	100
Ozmus, Philip			200
Phillipps, Gabl.	1		100
Pitner, John	1		200
Price, Mordeca	1		400
Rader, Adam	1		540
Rogers, Thos	1		
Rose, Hosea	0	0	320
Ruble, John	1		200
Scott, Absolem	1		
Smith, Ed	1	1	218
Tipton, Jonathan	1		
Watson, William	1		600
Young, Charles	1	1	320
Young, Joseph	1	3	915

....

1793

A List of the Taxable Property of the people within the district of Captain Scott's Company for the year 1793 - Taken by self

Allison, Frank	2	320
Bailes, Samuel	1	1400
Baker, Francis	2	300
Baxter, Francis	1	
Beaty, Robert	1	
Beaty, William	1	
Brown, Abraham	1	150
Brown, Jacob	1	100
Buhanon, Ezekiel	1	
Calvert, William	2	127
Cash, James Junr	1	
Cash, James senr	2	328
Cresselis, Isaac	0	100
Charter, James	1	138
Cloyd, William	1	160
Doak, Samuel	3	180
Evens, Thos	1	
Finch, Colvin	1	150
Frier, Robert	1	100
Hair, Isaac	1	130
Hall, James	1	
Harmon, Abraham	1	
Harmon, Adam	1	100
Herris, Joshua	1	
Harrison, Michael	1	145
Hathhorn, Noah	1	
House, George	3	50
House, Thomas	1	
Humberd, John	1	172
Hunter, Abraham	1	150
Larkins, James	1	87
Lilburn, Andrew	1	450
Miller, Henry	1	190
Million, Edward	1	162
Nody, William	6	300
Pean, Jesse	2	120
Reed, James	1	250
Rymal, John	1	230
Scott, James ex Charles Hays	0	175
Scott, James	1	200
Sevier, Jack	2	
Sevier, John junr	3	
Shanan, William	1	160
Slaiger, Gasper	1	100
Slaiger, John jr	1	
Slaiger, John senr	0	350
Smith, John	1	250
Smith, Robert	1	50
Taylor, Christopher	2	305
Waddill, John	1	
Walter, Peter	1	100
Wood, Samuel	1	272

....

Torn Scrap--- James Allisons Return. 1793
------- 1793
---- the Taxable property-- Allison Esquire----
--res of land two poles---------------
---- pounds worth of Town lots in Jonesborough.

....

1793-- The Delinquents for the year 1793

Names	Doll	cents
-aith, John (?)		50
Beaty, Wm		50
Borin, Doosy		50
Bradley, Andrew		50
Breeden, James		50
Brookshear, Joseph		50
Buckannon, Ezekiel		50
Burden, Charles		50
Christian, John		72
Conklin, David		50
Cooper, John		50
Crouch, James		58
Dobbins, Even		50
Dunn, Thomas		50
Easton, Abraham		75
Graves, Thomas		50
Green, John		50
Green, W		75
Hall, James		50
Hampton, James		50
Hanna, Samuel		67
Harper, Jeremiah		50
Hart, Hardy		50
Hatcher, John		50
Headrick, Jacob senr		50
Headrick, Peter		50
Hiter, Michael		25
Humphreys, John		50
Irwin, John		50
Jinkins, Hugh		50
Larkins, James		65
Little, John		25
McCloud, Thomas		50
McKinna, Henry		50
Miers, Frederick		50
Miller, Adam		50
Payne, Charles		50
Payne, John		50
Shields, Henry	1	18
Simerly, Adam		50
Starback, Michael		50
Swiney, Wm		50
Terry, John		50
Wallice, Aron		50
Wallin, John		50
Young, John		58
	$23.80	

On Back-- Return of Taxables- Returned by me- George Gillespie

TAX FOR THE YEAR 1794

50 cts on poles & 17 cents per hundred on land for the purpose of erecting the public buildings and defraying the contingent charges of the county.

And the same justices to receive the lists that took them in for the year 1793, Except that

Reuben Thornton Esquire take them in place of Richard White Esq,

Joseph Crouch Esquire, take in the list in Captain Melvins Company,

John Sevier in place of Samuel Handley Esquire,

James Stuart Esquire, to take in the list of Capt Scotts company,

James Allison to take in Norths & Browns companies in room of Ch. Roberson, Esquire,

Captain Nathl Taylor to take in the list of the Greesy and Limestone Coves for the years 1793 & 94.

Returns to be made to the next Court.

....

A List of the Taxable Property in Capt Blair's Company for 1794 - Taken by self

Names	Acres	wh pole	bl pole
Alexander, Frances	125	1	
Alexander, John	125	1	
Bell, James	100	1	
Biddle, Thomas	500	1	
Blackley, Daniel	130	1	
Blackley, Robert	370	1	
Blair, John	300	1	
Blair, Coln John	279	1	1
Blair, Capt. Robert	175	1	2
Boid, George	200	1	
Brown, David	200	1	
Brown, William	100	1	
Burk, John	173	1	
Campbell, Hugh	180		
Campbell, John Esq.	185	1	
Campbell, Robert	0	1	
Carmicheal, John	200	0	1
Carson, Moses	350	1	
Coson, John	700	1	
Davis, George	100	1	
Davis, Samuel	100	1	
Gamble, Andrew	0	1	
Kelsey, William	300	1	
King, Henry	170	1	
Lord, Abel	0	1	

Capt Blair's Company (cont'd)

Names	Acres	wh pole	bl pole
McConnel, John	300	1	
McWhorter, James	150	1	
Martin, Joseph	100	1	
Miller, John Blair	250	1	
Patterson, James	143	1	
Ramsey, Robert	0	1	
Richards, David	0	1	
Robertson, James	0	1	
Sands, Benjamin	365	1	
Shanks, James	350		
Shanks, William	0	1	
Shields, George	177	1	
Shields, Joseph	225	1	
Smith, Richard	0	1	
Tedlock, Lewis	0	1	
Tiffin, Henry	250	1	2
Williams, John	200	1	

....

Capt. Depews Company for 1794 is in same booklet.

....

A List of the Taxable Property in Captain Brown's Company agreeable to the order of the Cort. for 1794. May ye 16 -Taken by self

Names	Acres	Poles
Acton, James	0	1
Alison, Frances of Meriland returned by James Alison	234	0
Belis, Rubins	170	1
Boy, Henry	0	1
Brown, Benjamin	300	1
Brown, Capt. Jacob	326	6
Brown, John	326	1
Brown, Thomas	326	2
Colyar, William	0	1
Freintch, Peeter	200	
Hamond, Christofor	100	1
Hamton, Robert	200	1
Handley, George	0	1
Ingell, William	60	0
Jones, Richard	130	1
Keel, James	121	1
Keill, Jse	0	1
Kell, John	178	-1
Lamons, Christefor	0	1
Lemans, David	200	
Lemans, Jacob	0	1
Rodgers, John	100	1
Rodgers, Joseph	50	1
Shanon, John	100	1
Sinclear, Alexander	300	2

1794

A List of the Taxable Property in Capt. Carrigers Company for the year 1794

Names	Acres	Poles White	Black
Arrondell, John	200	1	
Bass, Jeremiah	280	1	8
Bowers, Leonard	50	1	
Carriger, Godfrey	2324	0	2
Carriger, Godfrey Jr.	222	1	
Carriger, Michael	150	1	
Carriger, Nicholas	450	1	
Carter, John	0	1	2
Carter, Landon	2240	1	6
Cobb, Pharoah	1000	1	7
Cooper, James	0	1	
Cox, Richard	0	1	
Drake, Abraham	400	1	
Duncan, Thomas	0	1	
Emmert, George	297	1	
Flannery, William	100	1	
Forbush, Hugh	0	1	
Garland, Humphrey	0	1	
Garland, John	200	1	
Gillam, William	0	1	
Greer, Alexr	0	1	5
Greer, Andrew	1700	0	3
Greer, Thomas	0	1	
Harden, William	0	1	
Hanry, William	0	1	
Heatherick, John Jr.	0	1	
Helton, Abraham	0	1	
Helton, John	0	1	
Helton, Peter	0	1	
Humphreys, Elisha	360	1	
Humphreys, John	0	1	
Ivey, James	50	1	
Johnston, Robt.	0	1	
Keer, John	0	1	
Kite, Isaac	0	1	
Kite, Richard	150	1	
Lacey, James	0	1	
Lacey, Philemon	0	1	
Large, Joseph	0	1	
Large, Robert	0	1	
Lincoln, Isaac	670	1	
Little, Thomas	0	1	
Matlack, Gideon	544	1	
Matlock, William	0	1	
Millard, Thomas	0	1	
Moore, John Parker	0	1	
Musgraves, John	0	1	
Musgraves, Robert	640	1	
Nave, Abraham	0	1	
Nave, Teter	350	1	
Nowlan, John	0	1	

Capt. Carrigers Company (cont'd)

Names	Acres	Poles White	Poles Black
Patrick, James	0	1	
Peters, Christian	0	1	
Price, James	210	1	
Redman, Stephen	0	1	
Right, James	0	1	
Roberson, John	50	1	
Sevier, Abraham	142	1	
Sevier, Valentine Sr.	410	0	0
Shoultz, Christian	0	1	
Shoultz, Christian Jr.	0	1	
Smithpeters, John Michael	745	1	
Stover, Christian	0	1	
Tipton, Samuel	890	1	
Tipton, Thomas	386	1	
Worley, John	100	1	

....

A List of Taxable Property in Capt. Depews Company for 1794

Names	Land	wh pole	bl pole
Allien, Robert	750	1	1
Allison, Ann	145	0	
Allison, Robert	400	1	4
Anderson, John	200	1	
Archer, John	0	0	0
Bails, David	0	1	
Bails, Isaac	130		
Balis, Richard	63	1	
Bell, Elizabeth			
Bell, George	135	1	
Blair, Brice	100	1	
Blair, Joseph, Junr	0	1	0
Blair, John, senr	300	0	1
Burk, William	0	1	
Carmichael, James	350	1	1
Carr, Thomas	90	1	
Carson, David	58	1	
Carson, David, senr	100	1	
Carson, David wd.	250	1	
Carson, Robert	0	1	
Carson, William	150	1	
Cowen, John	740	1	1
Craig, Thomas	90		
Depue, Isaac Cpt.	118	1	
Duncan, Andrew	229	1	
Duncan, Joseph	321	1	
Farguson, Alexander	0	1	
Farguson, John	300	1	
Farler, Obediah	50	1	
Glass, William	434	1	
Henderson, Joseph	140	1	

Capt. Depews Company (cont'd)

Names	Land	wh pole	bl pole
Hunt, Uriah	940	1	1
Hunter, James	0	1	
Johnston, Samuel	75	1	
Jones, Nathanl	90	1	
McCord, David	0	1	
McCord, James	400	1	
McCorkle, Joseph	200	1	
McLand, Alexr	200	1	
McNitt, Anthony	150	0	
McNitt, John	0	1	
Machlin, Robert	200	1	
Montgomery, William	100	1	
Neell, Samuel	113	1	
Newel, Joseph	0	1	
Pursley, William	240		
Richey, James	0	1	
Russel, David	282	1	
Shanks, Holden	222	1	
Shaw, Samuel	300	0	1
Shipley, Thomas	200	1	
Smith, Abraham	400	1	
Stewart, Alexander	0	1	
Stewart, David	341	1	
Stewart, David	50	1	
Stewart, John	30		
Taylor, Leeroy	241	1	2
Thompson, Andrew	167	1	2
Thomson, David	100	1	
Trotter, Alexander	99	1	
Tucker, Joseph	305	1	
Tucker, Nicholas	70	1	
Walker, William	184	1	
Woods, William	150	1	

....

Captain Blair's Company for 1794 is in the same booklet.

....

A List of Poles and Taxable Property in Capt. Joseph Fords Company for 1794

Names	Poles	Land
Abner, Elisha	1	0
Anderson, Thomas	1	200
Asher, John	1	200
Bishop, Joseph	1	100
Burk, Arthur	1	
Campbell, Isaac	1	50
Campbell, James	1	100
Campbell, Jeremiah	1	200
Campbell, Zachriah	0	100

Capt. Joseph Fords Company (cont'd)

Names	Poles	Land
Campbell, Zachriah Jr.	1	150
Cook, William	0	50
Davis, James	1	100
Dugger, Julius	1	100
Dugger, William	1	250
Duncan, Lance	1	140
Duncan, Patrick	1	
Grimes, John	0	100
Grindstaff, Catherine	0	100
Guin, Champ	1	100
Hog, Obediah	1	
Hoskins, Thomas	1	
Jones, Lewis Jr.	1	0
Jones, Lewis Sr.	0	200
Lord, Joseph	1	100
McGee, Thomas	1	50
Millsaps, James	1	
Moreland, William	1	150
Mullins, William	1	50
Mullins, William Jr.	1	
Perkesan, Mary	0	200
Polly, Edward	1	0
Potter, Hannah	0	100
Primmer, Mary	0	100
Ranbold, Adam	1	0
Ranbold, John	1	0
Ranbold, Widow	0	100
Richardson, Daniel	1	
Richardson, John	1	150
Simerley, John	1	300
Smith, Edward	0	450
Smith, Jacob	1	100
Smith, John	1	50
Smith, Nicholas	1	150
Smith, Samuel	1	
Smith, William	1	100
Starns, Conrad	1	100
Starms, John	1	50
Tate, John	1	50
Tate, Sameul	0	175
Vantrece, John	1	325
White, Richard	6	500
Yates, Samuel	1	

This List is on the back of Captain Thornton's Company for 1794.

....

A List of the Taxable Property in Captain Hale's Company for the year 1794

Names	Land	w pole	b pole
Acton, James	100	1	
Anderson, William	150	1	

1794

Captain Hale's Company (cont'd)

Names	Land	w pole	b pole
Colyer, Charles	66	1	
Culbertson, Samuel	650		
Dickins, James		1	
Dickins, Richard	173	1	
Diel, Patrick	109	0	
Dillard, Martha	200	0	8
Evens, John	125	1	
Evins, Thomas	45	0	
Garlan, Gutridge	150	1	
Hale, Capt.	56	1	
King, Henry	130	1	
Lewis, William		1	
Longmires, Charles	600	1	
McCray, Charels Esq.	100	1	
Mecray, James	366	1	
McInturff, Gasper	100	1	
Pohon, Wiliam	67	1	
Roberts, Jesse	50	1	
Samms, James	100		
Samms, John	261	1	
Smith, Henry		1	1

This list is copied on back of Hales for 1793.

....

A List of the Taxable Property of the people within the District of Captain Samuel Handleys Company for the year 1794 - Taken by self

Names	Poles	Land
Beard, Andrew	2	280
Bitner, John	1	100
Blackburn, Archabald	3	160
Broiles, Adam	1	
Broiles, Adam Bl Smith	1	300
Broiles, Daniel	1	110
Broiles, Reubin	1	
Broiles, Samuel	1	250
Broiles, Syries	2	100
Broiles, Tobias	1	
Brown, William	2	150
Clark, Jesse	1	
Clarke, John	1	200
Clarke, William	4	300
Collam, George	1	
Collan, Jonathan	1	200
Condren, William	1	160
Galliher, John	2	400
Gann, Adam Jr.	1	
Gann, Adam Sr.	0	150
Gann, Clamins	0	100
Gann, John	1	100

Captain Samuel Handleys Company (cont'd)

Names	Poles	Land
Gann, Nathan	1	220
Gann, Thomas	1	
Greenaway, William	1	112
Harbison, William	1	
Humphries, Richard	1	400
Lamon, John	1	
McFarlin, Robert	1	
McGee, John	1	
McGee, William	1	
McKee, John	1	100
Miller, James	1	100
Miller, Peter	0	400
Moore, Alexander	1	
Moore, William	1	358
Panther, Adam	2	164
Sherp, Joseph	1	150
Waddill, John Sr.	0	330
Waddell, Seth Cue	1	200
Woods, Michael	8	640

....

Scrap---

Memo of Tax of Captain Handley's Company for 1794.

D.	Cts.
36.	71

....

A List of the Taxable Property in Capt. Melvans Company for the year 1794.

Owners Names	Poles white	Poles black	Acres land
Bacon, Isaac			200
Bacon, John	1	0	190
Bacon, Jonnathan	1	0	200
Bard, Hobart	1	0	142
Barns, Joseph	0	0	100
Braden, James	1		
Brown, John	1	0	320
Brown, Peter	0	0	50
Carney, John	1	2	0
Carney, Thomas	1	3	3-30
Carney, Thomas Sr.	0	1	520
Carr, Thomas	1	0	1-9
Cox, James	1	2	50
Cowen, John	1	0	107
Crabtree, Barnett	1		
Crabtree, John	0	0	100
Croch, Joseph	1	0	355
Dier, John	1	0	90
Dungworth, Charles	1	0	110
Dunham, David	1		100
Ellis, William	2	1	715

Capt. Melvans Company (con't'd)

Owners Names	Poles white	Poles black	Acres land
Fraley, Christian	1	0	0
Gates, Jacob Sr.	2	0	200
Gates, Richard Sr. (?)	1	0	1-11
Genkins, George	2	0	500
Gray, Absolam	1		
Gray, John	1		
Hail, Abednego Jr.	1	3	150
Haines, Samuel	1		
Hall, Nathl	1	0	291
Hall, Samuel	1	0	100
Hall, Thomas	1	0	100
Hall, William	1		
Hammor, Baltis	1		
Hammor, Richard	1		
Hoss, John Sr.	2	1	520
Hoss, Jacob	1	0	700
Humphreys, Moses	1		
Hunt, Simon	1		
Hunt, Thomas	1	0	275
McCloud, John	1		115
McCloud, William	1		
McCloud, William Sr.	0	0	132
Meains, Isaac	0	0	200
Meains, Thomas	1		
Medlock, Zachriah	0	0	150
Melvain, Samuel	1	0	100
Melvan, Joseph son of Thomas	1		
Melven, Thomas	0	0	150
Melvin, John	1	1	150
Millburn, Samuel	1		
Miller, Peter	1	0	200
Nelson, John	1	0	100
Oldham, Henry	1	1	180
Pitcock, John	1		
Pretchard, Charles	1	0	150
Shaw, Benjamin	0	0	186
Starns, Peter	1	0	150
Stone, Robert	0	0	243
Stone, William	1	0	241
Thompson, Richard	1	0	130
Whethers, William	1	0	137
Wright, Thomas	1	0	0

Returned by me-- J. Crouch J.P.

....

List of Taxable Property in the bounds of John Milliken, for the year 1794.

Names	Poles	Acres
Adams, William	1	200
Ball, Thomas	1	

Property in the bounds of John Milliken (cont'd)

Names	Poles	Acres
Bottles, Henery	1	125
Breeden, William		100
Broyls, Abraham	2	200
Broyls, Nicholes	2	130
Cain, Hugh	1	0
Cleck, Lewis	0	200
Cunningham, Hugh	1	300
Cunningham, John	0	0
Crookshanks, George	1	133
Denton, Jonathan	1	100
Doak, Samuel	2	180
Embree, John	1	220
Gillespie, Thomas	3	1290
Green, Joshua	1	170
Grimes, James	1	0
Hall, Alex	1	
Hall, James	1	
Hannah, Andrw	1	320
Jurden, Lewis	1	300
McBeath, Andrew	1	250
MaCalistor, John	1	625
McCuen, Alex	1	312
Mathews, Alexander	4	460
May, Casimor	1	
Messer, Joseph	1	225
Millikin, John	1	200
Montgomery, Alex	1	100
Montgomery, James	2	180
Montgomery, Thomas	1	100
Nelson, Henry	2	190
Nelson, John	2	200
Roberts, John	1	0
Scott, Thomas	1	200
Smith, John	1	0
Stephenson, William	1	467
Taylor, David	1	150
Wallas, James	1	
Yeager, Solomn	2	100

June 30, 1794 -

I do hereby certify that the foregoing is a true Return of Taxables though there is some that have not made their return to me.

John Millikin.

....

Capt. Morrison's Co. - See 1793 List.

....

Return of the Taxable Property in Captain Murray Company for the year 1794.

Owners Names	Poles White	Poles Black	Acres Land
Austin, John	1	0	145

And as John Austin was out of the way last year gives in the same for 1793 & 1794.

Captain Murray Company (cont'd)

Owners Names	Poles White	Poles Black	Acres Land
Barron, Walker	1	0	130
Barron, Joseph	1	0	370
Barron, William	1	0	100
Britten, Joseph	1	0	318
Britten, the Estate of William	0	0	100
Bull, Jacob	1	1	225
Bullington, William	1		150
Burch, Richard	1	0	140
Chamberlain, James	1	1	160
Chapman, John	1	0	100
Christie, Ezzarel	1	0	200
Crouch, John Jr.	1	0	100
Crouch, John Sr.	0	0	50
Denham, Charles	1		
Dodson, William	1		
Dunn, James	1	0	100
Ellis, John	1	0	100
Emberton, Richard	1		
Ensor, Thomas	1	0	250
Epperson, Anthoney	1	1	250
Epperson, Peter	1	0	200
Epperson, Samuel	1	0	250
Ford, James	1		
Ford, John	1	1	200
Ford, Loyd Jr.	1	0	120
Ford, Loyd Sr.	0	2	100
Ford, Mordecai	1	0	100
Ford, Thomas	1	0	200
Ford, William	1	-	100
Glascock, Archable	1	1	240
Gott, Anthony	0	0	570
Gott, John	1	0	120
Gray, George	0	1	338
Gray, Robert	1	1	0
Gristham, Thomas	1	1	184
Haile, Abednego, the older	1	1	320
Haile, Alexander	0	0	100
Haile, George Jr.	1	2	220
Haile, George Sr.	0	1	200
Haile, John	1	0	92
Haile, Joseph the younger	1	0	100
Haile, Joseph the older	2	2	836
Haile, Joshua	1	0	
Haile, Meshack of George	1	0	420
Haile, Nathan	1	0	200
Haile, the estate of Nicholas Jr.	0	2	700
Hile, Nicholas Sr.	0	1	272
Haile, Richard	1	0	330
Haile, Samuel	1	1	200
Haile, Shadrack	1	0	100
Haile, William	1	0	200
Holland, Benjamin	1	4	550
Hunt, Jesse	1	0	420

Captain Murray Company (cont'd)

Owners Names	Poles White	Poles Black	Acres Land
Jackson, George	1	0	50
Jackson, William	1	0	152
Kincheloe, Charles	1	1	200
Kincheloe, George	1	2	-
Kincheloe, John	0	6	450
King, Kirbe	1	0	150
Lane, Tidance	0	0	250
McCubbin, Zacheriah	1	1	200
McFerson, Barten	1		
McFerson, Daniel	1	1	150
McFerson, Henry	1	0	120
Maden, Andrew	1		
Martin, James	1	0	170
Melvan, Joseph son of John	1	0	100
Miller, Adam	1		
Moore, Samuel	1	0	234
Mulkey, John	1		
Mulkey, Johnathan	1	0	100
Murrey, Morgan	1	0	200
Murray, Shadrack	1	0	150
Murrey, Thomas Sebnr.	0	0	290
Nolan, James	1	0	100
Nolan, George	1	4	300
Norwood, John	1		
Owen, James	1	0	100
Pearce, Philip Froford	1	0	200
Rector, George	1		
Rector, George	1	0	100
Shipley, Benjamin	1	0	170
Shipley, Edward	2	0	490
Shipley, Peter	1	0	150
Smith, Anderson	1	0	250
Whelock, John	1	1	650
White, Archable	1	0	200

Returned by me J Britten J P

....

A List of Capt. Norths Company for the year 1794 - Taken by self

Names	Land	Poles
Anderson, Fredrick	143	1
Antoney, Abrm	230	1
Belis, Danel	100	0
Bell, John	200	1
Bleyth, Samuel	0	1
Boring, Absalam	0	1
Boring, James Jr.	0	1
Boring, James Sr.	75	0
Boring, Zecall	70	0
Brooks, Giles	300	1
Buley, Antony	250	1

1794

Capt. Norths Company (cont'd)

Names	Land	Poles
Colet, Hack	0	1
Comton, Geremiah	0	1
Fine, John	250	1
Fitzchgeral, Geary	23	1
Goddpasture, Isaac	0	1
Goodpasture, Solomon	62	0
Gott, John	0	1
Graposts, Abraham (?)	200	0
Gree, Willis (?)	0	1
Hedrick, Charles	140	0
Henderson, John	250	1
Hunter, Henery	0	1
Hunter, John	619	0
Leman, Abraham	0	1
Leman, John	0	1
Lillburn, William (?)	100	0
Moor, James	105	1
North, Capt, George	100	1
Ozamus, Philip	200	0
Parker, John	0	1
Philaps, Gabrell	100	1
Pitner, John	200	1
Price, Mordecai	400	1
Reader, Adam	540	1
Rose, Hosea	320	1
Rodgers, Thomas	0	1
Rubell, John	200	1
Smith, Ewd	218	1
Tipton, Jonathan	0	1
Walker, Barbra widow	264	0
Watson, Jonathan	115	0
Watson, William	600	1
Young, Charles	320	2
Young, Joseph	915	5
Young, Thomas	318	4

This is to certify that this is a true list of all Capt. Norths Company.

....

A List for Capt Scott's Company for the year 1794 as follows Taken by James Stuart

Names	Land	Poles
Adams, John -1 lot in Jonesboro		1
Alison, Frances	314	3
Alison, James	700	1
Baker, Frances	200	1
Balis, Daniel	100	1
Balias, John	300	1
Baxtor, Frances		1
Belis, Samuel	1780	1

Capt Scott's Company (cont'd)

Names	Land	Poles
Bromit, Samuel	50	1
Brown, Abraham	150	1
Brown, Jacob	100	1
Calvinn, Capt J Pelam	127	2
Cash, Jams, Jr		1
Cash, Jams Sr	328	2
Crerslas, Isac	100	1
Ervin, Samuel	100	1
Evins, George	57	1
Fain, Wilam	850	1
Fintch, Calvin	150	1
Frier, Robert	100	1
Hall, James- 1 acre lot in Jonesborow		1
Harmon, Abraham		1
Hathorn, Noah		1
Hear, Isac	130	1
Humberd, John	172	1
Hunter, Abraham	150	1
Ingell, Mical		1
Joans, Isac		1
Kindell, George	100	1
Megies (?), J. John	430	1
Miller, Henery	240	
Milion, Edward	162	1
Noding, Wilam	300	6
Pain, Jese	200	
Remar, John	230	1
Robson, Col Charles	300	5
Scroggs, Ebnesor	200	
Sevier, James	179	3
Sevier, John Jr- 8 lots- 160 acres land- 3 poles		
Shanon, Wilam	150	1
Sidner, Martin	100	1
Sliger, Jasper	100	1
Sliger, John Jr	100	1
Sliger, John Senor	250	
Smith, James		1
Smith, John	25	
Spring, Nikels		1
Taylor, Critefor	305	2
Telor, Henery		1
Walter, Peeter	100	1
Woods, Samuel	273	

....

A List of the Taxable Property of Nathaniel Taylor Company for the year 1794

Name	Land	White poles	Black poles
Archer, William		1	
Baley, Coterel	500	1	
Bogart, Henery		1	
Clark, Josiah	270	1	

1794

Nathaniel Taylor Company (cont'd)

Name	Land	White poles	Black poles
Cooper, Abraham	100	1	
Cooper, Edward		1	
Cooper, Jobe	200	1	
Cooper, Joel Jr.		1	
Cooper, Joel Sr.	177	1	
Cooper, John son of widow Cooper		1	
Cooper, Nathan		1	
Cox, Abraham		1	
Crosen, Samuel		1	
Crouch, John		1	
Cunningham, Marey	580		
Davice, Nathan	260	1	
Davice, William	340	1	
Denton, Isaac	70	1	
Dungens, Jeremiah	1100		3
Eden, Austin		1	
Eden, James	580	1	
English, Robert	496	1	
Evens, Archer	160	1	
Franks, Richard	55	1	
Garland, Joseph	265	1	
Hagen, Barney	200	1	
Hagen, James		1	
Hale, John	349	1	
Hanes, George	300	1	
Hanery, Abraham	100	1	
Hendricks, Solomon	113	1	
Hone, Abraham		1	
Hone, Adam	150	1	
Hone, Christopher	100	1	
Hone, Mathias	100	1	
Hone, Sabaustian	550	1	
Hudeburk, Thomas	140	1	
Hufman, James	100	1	
Humfris, Jess	296	2	
Hyder, John	460	1	
Hyder, Michel	150	1	
Lackey, Thomas	200	1	
Lockerd, Robert		1	
Lockerd, William		1	
Luck, Robert	222	1	
Luces, George		1	
McEnturff, John Jr	218	1	
Mcfall, Frances	235	1	
McNabb, Baptist		1	
McNabb, David	250	1	
McNabb, William	394	1	
Mackenturff, John Sr.	250	1	
Mecay, John		1	1
Mackenturf, Christopher	232	1	
Maxwell, Capt. Thomas	180	1	
Micormack, Robert	55	1	

Nathaniel Taylor Company (cont'd)

Name	Land	White poles	Black poles
Milsaps, Thomas	100	1	
Moor, Absolom	50	1	
Moor, Daniel	100	1	
Nicholas, Daniel	92	1	
Peoples, John	160		
Peoples, William	100	1	
Poland, John	200	1	
Price, Solomon		1	
Price, Thomas	100	1	
Pue, William		1	
Range, James	270	1	
Resoner, Garet	238	1	3
Rockwell, Dosen		1	
Smith, Brooks		1	
Smith, Zebulon		1	
Taylor, Andrew	233	1	
Taylor, Issac	650	1	
Taylor, Mathew	150	1	
Taylor, Nathl	640	1	
Tipton, John		1	
Tipton, Col. John	1130		3
Tipton, Jonathan	200	1	
Tipton, Joseph	750	1	
Ward, William	250	1	
Whitson, Abraham		1	
Whitson, Jeremiah		1	
Whitson, Jess	298	1	3
Whitson, John		1	
Wiet, Thomas		1	
Wiet, William	200	1	
Williams, Frances		1	
Williams, George		1	

- - - - - - -

Scrap:
Inventory of Edmond Williams Taxable Property for 1794
April 1, 1794
To 1178 acres of land) Attest
To 4 males black) Edmd Williams
To 2 black females)

(Note: It is likely that Edmond Williams' list belongs in Capt. Nathaniel Taylor's Company. MHMcC)

....

A List of the Taxable Property in Capt. Thorntons Company
Taken by me - Reubin Thornton - 26th Aug. 1794

Names	Poles	Land
Adams, Jesse	1	
Arnnold, Nathal	1	
Arnnold, William	1	
Baker, John	1	100

Capt. Thorntons Company (cont'd)

Names	Poles	Land
Branstutter, Peter	1	200
Buckner, William	1	
Cain, Peter	1	
Cutberth, Daniel	1	
Dugglass, James	1	
Eastridge, Richard	1	0
Garland, Samuel	0	125
Gentry, Joseph	1	110
Graves, James	1	0
Griffen, William	1	200
Grindstaff, John	1	300
Guinn, James Sr.	0	178
Heatherley, Ewings	0	22
Heatherley, John	1	
Heaton, John	1	0
Howard, John	1	
Jackson, William	1	300
Jenkins, Rowland	1	248
Lindsey, Matthew	0	78
McQueen, John	1	207
Mullins, John	1	
Peevehouse, John	0	200
Perkins, George	1	200
Perkins, Jacob	1	200
Prophet, John	1	
Roberts, Aaron	1	
Roberts, Moses	1	
Roberts, Reuben	1	
Roberts, William	1	
Robertson, John	0	155
Sands, John	1	20
Sheffield, George	1	0
Snider, Elezabeth	0	115
Shoun, Leonard	1	
Slimp, Michael	1	
Snider, Peter	0	133
Storm, Peter	0	360
Stout, Daniel	1	300
Thornton, Rn.	1	400
Vaught, John	1	961
Waggoner, David	one white pole & three black	672
Waggoner, Mathias	one white, 2 black	765
Walthers, John	1	
Wheeller, Stephen	1	100
Whitson, Thomas	0	400
Widby, William Jr.	1	
Willson, Garland	1	
Willson, Samuel	1	150
Wilson, John Jr.	1	73
Wilson, John Sr.	1	100
Wilson, Joseph	1	
Wilson, William	1	0

Capt. Thorntons Company (cont'd)

Taken in by me - Reubin Thornton
for the year 1794 this 26th August.

This list is on the back of Captain Ford's Company for 1794.

....

The Delinquents in the Duplicate for 1794

	Land	Pole	£	S	D
Adams, Jesse		1-		4	
Anthony, Abraham	230	1-		7	
Arnel, John	200	1-		6	8
Arnel, Nathen		1-		4	
Arnell, William		1-		4	
Bermingham, James		1-		4	
Campbill, James	50	1-		4	8
Campbill, James	100	1-		5	4
Dodson, Wm.		1-			4
Dunan, Patrick		1-			4
Emberton, Richard		1-			4
Goodpaster, Solomon	62				-10
Grimes, John	100	1-			4
Hall, James		1-		4	
Heatherly, John		1-		4	
Helton, Peter		1-		4	
Henry, William		1-		4	
Hopkins, Thomas		1-		4	
Ivy, Howie		1-		4	
Kerr, John		1-		4	
Lemons, Jacob		1-		4	
Loyd, Abel		1-		4	
Mcgee, Thomas	50	1-		4	8
McQueen, John	207	1-		6	9
Miller, Adam		1-		4	
Mulky, John		1-		4	
Oldham, Henry	180	2-		10	5
Pearce, Phil G.	200	1-		6	8
Raignbolt, John		1-		4	
Ramsey, Robert		1-		4	
Ritchey, James		1-		4	
Roberts, Aron		1-		4	
Sharp, Joseph	150	1-		6	
Shoults, Christian, Junr		1-		4	
Smith, James		1-		4	
Tate, Samuel	175			2	4
Ward, Dr Wm.		2-		8	
Wheler, Stephen	100	1-		5	4
Ingle, Michael		1-		4	
Forbush, Hugh		1-		4	
Haile's Company- for the years 1793 & 94.					
Anderson, Wm-	300-	2 poles-		12	
Roberts, Jesse-	100-	2 "		9	4
Smith, Henry-	-	2		8	
			11	3	4

1795

Captain Calverts Company for 1795

Names	Poles wht	Poles bl	Stud	Land
Ball, Thomas	1			
Baxter, Francis	1			
Bayless, Saml	1			1867¼ or 186 3/4
Bohanan, Ezekiel	1			
Botles, Henry	1			125
Brown, Abraham	1			150
Brown, Jacob	1			100
Brown, Joel	0			179
Calvert, William	1	1		127
Cash, Jas jr	1			
Cash, Jas senr	0	1		328
Cloyd, William	1			210
Cowan, Nathl	1	1		
Creseless, Isaac	1			100
Creseless, John	1			100
Deakins, Jas	1			
Deedrick, David	1	1		
Emeby (?), John	1			100
Ensor, Frances	1	1		79
Evans, George	1			57
Faine, William	1			350
Finch, Calvin	1			150
Fryer, Robert	1			
Gier, Jacob	1	0		124
Gray, Josheway	0			300
Harle, Baldwin	1	0	1	
Harman, Adam	1	0		100
Harmon, Abraham	1			
Hadlor, Sabastan	0	1		300
Hair, Isaac	1			180
House, George	1	1		860
Humbert, John	1			172
Ingle, Michael	1			
Irwin, Saml	1			
Kindle, George	1			100
Lilburn, Andrew	1			100
McGines, John	1	0	1	430
Meser, Joseph	1			250
Miller, Henery	0			240
Millikin, John	1			100
Million, Edward	1			162
Munson, John	0			162
Neal, William	1			96 2/4
Nodding, William	0	6		300
Payne, Jesse	1	1		630
Rymal, John	1			230
Scroggs, Ebenezer	0			20
Sevier, Jas.	1	4		650
Sidney, Martin	1			100
Sidner, Martin	1			100
Slyger, Casper	1			100

Captain Calverts Company (cont'd)

Names	Poles wht	Poles bl	Stud	Land
Slyger, Henry	1			20
Slyger, John	0	0	0	250
Slyger, John Jr.	1			100
Smiley, Thomas (?)	1			
Smith, Robert	1			
Spring, Nicholas	1			
Stuart, James	1	8	The same land as 1794 & 300 to be aded	
Taylor, Christ.	1	1		305
Taylor, Henry	1			
Thomas, Wealam	1			110
Tucker, Abraham	1			
Tucker, Elizabeth	1			395
Tucker, Joseph	1			
Waddill, John	1			
Wagoner, Phillip	1			
Walters, Peter	1			100
Woods, Samuel				273
Woods, William	1			

Recorded - Jas. Sevier

....

A Return of Taxable Property in Captain Nicholas Carriger's District, in the County of Washington and Territory of the United States south of the River Ohio for the year 1795

Name	Acres	Situation	Poles wht	Poles bl	Stud
Bass, Jeremiah	280		1	10	
Bird, James	0		1		
Bowers, Leonard	50		1		
Brown, Moses	no return		1		
Carriger, Godfrey	2444		0	2	1
Carriger, Godfrey Jr.	322		1		
Carriger, Micheal	156		1		
Carriger, Nicholas	450		1		
Carter, John	400		1	3	
Carter, Landon	3716		1	7	1
1 Town Lot,	1280	in Sevier Co.			
in Nashville	2180	in Knox Co.			
	228	in Davidson Co.			
	7028	acres			
Cobb, Pharoah	1050		1	8	1
Cooper, James	0		1		
Cox, Richard	0		1		
Drake, Abraham	640		1		
Duncan, Thomas	no return		1		
Emmet, George	297		1		
Evons, Samuel	0		1		
Frazer, Alexander	0		1		
Garland, John	200		1		
Gillum, William	0		1		
Greer, Alexander	0		1	3	1

Captain Nicholas Carriger's District (cont'd)

Name	Acres	Situation	Poles wht	bl	Stud
Greer, Andrew, Esquire	1525	in Sullivan County		no return	
" & Genl Sevier	300	joining Shelby's Old Patent land		3	1
Greer, Andrew, Jr.	0		1	2	
Greer, Thomas	100		1		
Harden, William	0		1		
Hetherie, Jacob			1		
Hinks, George	0		1		
Hooker, William	0		1		
Humphreys, Elisha	368		1		
Ivy, James	50		1		
Kite, Richard	150		1		
Lacey, James			1		
Lacey, John	0		1		
Lacy, Philemon	0		1		
Large, Joseph	0		1		
Lincoln, Isaac	759		1	3	1
Matlock, George	420		0		
Matlack, Gideon	300		1		
Matlock, William	100		1		
Maxfield, Thomas	280		1		
Moore, John Parker	120		1		
Musgrave, John	0		1		
Musgraves, Robert	0		0		
Musgraves, Samuel	320		1		
Nave, John	100		1		
Nave, Teter	250		1	0	1
Nowlen, John	0		1		
Patrick, Jesse	0		3		
Perkins, George	0		1		
Peters, Christian	100				
Peters, Michael S.	742		1	0	1
Price, James	225		1		
Redmun, Steven	0		1		
Right, James	0		1		
Right, Robert	0		1		
Sevier, Abraham	142		1		
Sevier, Valentine, senr.	420		0	0	
Sharp, William	400	Stony Creek		no return	
Shultz, Christian	0		1		
Stover, Christian	0		1		
Tipton, Samuel	742		1	1	1
do	149	back lands			
Tipton, Thomas	386		1		
Western, Joseph			1		
Western, William			1		
Whitson, Charles	0		1		
Williams, Thomas	0		1		
Worley, John	100		2		

Sworn to before me
Feb. 20, 1795

Landon Carter, J. P.
Washington County

Rec'd Jas Sevier

A Return of the Taxable Property in Captain Fords District in the County of Washington & Territory of the United States south of the River Ohio for the year 1795

Names	Acres	Poles white	Poles black	Studs
Abner, Elisha	170	0		
Anderson, Joshua	0	1		
Anderson, Thomas	150	1		
Anderson, Thos	0	1		
Asher, David	0	1		
Asher, John	100	1		
Asher, Roberson	100	1		
Beams, James	0	1		
Bishop, Joseph	100	1		
Bolish, John	150	0		
Brown, Austin	0	1		
Buckner, Michel	100	0		
Bullinger, Peter	150	0		
Burk, Arthur	0	1		
Campbell, Isaac	50	1		
Campbell, James	0	1		
Campbell, Jeremiah	100	1		
Campbell, Solomon	200	1		
Campbell, Zachariah	0	1		
Campbell, Zachariah	100	0		
Collet, James	0	1	no return	
Cook, William	50	0		
Davis, James	0	1		
Duncan, Lawrance	240	1		
Duncan, Patrick	0	1		
Duggard, Julius	175	1		
Edwards, James	100	1		
Ferguson, John	0	1		
Ford, Joseph	200	1		
Grindstaff, Catherin	100	0		
Guin, Champ	100	1		
Guinn, James Jr.	0	1		
Guinn, James Sr.	76	0		
Hogg, Obediah	0	1		
Hoskins, Ninean	0	1		
Ingle, George	100	1		
Jones, James	200	1		
Jones, Lewis	50	0	0	1
Jones, Lewis Jr.	0	1		
Jones, William	100	1		
Lay, Jesse	0	1		
Logan, George	0	1		
Loyd, James	50	0		
Loyd, John	0	1		
Loyd, Levy	200	1		
Lynch, John	100	1	1	
Megee, Thomas	50	1		
May, John	50	1		
Miller, Christley	100	1		
Miller, Daniel	150	1		
Miller, George	60	0		

1795

Captain Fords District (cont'd)

Names	Acres	Poles white	black	Studs
Miller, Henry Jr.	0	1		
Miller, Henry Senr.	200	0		
Miller, John Jr.	0	1		
Miller, John Sr.	150	1		
Millsaps, James	0	1		
Moreland, Wm	100	1		
Mulkey, James	100	0		
Mulkey, Philip	150	1		
Mullins, William	50	0		
Mullins, William Jr.	0	1		
Parsons, Jesse	0	1		
Pauley, Edward	0	1		
Petree, Adam	0	1		
Petre, Daniel	50	1		
Philips, -----	0	1	no return	
Potter, Hanna	100			
Premmer, Mary	100	0		
Rainbolt, Adam	100	1		
Rainbolt, Elisha	0	1		
Rainbolt, Susanah	100	0		
Ray, William	0	1		
Reynolds, Henry	0	1		
Richardson, John	100	1		
Roberts, Moses	0	1		
Roberts, Reuben	50	1		
Runnals, Moses	150	1		
Semerlin, John	300	1		
Skyler, Joseph	0	1		
Smith, Edward Esquire	600			
Smith, Jacob	100	1		
Smith, John	150	1	0	1
Smith, Nicholas	0	1		
Smith, Samuel	0	1		
Smith, William	100	1		
Storm, Coonrad	100	1		
Storm, John	100	1		
Strivil, William	0	1		
Suet, Thomas	0	1		
Tate, John	50	1		
Tate, Samuel	175	0		
Vandergriff, Leonard	0	1		
Vintrees, John	325	1		
Watson, Stephen	0	1		
Whitson, John	0	1		
Whitte, Richard	500	1	no return, living out of Government	
Wilder, Joab	100	0		
Wilson, Samuel	100	1		
Yates, Samuel	0	1		

Signed by John Carter R. T. L.

Rec. Ja. Sevier

A List of the Taxable Property in the District of Captain Samuel Handley's Company March 28th 1795

Names	Poles wht	Poles bl	Stud	Acres Wash Co.	Acres Greene Co.
Beard, Andrew	1	2	1	280	
Bitner, John	1			100	
Blackburn, Archd.	2	2		160	400
Breeden, Brian	1				
Broiles, Adam	0	2		100	
Broiles, Adam B. Smith	1			300	
Broiles, Daniel	1	1		110	
Broiles, James	1				200
Broiles, Reuben	1				
Broiles, Samuel	1			250	
Broiles, Syries	0	2		100	
Broiles, Tobias	1				
Brown, William	1	1		150	
Clark, Jesse	1				
Clarke, John	1			200	
Clarke, William	0	4		300	
Collam, George	1				
Collam, Jonathan	1			200	
Condren, William	1			160	
Gallaher, John	1	1		400	
Gann, Adam, junr	1				
Gann, Adam senr	0			150	
Gann, Clemens	0			100	
Gann, Isaac	1				
Gann, John	1			100	
Gann, Nathan	1			220	
Gann, Thomas	1				
Greenway, William	1			112	
Harbison, Samuel	1				
Harbison, William	1				
Hall, Henrey	1				
Humphries, Richard	1			400	
Jurden, John	1				
Lamon, John	1				
McFarlin, Robert	1				
McGee, William	1				
McKee, John	1				
Miller, James	1			100	
Miller, Peter				400	
Moore, Alexander	1		1	0	
Moore, William	0	1		358	
Nunn, Warten	1				
Panther, Adam				364	
Prethero, Alexr	1			100	
Sharp, Joseph	1				
Waddill, John senr	2			330	
Waddill, Seth Que	1			200	
Woods, Michial	1	9		640	
do					600

- - - - - - - -

1795

Scrap:

Handley's Company 1795

Court House Tax 31.60
County Tax 16.66 3/4

....

Captain Melvane's District in Washington County 1795

Names	No. Acres	Place where lies	Water Course	Poles wht	bl	Studs
Barns, Joseph	(740	(Sumner)	Cumberland			
	(100	Wash Co.	Sinking			
Bacon, Isaac	200	"	Boons Creek			
Bacon, John	197	"	" "	1		
Bean, Edmund	0			1		
Beard, Robert	140	"	Boons Creek	1		
Bierd, Henry				1	0	1
Braden, James				1		
Brown, John	350	"	Boons Creek	1		
Brown, Peter	50	"	" "	0		
Carney, John	0			1		
Carney, Thomas Junr.	300	"	Wattaga River	1	3	
Carney, Thomas Snr.	520	-	Redy Branch	0	1	
Carr, Thomas	100	"	Reedy Branch	1		
Cowen, John	107	"	Boons Creek	1		
Cox, James	70	"	" "	1	2	1
Crabtree, John	103	"	" "			
Crabtree, William	0			1		
Denham, David	100	"	Sinkin Creek	1		
Dungworth, Charles	100	"	Boons Creek	1		
	640	Somner Co	Cumberland			
Dyer, John	90	Wash Co.	Wattaga river	1		
Ellis, William	715	"	Boons Creek	1	1	0
Gates, Jacob	200	"	"			
Gates, Richard	111	"	Reedy branch	1		
Genkins, George, jr	0			1		
Genkins, George, sr	500	"	Boons creek			
Gholson, Anthony	53 2/4	"	"			
Gray, Absolum	195	"	"	1		
Hagin, Arter	200	"	"	1		
Haile, Abednego	237	"	"	1	4	
Hall, Samuel	100	"	"	1		
Hall, Thomas	100	"	Wattaga river	1		
Hammor, Balties	100	"	Redy branch	1		
Hoas, Jacob	700	"	Boons creek	2		
Hodges, John, jr	190	"	Wattaga river	1		
Hodges, John, snr.	330	"	"	1	1	
Hunt, Thomas	305	"	Boons creek	1		
Keer, Philip	100	"	"	1		
Mapols, John	0			1		
Matlock, Zachariah	150	"	"			
Meins, Isaac	200	"	"			
Meins, Thomas				1		
Melvan, John	250	"	"	1	1	
Melvan, Joseph the younger				1		

Captain Melvane's District (cont'd)

Names	No. Acres	Place where lies	Water Course	Poles wht	bl	Studs
Melvan, Samuel	100	Wash Co.	Sinking creek	0		
Melvan, Thomas	150	"	Boons creek			
Milburn, Samuel	0			1		
Miller, Peter	200	"	"	1		
Mcclowd, James	0			1		
Mccloud, John	115	"	Redy creek	1		
Mcclowd, Robert	0			1		
Mcclowd, Thomas	0			1		
Mcclowd, William, jr	0			1		
Mcclowd, William, senr.	130	"	Boons creek			
Nelson, John	100	"	Sinking Creek	1	0	0
Oldham, Henry	180	"	Wattago River	1	1	2
Prichett, Charles	323	"	Boons Creek	1		
Starnes, Peter	200	"	"	1		
Stone, Robert	243	"	"	1		
Stone, William	243	"	"	1		
Thompson, Richard	230	"	Redy Branch	1		
Weathers, William	137	"	Boons Creek	1		
Wiley, Thomas	0			1		
York, William	200	"	"	1		

Recorded by Jack Sevier D.C.

....

Capt. John Millikins Company for 1795

Names	Poles wht	bl	Stud	Land
Aikens, James	1	2		130
Blair, Brice	1			107
Blair, John senr	0	2		288
Blair, Richard	1			63
Breedin, William	1	1		100
Broils, Abraham	1	1		100
Broils, Nicholas	0	3		100
Collam, Jonathan	1			
Crookshanks, George	1			133
Cunningham, Hugh	1			150
Cunningham, John	2	0		150
Denton, Jonathan	1	0		100
Doak, Rev. Saml	1	1	1	180
Embree, Thomas	1	0		350
Gillespie, George	3	11		900
Gillespie, Thomas	1	2		1290
Hannah, Andrew	1			320
Hannah, John	0	0		200
Jodan, Lewis	1			350
Keowan, John	1			
Logan, Charls	1	0		100
Lowry, Adam	1			
McBeath, Andrew	1	0		250
McCallister, John				625
McEwen, Alexr	1			345
McFerran, Andrew	0			200

Capt. John Millikins Company (cont'd)

Names	Poles wht	Poles bl	Stud	Land
Mathews, Alex	1	3	1	500
May, Cassemor	1			
Montgomery, James	1			176
Nelson, Henery	1	2		394
Nelson, John	2	1		200
Rasor, William	1			
Scott, Thomas	1	1	1	200
Shields, Patrick	0			278
Smith, John	1			
Stephenson, William	0			467
Telford, Thomas	1			
Vickery, Francis	1			
Wallas, James	0	1		
Yeager, Solomon	1	1		200

I do hereby certify that the foregoing is a true of the persons retruend to me forthe year 1795. John Millikin

Rec'd Jas. Sevier

....

A List of Taxable Property Belonging in Capt. Morrison's Company for the year 1795 Recorded by Jack Sevier, D.C. Undated- Most likely 1795. It can't be later than 1795 for the widow of John Fain married John Hammer in 1795. MHMcC & NEJS.

Name	White poles	Black poles	Horses Stud	Acres Land	
Baller, Amos	1			306	on Sinking Creek
Bean, John	1			7.53	Watauga
Birmingham, James	1				
Bogard, Henry				400	Knob Creek
Bogart, Samuel	1				
Boman, Jacob	1			240	Brush Creek
Boren, William				76	do
Boughran, Elijah	1				
Caruthers, Johnathan	1	2		242	do
Carr, John		2		232	Nob Creek
Carr, John	1				
Collins, Joshua	1				
Collens, Joseph	1			100	Wattauga
Creson, John	1				
Cumpton, John	1				
Daneis, William				260	Brush Creek
Daniels, John	1				
Davis, Thomas	1				
Denton, Isaac	1				
Denton, Jeremiah	1				
Denten, Joseph	1			185	do
Denton, Samuel	1			400	Nob Creek
Duncan, Charles	2			460	do
Engle, John	1			350	Ceder Creek
Fain, Agnes		1		240	Nob Creek

Capt. Morrison's Company (cont'd)

Name	White poles	Black poles	Horses Stud	Acres Land	
Gibson, Thomas				117½	on Nob Creek
Gray, John	1				
Great, David	1			100	Cinking Creek
Hammer, Isaac	1				
Hammer, Jacob	1				
Hammer, John	1			349	Nob Creek
Hines, Samuel	1				
Humphreys, George	1				
Humphreys, John				100	Watauga
Huston, John	1				
Job, David		4		280	Brush Creek
Jones, Darling	1			200	do
Kelley, Kinchen				200	Nob Creek
Leathem, John	1				
Lee, Clemment	1			100	do
Little, John	1				
Little, Jones				320	Brush Creek
McMahan, John B.	1	2		400	Nob Creek
Masengill, Hennery	1	5		900	Wattaugau
Melven, Joseph	0	0		250	Nob Creek
				& 200	in Knox County
Miller, John	1			142	Nob Creek
Mitchell, Adam	1			200	do
Mitchell, Robert	1			100	do
More, Reuben	2			386	Brush Creek
Morrison, Joseph	2			200	do
Mury, Gerimiah	1				
Nelson, Jean		2		100	Sinking Creek
Nelson, William	2	3		500	Nob Creek
Pearcefiel, Samuel				125	do
Range, Peter	1			500	do
				& 259	on Sinking Creek
Reno, John	1				
Runo, Charles	1			91½	Brush Creek
Ryan, James	1			250	Nob Creek
Steveson, Henry	1	1		430	Cedar Creek
Thomas, John	1				
Tullis, Jonathan	1			399	Brush Creek
Ward, William	1				
White, James	1				
White, John	1			360	Nob Creek
Whittecar, Mark	1			50	Knob Creek
Wood, William				177	Sinking Creek
Wright, Thomas	1				
Young, John	0			252½	Nob Creek
				& 400	in Jefferson Co.
Young, Robert	1			640	Brush Creek

....

A List of Taxable Property in Captain Murey's Company - 1795

Note by Capt. Murey: As there is two Sinking Creeks in the vicinity of this company I distinguish them by the letters E and W for East and West. One is on the East side of Buffalow Ridge the other west.

Captain Murey's Company (cont'd)

Owners names	Acres in each tract	Place where tract lies County	Water Course	Poles wh	bl	Studs
Austin, John	100) 45) 145	Wash	E Fork-Cedar Cr Redy Branch	1		
Bacon, Jonathan	200	do	W Sinking Cr	1		
Barron, John				1		
Barron, Joseph	200	do	do	1		
Barron, Walker	130	do	do	1		
Barron, William	100) 25) 125	do	do	1		
Billingsley, Samuel	200	do	Dry Fork of W Sinking Cr	1	2	
Bull, Jacob	225	do	Sinking Branch	1	1	
Bullington, William				1		
Burch, Richard	130	do	Dry Fork of W Sinking	1		
Chamberlain, James	110) 50) 160	do	Cedar	1	1	
Chapman, John	100	do	East Sinking	1		
Chinueth, Nicholas	49	do	Buffalo Ridg			
Christian, Israel	200	do	West Sinking			
Cox, Elijah				1		
Crofford, Thomas	150) 30) 180	do	Cedar			
Crouch, Elijah				1		
Crouch, John Jr.	50) 50) 100	do	Waters of Boone	1		
Crouch, John Snr.	50	do	Boone			
Denham, Charles	120	do	Head W Sinking	1		
Dun, Daniel	100) 60) 160	do	Head of Lick	1	1	
Duncan, Elezebeth	300	do	North Watauga River			
Ellis, John	100	do	East Sinking	1		
Emberton, Richard				1		
Ensor, Thomas	100) 150) 250	do	Waters of Watauga River			
Epperson, Anthoney	250	do	W Sinking Cr	0	1	
Epperson, Peter	200	do	Kindricks Cr	1		
Epperson, Samuel	200) 50) 250	do	W Sinking Cr	1		
Forbush, Andrew				1		
Forbush, Hugh				1		
Ford, James				1		
Ford, John	50) 168) 218	do	W Sinking Cr	1		
Ford, Loyd, Jr.	121 3/4	do	do	1		
Ford, Loyd, Sr.	100	do	do		2	
Ford, Mordicai	150) 100) 250	do	do Little Limestone			
Ford, Thomas	120) 100) 220	do do	W Sinking Cr Dry Fork of "	1		
Ford, William	50) 50) 100	do	W Sinking	1		

Captain Murey's Company (cont'd)

Owners names	Acres in each tract		Place where tract lies County	Water Course	Poles wh	bl	Studs
Fraley, Christian					1		
Giffort, John					1		
Glascock, Archable	40)						
	200)	290	Wash	Kindricks	1	1	
	50)						
Gott, Anthony	300)						
	150)	570	do	W Sinking			
	10)						
	110)			Buffalo Ridge			
Gott, John	120		do	Head of Cedar	1		
Gray, George	338		do	Cedar		1	
Gray, Robert					1	1	
Grille, Richard					1		
Gristham, Thomas	184 2/4		do	do	1	1	
Haile, Abednego	300)						
the older	45)	345	do	Waters of Cedar			
Haile, George Jr.	226		do	E Fork of "	1	2	
Haile, George Sr.	50)		do	do	0	1	
	150)	200					
Haile, Jamima							
Adm. of Nicholas	200)		do	W Sinking Cr			
Haile Estate	500)			Kindricks Cr			
Haile, John	92		do	W Sinking Cr			
Haile, Joseph	836		do	Cedar	1	3	
the older							
Haile, Joshua					1		
Haile, Little Meshach	100		Green Lick		1		
Haile, Meshack	420		Wash	E Sinking	1		
Haile, Nathan	200		do	W Sinking	1		
Haile, Nicholas Sr.	200)		do	do	1		
	40)	272					
	32)						
Haile, Richard	110)		do	W Sinking	1		
	120)	230	Sullivan	do			
Haile, Samuel	100)		Wash	do	1	2	
	100)	200		E Sinking			
Haile, Shadrack	100		do	head of Clear Fork Lick	1		
Haile, William	200		do	W Sinking Cr	1		
Hale, Joseph	100		do	do	1		
son of George							
Hall, Nathaniel	291		do	Watauga River			1
Hall, William					1		
Holland, Benjamin	550		do	Kindricks Cr	1	3	1
Holland, Peter					0	1	
Hunt, Jesse	206)						
	100)	422	do	Sinking Creek	1		
	80)						
	36)						
Hickey, David	50		do	E do			
Jacson, William	110)	160	do	W Sinking	1		
	50)		Sullivan	Kindricks			

Captain Murey's Company (cont'd)

Owners names	Acres in each tract		Place where tract lies County	Water Course	Poles wh	bl	Studs
Jackson, George	80		Wash	W Sinking			
Kincheloe, Charles	200		do	Kindricks	1	2	1
Kincheloe, George	100)	150	do	do	1	2	
	50)						
Kincheloe, John	140)	280	do	do		7	
	140)						
Laine, Tidence	244)	284	do	Cedar Cr			
	40)						
Low, Andrew					1	0	1
McCubbin, Zachariah	200		do	E Fork Cedar	0	1	
McFerson, Daniel	150		do	Kindricks	1	2	
McFerson, Henry	100)						
	50)	170	do	do	1		
	20)						
Maden, Andrew					1		
Martin, James	99)						
	21)	170	do	Little Sinking Branch	1		
	50)						
Melvan, Joseph son of John	100		do	Buffalo Ridge	1		
Moor, Peter	100		do	Kindricks	1		
Moore, Samuel	204		do	E Fork of Cedar	1	0	1
Mulkey, Reverat Jonathan	100		do	Big Limestone	1		
Murrey, Christopher							
Murrey, Morgan	100)						
	50)	205	do	W Sinking	0	1	
	55)						
Murry, Shadrack	150		do	do	1		
Murrey, Thomas, jnr					1		
Murrey, Thomas, Sr	200)	290	do	do			
	90)						
Nolan, George	270)						
	60)	380	do	E Sinking Cr	1	4	
	50)						
Nolan, James	150		do	Kindricks Cr	1		
Norwood, John					1		1
Owen, James	87)	91	do	E Fork of Cedar	1		
	4)						
Pearce, Joshua					1		
Porter, Charles					1		
Recor, John					1		
Rector, George					1		
Rector, Uriah					1		
Shaw, Benjamin	189		do	Wolf Branch			
Shipley, Benjamin	125)		do	Head of E Fork			
	15)	195		of Cedar			
	55)						
Shipley, James					1		
Shipley, Edward	490		do	Head Cedar	1		
Shipley, Nathan					1		
Shipley, Peter	150		do	Waters of Cedar	1		
Smith, Anderson	250		do	Kindricks			

Captain Murey's Company (cont'd)

Owners names	Acres in each tract		Place where tract lies County	Water Course	Poles wh	bl	Studs
VanVactor, Benjamin					0	1	
Weelock, John	200)						
	200)						
	100)	750	Wash	Kindricks	1	2	
	50)						
	200)		do	Horse			
White, Archable	200)	300	do	Big Spring			
	100)						
White, Isaac	400		do	Horse	1	1	
Woods, Whiley	140)	215	do	Kindricks	1		
	75)						

Returned by Joseph Britten, J.P.

	W	B	S
2119 1/4	15	4	1
5116	24	13	4
4815	21	21	0
5842 3/4	21	13	1
17893	81	51	6

Recorded by J. Sevier, D.C.

....

A List of Taxable Property made out by Nathaniel Taylor - 1795

Names	Location	Acres	Poles white	black	Studs
Archer, John	Waters of Buffaloe creek	200			
Archer, William			1		
Bayley, Cotrel	do	400			
" "	do	100			
Clark, Josiah	Gap creek	200			
Cob, Ethelred	North side of Watago river	53	1		
Conner, Julius			1	1	
Cooper, James			1		
Cooper, Joab	Dry creek	160	1		
Cox, Abraham			1		
Crouch, James	Sinking creek	100	1		
Cunningham, Mary	Buffalo creek	590			
Davis, Nathan	Sinking creek	261	1		
Davis, William	Buffalo creek	200		1 female	
Dungan, Jeremiah	both sides of Watago	1000		3 (2 m, 1 f)	1
Dungan, Jeremiah	Sinking creek	140			
Eden, Austin			1		
Edwards, Solomon			1		
Evans, Archibald	North side of Watago river	160	1		
Franks, Richard			1		
Haun, Sebastian	Waters of Buffaloe creek	400			
	Waters of Doe river rock camp	320			
	Roans creek	266			

1795

List by Nathaniel Taylor (cont'd)

Names	Location	Acres	Poles white	Poles black	Studs
Hendricks, Solomon	Sinking creek	110	1		
Humphreys, Jesse	Waters of Sinking creek	150			
Lockert, Robert			1		
Lockert, William			1		
McCormack, Robert	North side of Watago River	50			
McEnturf, Christopher	Buffaloe	232			
McFall, Francis	Sinking creek	235			1
McNabb, Baptist			1		
McNabb, David	on Buffaloe creek	255			
" John P.	Waters of Gap creek	430			
Maupin, John	Watago		1		
Milsap, Thomas	Gap creek waters	100	1		
More, Daniel			1		
Peoples, John	Waters of Buffaloe creek	160	1	1 female	
Peoples, William	do	100			
Reasoner, Garret	Sinking creek	2008		3 (2male, 1female)	
Rogers, Robert			1		
Sharp, William	Gap creek	540			
	Rones creek	200			
Taylor, Andrew	Waters of Buffaloe creek	238	1		
Terrey, Fanny				1 male negroe	
Terrey, William			1		
Tipton, John			1		
Tipton, Jonathan	Waters of Gap creek	217	1		
Tipton, Joseph	Mouth of Buffaloe creek	500		1 fem	2
	joining said land	250			
	do	742			
Whitson, Abraham			1		
Whitson, Jeremiah	Buffaloe	145	2		
Whitson, Jesse	Sinking Creek	237	1	3	
	adjoining sd land	35			
Whitson, John	Waters of Sinking creek			1	
Whitson, Tho	on Little --------	100			
	joining that tract	100			
	The second branch above the Laurel of Little Doe	50			
Wiles, John			1		

Nathl Taylor

\- - - - - - -

On reverse side:

This day came Edmond Williams and gave in his taxable property.

one white pole 1
4 male black poles 4
2 female black poles 2
Land 1376 acres

Matthew Talbott for Agnes Hay on Watago River 300 acres
David Hay adjoining sd land 200

February the 5th 1795
(signed) William McNabb

List by Nathaniel Taylor (cont'd)

Up side:
Thos. Whitson
The rich land at the foot of the Iron Mountain
waters of Little Doe 100 acres
On the third branch of Little Doe above the
Laurel (Benj. Brown old place) 50 acres
for son John Whitson 1 pole

- - - - - - -

Scrap:

A List of Capt. Taylor's Company taxes, 1795

Govt. Tax	52.82
Court House	44.88
County tax	22.15

....

Captain Reuben Thornton's Company - 1795 - Territory South of the River Ohio - Washington County

Names	Wh polls	Land	Bl polls	Studs
Adams, Jose	1			
Baker, John	1	155		
Beckner, William	1			
Boone, Sollomon	1	30		
Branstten, Peter	1	200		
Buck, Abraham	1			
Cone, Peter	1			1
Cutbarth, Banjn Sen.			1	
Culbouth, Bugn (?)	1			
Cutbuth, Donnel	1	100		
Crosswhite, Abraham	1	100		
Daase, John	1			
Estridge, Richard	1			
Garland, Samuel		300		
Grave, James	1			
Grifin, William		300	3	1
Grinstaf, John	1	100		
Hanson, John	1			
Handricks, Jonithan	1			
Hatherley, Evans		2		
Haton, John	1	100		
Hawar-, John	1	1007		
Jackson, William		300	second page	
James, Roland	1	517		
Janttry, Joseph	1	100		
Jenkins, Roland	1	1	B.	
Linsday, Samel		82		
McOueen, Hannah (wd)		310		
Mulans, John	1			
Profftt, John	1	400		
Puchase, John		300		
Purkins, Joab	1	200		
Richardson, John	1	100		
Robinson, John		100		

Captain Reuben Thornton's Company (cont'd)

Names	Wh polls	Land	Bl polls	Studs
Sands, Joseph	1	30		
Seule, Joseph	1			
Shone, Lonard	1			
Shuffield, George	1			
Slemp, Michal	1			
Snider, Peter		133		
Starns, Peter		300		
State, Donnal	2	300		
Suele, Abraham	1			
Suele, Dosson	1			
Thornton, Reuben	1	400		1
Tompkins, Joseph	1			
Tulley, Samel	1	400		
Vast (?), Genge	1			
Vaught, John	1	8005 (?)		
Wagnar, David	1	572	3	
Wagner, Mathias	1	785	3 (?)	
Walters, John	1			
Walters, Robert	1			
Wherlen, Shepp (?)	1	400		
White, James		1300		
Willson, John	1	13		
Willson, John		--3	1	
Willson, Joseph	1			
Wimon, Honney		400		
Woodly, William	1	100		
------, William	1	150		

A list of the persons failing to turn in their taxes for this present year -

Joseph Jenkins - his pole and 1 stud horse
Thoms Jackson - land 300 acres
Mathias Wagner - 1 stud horse only

The whole of the land lies in Washington County and territory as satisfied by me this 20 of fabarey 1795.

Rn Thornton, J.P.

....

A List of Taxable Property in Captain Joseph Young's Company

Note: Undated but likely 1795 as Young's company is missing for that year and the form is similar to tabulation of 1795. It is before 1798 as Charles Robertson, Sr. who is listed below died in 1798. MHMcC & NEJS.

Name	White Pole	Black Pole	Acres Land	
Anderson, Frederick	1		143	on Cherokee Creek
Anthony, Abraham	1		100	do
Atkinson, Robert	1			
Ausimas, Philip			200	do
Baker, Frances		1	200	Little Limestone
Bayles, Daniel Jr.	1		100	Cherokee Creek
Bayles, Daniel Sr.			100	do

Captain Joseph Young's Company (cont'd)

Name	White Pole	Black Pole	Acres Land	
Bayles, John	1		296	on Cherokee Creek
Bell, John	1		200	head Brush Creek
Blythe, Samuel	1			
Boran, Ezekiel			70	Cherokee Creek
Boran, James Jr.	1			
Boran, James Sr.			750	head of Brush Cr.
Borin, Absolam	1			
Brooks, Giles	1		300	Cherokee Creek
Brummer, Samuel	1		50	head of Little Limestone
Buley, Anthony			250	Cherokee Creek
Chasady, Robert	1			
Compton, Jeremiah	1		25	do
Conne, James	1			
Cooper, Joseph			70	
Disney, Thomas	1			
Fine, John	1		250	Cherokee Creek
Gaut, John	1		100	
Gaut, John	1		100	Cherokee Creek
Gaymon, Abram	1			
Goodpasture, Isaac	1			
Gray, Willis	1			
Greene, Richd	1			
Haggard, William	1			
Hartsell, Hannah			60	Cherokee Creek
Headrick, Charles			140	do
Henderson, John	1		200	do
Henderson, Joseph	1		200	do
Hufman, David	1		236	do
Hunter, Abraham	1			
Hunter, Henery	1			
Hunter, John Sr.			630	Cherokee Creek
Irwin, James			200	do
Laymon, Christopher	1			
Laymon, John Jr.	1			
Leach, Wm.			100	Cherokee Creek
Moore, James	1		305	do
Murry, Ephrm.	1		255	do
North, George	1		100	do
Ob?es, Thomas	1		208	do
Parker, John	1			
Phillips, Gabriel	1			
Pitner, John	1		200	do
Price, Mordicka	1		400	Sinking Creek
Rader, Adam	1		540	Brush Creek
Roberson, Charles Sr.		5	200	Cherokee 1 Stud Horse
Rogers, Thomas	1		62	do
Rose, Osey			320	do
Rubil, John	1		200	Brush Creek
Rubil, Peter	1		553	Cherokee Creek
Smith, Edward	1		218	do
Tipton, Jonathan	1			
Watson, William	1		600	Sinking

Captain Joseph Young's Company (cont'd)

Name	White Pole	Black Pole	Acres Land	
Witt, Burgess	1			
Young, Jos	1	5	915 on Brush Creek	
Young, Mary		3	343 do	1 stud horse

Recorded by J. Sevier

....

List of Taxable Property for the Year ____ - No Captain Listed

(Note: The form of this list resembles the year 1795. MHMcC)

Mens Names	Quantity	Situation	Title	Wh	Bl	Townlot	Stud
Barger, Jacob	100	big limestone	deed				-I at
Biddle, James				1			one doll
Biddle, John				1			
Biddle, Thos.	100	N big Limstone	Warrant				
	300	" "	deed				
Blackly, Daniel	130	Blair Branch big limstone	deed	1			
Blackly, Robert	145	Blairs branch big limstone	grant				
Blackly, Thos				1			
Blackly, William	236	blairs branch big limstone	deed	1			
Campbell, Hugh	219	N big limstone	deed	1			
Carmicle, Arch				1			
Carmicle, Isbel	204	North branch big limstone	deed		2		
Cumings, Hugh	100	Mill Creek	deed	1			
Davis, George	120	Mill Creek	deed	1	1		
Gilworth, John	100	Mill Creek	deed	1			
Henderson, John	101	Mill Creek	deed	1			
Humphreys, David	160	N side big limestone	deed	1			
Hunphreys, Lesly	130	N big limstone	deed	1			
Kelsey, John							
Kibble, Jacob				1			
McWhorter, James	150	Mill Creek	deed				
Martin, Joseph							
Roberts, Jas	158	Mill Creek	deed				
Robison, John							
Rodgers, James				1			
Rodgers, Sml	100	Mill Creek	deed	1			
Sands, Benjamin							
Sehorn, Nansy	140	Mill Creek	Occupancy				
Shanks, William							
Snider, Daniel							
Thompson, Adam				1			
Tweedy, Jas.	118	blairs branch big limstone	deed	1			
Williams, John	200	big limstone N branch	deed				

Different Men's Taxes for 1795

Note: There seems to have been a government tax, a court house tax, and a county tax in 1795. MHMcC & NEJS.

57.32 1/2	28.6 3/4	50.38 3/4
58.73	21.72	38.4 1/2
52.9	23.28	41.36
35.69	13.70	24.98
116.61	46.76	73.76
69.91	30.78	57.8
49.42	22.76	43.50
123.14	? 46.11	72.89
61.73	31.11	41.73
50.89	22.92	40.90
72.69	22.36	58.5
35.22	17.48	30.10
55.44	21.21	42.22
30		
873.70	350.85 3/4	620.0 1/4
		873.70
		1493.70
		350.25
		1843.95

....

A List of the Mistakes in taxing property for the Year 1795

Returned by Geo. Gillespie (Sheriff)

	Doll	Cents
Ecton, James mist. in land		62½
Cash, James Sr. mist in a pole		62½
Doak, Rev. Samuel, mistaken one negro & stud	5	12½
Jones, Nathaniel, mist. in land	5	6
Reasoner, Garret, mist. in land	10	25
Tucker, Elizabeth, mist. in land	3	12½
Tucker, Joseph, mist. in a pole		62½
Weelock, John, mist in land		62½
total amount	26	6

....

Scraps in 1795 File - Personal Lists

List of Joseph Brittons Taxable property for the year 1795

179)
100) acres in Washington County on East Sinking Creek
72)

1 white pole

Joseph Britton as administrator of the estate of William Britton, dec'd. 100 acres in Washington County on W. Sinking Creek.

- - - - - - - -

Taxable Property of Landon Carter

3340 acres of land in Washington County

1795

Taxable Property of Landon Carter (cont'd)

1280 acres of land in Sevier County
2180 acres of land in Knox County
torn 228 acres of land in Davidson County

920
Nashville Mero District, all my
believe to lie within the Indian Bound
Seven black poles and one stud horse

\- - - - - - - -

A list of James Charter taxable property

138 acres of land, 1 white pole
for 1795

\- - - - - - - -

A list of Wm. Colyers Taxable Property 1795

Three hundred acres of land in Washington
two Black poles

Test John Sevier

\- - - - - - - -

A list of James Stuart's taxable property for 179_

of land 5402
1 white pole
6 black poles

On the back:
James Stuart
Tax for
1795

1793 of land 5800 acres
1 white pole 300
6 black poles 6100

....

Names of the Delinquents in the Duplicate for 1795

	Land	Poles	D Cents	D Cents	D C
Anthony, Abraham	100	1	50	25	50
Asher, David		1	25	12½	25
Auston, John	145	1	62	31	62
Bishop, Joseph	100	1	50	25	50
Brown, Austin		1	25	12½	12½
Buckannon, Ezekeal		1	25	12½	25
Campbill, James		1	25	12½	25
Carney, John		1	25	12½	25
Collom, John		1	25	12½	25
Embert, Richard		1	25	12½	25
Forgason, John		1	25	12½	25
Gardner, James	50	1	37½	18	37½
Gaut, John	100	1	50	25	50
Haggert, Wm		1	25	12	25
Hoskins, Ninean		1	25	12½	25
Husk, Wm		1	25	12½	25
Kerk, John	175	1	68	34	68
Loyd, Abel	185		46	23	46
Mcgee, Thomas	50	1	37½	18	37½

Names of the Delinquents in the Duplicate for 1795 (cont'd)

		Land	Poles	D	Cents	D	Cents	D	C
Mcferson, Henry		170	1		67		35		67
Monson, John		162			40		20		40
Mullins, Wm, Jr			1		25		12½		25
Murphy, Patrick			1		25		12½		25
Neal, Samuel		113	1		53		27		53
Oldham, Henry	2 studs-	180	2	9	20		60		95
Phillipps, Gabreal			1		25		12½		25
Prattill, John		400	1	1	25		62½	1	25
Rector, John			1		25		12½		25
Rector, George			1		25		12½		25
Rector, Uriah			1		25		12½		25
Richards, David			1		25		12½		25
Roberts, Reuben		50	1		37½		18		37½
Russells, Henry			1		25		12½		25
Sands, Edmund		157	1		66		33		66
Shanks, James		200	1		75		37½		75
Sharp, Joseph			1		25		12½		25
Smith, Henry		50	1		37½		18		37½
Smith, Robert			1		25		12½		25
Stanton, Richard			1		25		12½		25
Tipton, Jonthen			1		25		12½		25
Ward, Wm, Doctor			1		25		12½		25
Watson, Stephen			1		25		12½		25
Wheler, Stephen		400	1	1	25		62½	1	25
Wilder, Jacob			1		25		12½		25
Woods, Whiley		215	1		78		39		78
				28	78	9	88	19	53

....

1796

Inventory of Brown's Company for the year 1796

Name	White pole	Black pole	Land	Stud
Balis, Rubin	1		291	
Booth, Joseph	1		100	
Brown, Benjamin	1	1	300	
Brown, Jacob	1	2	323	1
Brown, John	1		326	
Brown, Ruthe		4	326	
Brown, Thomas	1	1	326	
Campbell, Richard	1	1		
Casner ?, Jacob			300	
Colled, Isac	1			
Collem, William	1	2	328	
Debaben ?, Arter	2	8	233	1
Embree, Jacob	1			
Embree, Jobe	1		67	
Embree, Margaret			183	
Ervin, Samuel	1			
Ficke, John	1			
French, Petter			2	
Gier, Jacob	1		350	
Hammond, Cristefor	1		100	
Handley, Gorge	1			
Handley, James	1			
Handley, John	1		300	
Hanley, Samuel	1			
Hemton, Robert	1		200	
Hogatt, Solemon	1			
Ingle, William			200	
Jones, Richard	1		11	2
Keele, John			178	
King, Walter			499	
Lemmons, David			200	
Neal, Henry	1		84	
Neal, Jorge	1		300	
Neal, William			96¼	
Richmond, John	1			
Roberson, Charls	1		125	
Roberson, Jules	1		125	
Rogers, John	1		115	
Rogers, Joseph	1		50	
Sevier, Abram	1			
Sevier, James	1	3	737	
Sevier, John Gov.	1			
Shirrell, Samuel	1	8	2850	
Shannon, John	1		100	
Templin, William	1			
Wiley, Thomas	1			

....

Captain Calvert's Company - 1796

Names	White pole	Black pole	Land	Stud
Adams, Alexander	1		116½	
Adams, Jno.	1		75	

Captain Calvert's Company (cont'd)

Names	White poles	Black poles	Land	Studs
Alison, Elizabeth			175	
Alison, Frank	1	1	495	
Allen, John	1			
Bailey, Samuel	1		2092$\frac{1}{4}$	
Baily, William	1			
Brooks, William Lash	1			
Brown, Abraham	1		150	
Brown, Jacob	1		100	
Brown, Joseph	1	1		
Calvart, Capt. Wm.	1	1	127	
Cash, James		2	320	1
Chester, William	1			
Creselus, Isaac	1		100	
Disney, Thomas	1			
Ewen, John	1			
Fain, William	1		600	
Finch, Calvin	1		150	
Fraker, Michal	1		172	
Giar, Jacob jr.	1		141$\frac{1}{2}$	
Gordon, James	1			
Harmon, Abraham	1			
Harmon, Adam	1		220	
Harman, Michal	1			
Harrison, Edmond	1			
Headler, Sebastian		1	300	
House, George	1	2	470	
House, Thomas	1			
Ingle, Michal	1		6	
Jacobs, Dufty	1			
Kinard, John	1			
Kindle, Barbary			175	
McGinis, John	1		430	1
Mackin, Edward	1			
Mackin, John	1			
Millian, Edward	1		162	
Nodding, William		5	300	
Reed, James	1		200	
Reid, James	1			
Reymeal, Jno.	1			
Rice, Thomas	1			
Robeson, Charles		7	300	
Sevier, John	1	2	190	
Shannon, William	1		160	
Sidnor, Martain	1		175	
Sligar, Gasper	1		94	
Sligar, Henry	1		20	
Sligar, Jno. Jr.	1		100	
Sliger, Jno. Sr.		1	250	
Slone, George	1			
Smith, John			350	
Taylor, Cristiphar		1	305	
Taylor, Henry	1			
Waddill, John	1	1		

1796

Captain Calvert's Company (cont'd)

Names	White poles	Black poles	Land	Studs
Wair, John			110	
Walter, Petter	1		100	
Witt, Airs	1			
Witt, Burgess	1	1		
Witt, Jesse	1			
Wood, James	1		200	
Wood, William	1			
Woods, Samuel			400	

....

Capt. Handly's Company - 1796

Names	White poles	Black poles	Land	Studs
Alleson, Robert	2		280	
Alleson, Samuel	2			
Baxter, Francis	1		60	
Bitner, John	1		100	
Blackburn, Archd.	2	2	360	
Brown, James	1	1	200	
Brown, William	1	1	150	1 town lot
Broyles, Adam	1			
Broyles, Adam, B. Smith			300	
Broyles, Daniel	1	1	110	
Broyles, James	1		200	
Broyles, Ruben	1			
Broyles, Samuel	1		250	
Broyles, Syrus		2	100	
Clarcke, William		4	300	
Clarke, John	1			
Collam, George	1			
Collam, Jonathan	1			
Elleman, John	1			
Gallaher, John	1		400	
Gann, Adam			150	
Gann, Adam Jr.	1		160	
Gann, Clam			100	
Gann, Isaac	1			
Gann, John	1		100	
Gann, Nathan	1		220	
Gann, Thomas	1		50	
Harbison, William	1			
Heath, Jonston	1			
Heath, Richard	1	1		
Huffman, Anthony	1			
Huffman, Jesse	1			
Humphries, Jehue	1			
Humphries, Richard	1		400	
Hunt, Simon	1		200	
Jurden, John	1			
Kenidy, David Jr.	1		10025(?) or 125 (10025)	
Kenidy, David Sr.			705	
Layman, Jacob	1			
McGee, George	1			

Capt. Handly's Company (cont'd)

Names	White poles	Black poles	Land	Studs
McGee, John	1		100	
McGee, William	1			
McKee, Allexr.	1		550	
Miller, James	2		100	
Miller, Petter			200	
Milsaps, Thomas	1			
Nelson, Suthey	1			
Nunn, Wharton	1			
Pain, Rubin			200	
Pain, John				
Penney, John	1			
Penther, Adam			314	
Prethro, Alexander	1		100	
Rush, William	1			
Smith, Daniel	1			
Smith, John	1			
Smith, Phillip	1			
Waddill, John Sr.	2		334	
Waddill, Sethque	2		200	
Wardrip, James	1			
Weir, John	2	1	514	
Williams, John	1			
Woods, Michial	1	9	640	
Estate of Robert Cowan deceast			180	
Reubin Pain for year 1795			200	

....

Capt. Longmire's Company - 1796

Names	White poles	Black poles	Land	Studs
Acton, James	1			
Acton, James Sr.			119	
Biddlecom ?, William	1			
Branham, James	1			
Branham, Thomas	1			
Clouse, George	1		100	
Cooper, Joseph			69	
Culbertson, Joseph	1		500	
Culbertson, Samuel	1		900	
Deakins, James	1		110	
Deakins, John			50	
Deakins, Richard			113	
Dillard, Martha	1	12	500	
Dillard, Thomas	1	2	100	
Doyel, Patrick			119	
Eavans, John	1		80	
Eavans, Thomas			45	
Garreis, Alexander			50	
Harrell, John	1			
Haun, Adam	1		130	
Leamons, Joseph	1			
Lewis, William	1		100	
Longmire, Charles		1	600	

Capt. Longmire's Company (cont'd)

Names	White poles	Black poles	Land	Studs
Longmire, John	1			
McInturf, Gasper	1		100	
McCray, Charles	1		125	
McCray, Daniel			414	
Nelson, Benjamon	1			
Norton, Enoch	1			
Patterson, Wm.	1		100	
Phillps, Wm.	1			
Polley, James	1		100	
Polley, John	1			
Rigsby, Thomas	1			
Riply, John		1		
Riply, Peasent	1		871	
Sans, John	1		260	
Taply, Wm.	1			
Tinker, William	1			
Tittle, John	1		125	
Young, John			100	

....

Captain Melvin's Company - 1796 - Return by Joseph Crouch

Names	White poles	Black poles	Land	Studs
Bacon, Isaac			400	
Bacon, John	1		197	
Bean, Edmon	1			
Beard, Robart	1		140	
Brown, John	1		335	
Brown, Peter			50	
Carney, John	1			
Carney, Thomas Jr.	1	5	300	
Carney, Thomas Sr.		2	520	
Coarby, Cannel	1			
Cowen, John	1		17	
Cox, James	1	2	70	1
Crabtree, Barnat	1			
Crabtree, John			100	
Crabtree, Wm.	1			
Crouch, Elijah	1		40	
Crouch, Joseph	1		355	
Dungworth, Charles	1		110	
Ellis, Wm.	1	4	880	
Gates, Jacob			200	
Gates, John	1			
Gates, Richard	1		111	
Genkins, Gorge Jr.	1			
Genkins, George Sr.			500	
Gillis, John	1			
Hagan, Arther	1		175	
Haile, Abednego	1	5	232	1
Hall, Nathanel			290	
Hall, Thomas			100	

Captain Melvin's Company (cont'd)

Names	White poles	Black poles	Land	Studs
Hall, Wm.	1			
Hammar, Baltes	1		136	
Hoase, Jacob	1	1	750	
Hoase, Peter	1			
Hodges, John Jr.	1		190	
Hodges, John Sr.		1	330	
Hunt, Thomas	1		35	
Lyon, John	1		276	
Lyon, Zeakel	1		200	
McClowd, Anthony	1			
McClowd, James	1			
McClowd, Robart	1			
McClowd, William Jr.	1			
McClowd, William Sr.			137	
Mabury, Gorge Sr.		2		
Matlock, Zachariah			150	
Meins, Isea	1		200	
Meins, Thomas	1			
Melvin, John	1	1	250	1
Melvin, Joseph Jr.	1			
Melvin, Thomas			150	
Melvin, Joseph Sr.	1		300	
Milburn, Samuel	1			
Oen, James	1		136	
Prichet, Charles			323	
Starns, Peter	1		226	
Stone, Robart			140	
Stone, Wm.			140	
Tompson, Wm.	1		115	
Weathers, Wm.	1		137	
York, Wm.	1		651	

May Tun--- ?
Return by Joseph Crouch

....

Captain Millikin's Company - 1796

Names	White poles	Black poles	Land	Studs
Blackburn, Thomas	1			
Blair, Brice	1		107½	
Blair, John		2	200	
Bottles, Henry	1		125	
Bowman, Enoch	1			
Breding, William	1	1	100	
Broyles, Abraham	1	1	100	
Broyles, James	1		200	
Broyls, Nicholas		2	100	
Cleck, Lewis			245	
Cleck, Peter	1			

1796

Captain Millikin's Company (cont'd)

Names	White Polls	Black Polls	Land	Studs
Cummins, Hugh	1		60	
Cunningham, Hugh	1		150	
Cunningham, John	1		150	
Crookshanks, George	1		133	
Denton, Jonathon	1		100	
Doak, Rev. Samuel	1	1	100	
Dolphin, Will	1			
Embree, John	1		200	
Embree, Thomas	1		350	
Evins, George	1		57	
Falls, John	1			
Gallihar, William	1			
Gillespie, George	3	10	1900	
Gillespie, Thomas	1	3	690	
Greeneway, William	1		112	
Hannah, Andrew	1		320	
Harvy, James	1			
Holly, John	1			
Jordan, Lewis	1		675	
Lott, Gasper	1			
Lowry, Adam	1		176	
McAlister, John			625	
McBath, Andrew			250	
McBath, Robart	1			
McBath, William	1			
McCullick, James	1			
McEwen, Margaret			365	
McFerrin, Andrew			200	
McLin, Alexander	1		200	
Mathis, Alexander	1	3	460	
Messer, Joseph	1		225	
Millikin, John	1		225	
Nelson, Henry		2	394	
Nelson, John	1	1	200	
Payn, Jesse	1		720	
Scott, Robert	1		100	
Scott, Thomas		2	200	1
Shields, Patrik			270	
Slawter, William	1			
Squibb, John	1	1	204	
Stephenson, William			467	
Tilford, Thomas	1			
Tucker, Nicholas	1		70	
Wallace, James Jr.	1			1
Wallace, James Sr.		1		
Wallace, Thomas	1			
Wilhite, Samuel	1			
Wilson, Issack			350	

Captain Millikin's Company (cont'd)

Names	White Polls	Black Polls	Land	Studs
Woods, Archable	1			
Yegar, Solomon	1	1	200	

Finis

....

A List of Taxable Property - Capt. Morrison's Company - 1796

Names	Polls White	Polls Black	Land	Studs	Location
Ball, Amos	1		100		Little Dow Carter County
			307		Sinking Creek
Bean, John	1		640		Wattauger River
			100		Nobb Creek
Bogart, Henry			60		Wattuagaw River
Bogart, Samuel	1				
Boreing, William			73		Brush Creek
Carathers, Jonathan	1		100		Brush Creek
Carley, John	1				
Carr, John Jr.	1				
Carr, John Sr.		2	232		Nobb Creek
Collins, Joseph	1		100		Wattauger River
Crushon, John	1		91		
Daniel, William			260		Brush Creek District
Denton, Isaac	1				
Denton, James	1				
Denton, Jeremiah	1		60		Sinking Creek
Denton, Joseph	1		185		Brush Creek
Denton, Samuel	1		402		Nobb Creek
Duncan, Charles	2		460		Nobb Creek
Fain, John's Orfants			240		
Fain, Samuel's Orphans			400		Nobb Creek
Ford, Horatio	1	1	100		Brush Creek
Francis, John	1				
Gibbs, Thomas	1				
Gibson, Thomas			117½		Nobb Creek
Gray, John	1				
Greate, David	1		100		Brush Creek
Hammer, Jacob	1				
Hammer, John Jr.	1	1	240		Head Spring Nobb Crk.
Hammer, John Sr.			349		Nobb Creek
Humphries, George	1				
Huston, John	1				
Huston, William	1				
Job, David		4	280	1	Nobb Creek
Jones, Darling	1		195		
Kelley, Kinchen			200		Nobb Creek
King, Thomas	1		1180		3 Tracks Nobb Cr.
			300		Nobb all joining

Capt. Morrison's Company (cont'd)

Names	Polls White	Polls Black	Land	Studs	Location
McMachon, John Blair	1	2	400		Nobb Creek
Latham, John	1		1000		in Hawkins Co.
Little, John	1				
Little, Jonah			320		Brush Creek
Mapels, John	1				
Mapels, William	1				
Martain, John	1				
Massengell, Henry	1	5	100		Wattaugar & Brush Cr.
Melvin, Joseph	1		250		Nobb Creek
Millar, John	1		222		Nobb Creek
Mitchell, Adam	1		280		Nobb Creek
Mitchel, Robert	1		120		Nobb Creek
Morrison, James	1		50		
Morrison, Joseph	1		200		Brush Creek
More, Ruben	3		386		Brush Creek
Murry, Jeremiah	1				
Nelson, George	1				
Nelson, Jane		2	100		Sinking Creek
Nelson, William		3	500		Nobb Creek
Patrick, Jessey	1				
Percefield, Samuel			225		Nobb Creek
Pore, Benjamin	1				
Range, Peter	1		500		Nobb Creek
			259		Sinking Creek
Runo, Charles	1				
Ryen, James	1		258		Nobb Creek
Stevens, Henry	1	1	430		Ceder Run
Stover, John	1				
Tullis, Jonathan	1		399		Cain Creek
Whitteker, Mark	1		30		
Wood, William	1		177		Sinking Creek
Young, John		2	252½		on Nobb Creek
			200		in Knox County
Young, Robert	2		640		Brush Creek

Total William Nelson, J.P.

- - - - - - - -

John Engil and John White
Not Given in

- - - - - - -

An Addition to Capt. Morrison's Co. for 1796

Taken from Taylor's District

Names	Polls White	Polls Black	Land	Studs	Location
Dungan, Jeremiah		3	1000	1	Watauga River
Eagen, Barnebe			200		Sinking Creek
Eagan, James	1				
Lucas, George	1				
Smith, Absolam	1				
Wood, William			250		

August 12, 1796

Taken by me, William Nelson J.P.

List of the Taxable Property of Capt. Shipley's Co. - Late Murry's for 1796

Name	White pole	Black pole	Land	Stud
Allison, Charles	1		257	
Barron, John	1			
Barron, Joseph	1		200	
Barron, Thomas			125	
Barron, Walker	1		250	
Barron, William	1		100	
Billingsly, Samuel	2	2	200	
Braden, James	1			
Bull, Jacob	1		255	
Bullington, William	1		226	
Carr, Thomas	1			
Chamberlain, James	1	1	160	
Chinueth, Nicholas			49	
Chapman, John			100	
Cops, Thomas	1		149	
Cox, Elijah	1			
Crouch, John Sr.			50	
Denham, Charles	1		115	
Denham, David	1		115	
Dugglas, John	1			
Ellis, John	1		100	
Ensor, Thomas			250	
Epperson, Anthoney		1	400	
Epperson, Peter	1		350	
Epperson, Samuel	1		250	1
Forbush, Hugh	1			
Ford, Loyd	1		121 3/4	
Ford, Loyd Sr.		2	100	
Ford, Mordicai			220	
Ford, Thomas	1		200	
Ford, William	1		100	
Glascock, Archeble	1	2	300½	
Gott, Anthoney			588	
Gott, John	1		125	
Gray, George		1	530	
Gray, Robert	1	1	160	1
Grills, Richard	1			
Grimsley, William	1			
Gristham, Thomas	1	1	184½	
Haile, George Jr.	1	2	220	
Haile, George Sr.		1	200	
Haile, Henry	1			
Haile, Joshua	1			
Haile, Meshack	1		421	
Haile, Joseph the older		3	836	
Haile, Nathan	1		200	
Haile, Nicholas Sr.		1	272	
Haile, Richard Jr.	1		15	
Haile, Richard Sr.	1		180	
Haile, Samuel	1	1	175	
Haile, Thomas	1			
Haile, William of Nicholas	1		200	

1796

Capt. Shipley's Co. (cont'd)

Name	White pole	Black pole	Land	Stud
Haile, William of Richard Sr.	1		75	
Holland, Benjamin	1	4	550	
Holland, Peter		1		
Hunt, Jesse	1		422	
Jackson, George	1		80	
Jackson, William	1		160	
Kerby, Christopher	1			
King, Uruth			155	
Kintcheloe, Charles	1	2	200	
McCubbin, Zachariah			200	
McFerson, Daniel	1	2	150	
Maden, Andrew	1			
Martin, James	1		178	
Moore, Samuel	1		254	
Murry, Christopher	1			
Murrey, Morgan			205	
Murray, Shadrack	1		150	
Murray, Thomas Jr.	1			
Murry, Thomas Sr.			290	
Noland, James	1		150	
Norwood, John	1		146	
Nowland, Georg	1	4	380	
Porter, Charles	1			
Rusten, Jesse	1			
Shipley, Benjamin			195	
Shipley, James	1		245	
Shipley, Nathan	1		80	
Shipley, Thomas	1		200	
Van Vactor, Benjamin		1		
White, Archeble			300	

Returned by me at May turm 1796
Joseph Britten

List of the Taxable property of Joseph Britten
1 White pole 422 acres
as Administrator of the estate of
William Britten 100 acres
To 431
J. Britten

....

Joseph Young's Company, Year 1796

Name	White Pole	Black Pole	Land	Stud
Anderson, Frederick	1		143	
Ausmus, Henery	1			
Ausmis, Philip			200	
Baley, Daniel	1		100	
Baley, John	1		200	
Bales, John			173	
Bell, Thomas	1			
Bolinger, Frederick	1			
Boren, Ezekiel			70	

Joseph Young's Company (cont'd)

Name	White Pole	Black Pole	Land	Stud
Boren, Chana	1		750	
Borin, Absolam	1			
Borin, Nicholis	1		149	
Boriff, Phelty	1			
Brock, Christian	1			
Brooks, Jailes	1		300	
Buley, Anthony			200	
Cassidy, Robert	1			
Crissilles, John	1		100	
Cumpton, Jerimiah	1			
Desheart, Elisha	1			
Fine, John	1		250	
Gray, Willis	1			
Greene, Richard	1			
Headrick, Charles			140	
Heartsell, Hana			60	
Henderson, John	1		200	
Henderson, Joseph	1		200	
Hufman, David	1		250	
Hunter, Abraham	1			
Hunter, Henery	1			
Hunter, Jacob	1		230	
Hunter, John			389	
Inks, George	1			
Irwin, Benjamin	1		200	
Kirby, Mallaly	1			
Leach, William			100	
Lilborn, Andrew	1		100	
Mitchel, Andrew	1			
Moor, James	1		411	
Murry, Ephraim	1		255	
North, George	1		100	
Oar, Thomas			208	
Parker, John	1			
Pewit, Joel	1			
Pitner, John	1		200	
Potts, David	1			
Price, Mordica	1		400	
Rader, Adam	1		540	
Rhods, Elisha	1			
Rose, Hosea			320	
Ruble, John	1		200	
Ruble, Peter	1		553	
Smith, Edward	1		218	
Starmer, George			133	
Tipton, Col. John		5	947	1
Walker, Barbary			275	
Watson, John	1			
Watson, Jonathan			115	
Watson, William	1		600	
Young, Joseph	1	6	915	
Young, Mary relict of Thomas Young		3	340	
Young, Rebecca relict of Charles Young		1	220	

1796

A List of the Lots of Jonesborough for 1796

John Adams

To 1 Lott N.25

Francis Allison
To 1 lott N.14

Brown, Joseph
To 1 lott N.21

Brown, William
1 ditto

Cowan, Nathaniel
to 23 part of . . . N.30
To 1 lott N.32

Davis, John
To half of a lott . N.20

Davis, Nathaniel and
Charter, James Executors of
James Allison Dec'd.
To 8 lotts. . .

Deaderick, David
To 1 lot N.33
To 23 feet part of N.30

Harrison, Michael

To part of a lott N.18 after deducting 60 feet of the said lott

---

Herrl ?, Baldwin
to half of a lott . N.20

House, George
To 1 lott N.17
1 ditto 13
1 ditto 15
1 ditto 16

Jacobs, Dufty
to 60 feet in front of N.16

Kenarth, John ?
To 1 lott N.11

Reid, James
To 1 lott N.21

Rhea, John
To 1 lott N.22
To 1 lott N.40

James Scott
To part of a lott . . N.30
after deducting 46 ft of the full lott

Sevier, John Jr.
to 1 lott N.23
to 1 ditto N.24
to 1 ditto

Stuart, James
To 1 lott N.28
to 1 ditto N.29

By me James Stuart

Captain Biddle's Company - 1797

Names	Wh Poles	Bl Poles	Land	Studs
Alexander, Frances	1		125	
Alexander, John	1		125	
Alexander, Jonathan	1			
Allen, Robert	1		166	
Beas, Jacob			200	
Biddle, Thomas	1		500	
Blackly, John	1		130	
Blackly, Robert			290	
Blair, Brice	1		107	
Blair, Big John	1		250	
Blair, Hugh	1		520	
Blair, John	1	2	279	
Blair, John Senr	1	2	200	
Blair, John Md.	1		250	
Blair, William	1		210	
Brown, David			300	
Brown, William	1			
Campbell, George	1			
Campbell, Hugh	1		310	
Campbell, John Jun	1	3	175	
Campbell, John Sr			200	
Campbell, Robert	1		280	
Campbell, William	1	1		
Carmichael, John		2	200	
Carson, Andrew	1		50	
Carson, Moses			300	
Cason, Rev. John		1	726	
Cumins, Gibriel	1			
Davis, George	1	1	140	
Davis, Saml	1		124	
Gillworth, John	1		200	
Haile, Abednigo	1		100	
Humphreys, William	1	1	590	
Kelsey, William		1	291	
McCall, John	1		250	
McWhorter, James	1		150	
Martin, Joseph	1		148	
Patterson, James	1		100	
Patton, Anthony	1			
Richards, Lewis	1		100	
Rogers, Moses	1			
Rogers, Thomas			500	
Rogers, Thomas Jr	1			
Seehorn, James	1		140	
Shanks, William	1		115	
Shields, David	1		250	
Shields, George	1			
Shields, Henry	1		197	
Shields, Joseph	1		230	
Smetier (?) Peter	1			
Smith, Richard	1		130	
Stuart, Charles	1			
Stuart, John	1			

1797

Captain Biddle's Company (cont'd)

Names	Wh Poles	Bl Poles	Land	Studs
Blackly, Daniel	1		125	
Sams, Benjamin			200	
Sweet, John		1	27	
Tedlock, Lewis	1	2	300	
Thompson, Andrew		2	350	
Tiffin, Henry	1	2	250	
Trotter, James	1	1	100	
Tweedy, James	1		100	
Vance, Handale			155	
Williams, John	1		200	

....

Capt. Calvert's Company - 1797

Names	Polls Wh	Bl	Land	Situation	Studs	Town Lots
Adams, Alexander	1		116			
Adams, John	1		175			
Allen, John Sr.	1					(1) No. 25
Allison, Francis	1	3	175			
Ball, Thomas	1					
Bayles, Samuel	1		209¼			
Bayles, Willm	1					
Beard, John	1					
Brown, Abram	1		150			
Brown, Conrod	1					
Brown, Daniel	1		179¼			
Brown, David	1		80			
Brown, Jacob	1		124¼			
Brown, Jacob Senr			130			
Brown, John	3		324			
Brown, Joseph	1	2	100			(1) No. 11
Brown, Phillip	1					
Brown, Solomon	1					
Calvert, William	1	1	127	Wash.Co.		
Cash, James		3	328			
Cash, John	1					
Cash, Willm	1					
Chester, William P	1		150			(5) No. 26,55, 56,57,58
Cloyd, William	1		210			
Coppick, Aaron	1					
Creselus, Isaac	1		100			
Davis, John	1					(½) No. 20
Davis, Nathaniel						(10) No. 2,3,4,5, 10,12,28,42,45,50
Deaderick, David	2	2	89			(5) No. 13,33,59, 62,63
Disney, Thomas	1					
Donelly, Thomas	1					
Ellemon, John	1					
Faine, John						(1) No. 61
Finch, Calvin	1		150			

Capt. Calvert's Company (cont'd)

Names	Polls Wh	Polls Bl	Land	Situation	Studs	Town Lots
Gier, Jacob	1		141½	Wash.Co.		
Grimes, James	1					
Haire, Isaac	1		172			
Gilespee, Allen			200			
Harbison, Samuel	1					
Harrison, Michael	1	4	240			(1) No. 18
Harle, Baldwin	1					(½) No. 20
Hill, Willm	1		100			(1) No. 31
Hines, Samuel	1					
House, George	1	2	387			(3) No. 16,17,38
Ingle, Michel	1					
Jacobs, Dufty	1					(2) No. 51,60
Kindal, Barbary			175			
McGinnis, John	1		430		1	
McKim, Edward	1					(1) No. 9
May, Samuel Jr.	1	1	50			(2) No. 32,50
Million, Edward	1		162	Wash.Co.		
Mitchel, Robert	1	2	390			(1) No. 19
Naile, Jesse			100			
Nodding, Willm		5	300			
Parker, James	1					
Pipkin, John	1					
Reed, James	1		200			(1) No. 23
Rice, Thomas	1					
Robertson, George	1					
Salt, Henery	1					
Seuman, Jacob	1		262¼			
Severe, John Jun.						(4) No. 7,8,24,29
Shannon, Willm	1		160			
Sidner, Martin	1		175			
Sliger, Gasper	1		94			
Sliger, Henry	1		564			
Sliger, John junr.	1		100			
Sliger, John Sn.		1	250			
Smith, John Jun.	1					
Spring, Nicholas	1					
Starmer, John	1		150			
Stewart, James	not give in					
Taylor, Christopher		3	305			
Waddle, John	1	1				
Walter, Peter	1		85½			
Witt, Burgis	1					
Wood, Willm	1					
Weare, John			100			

....

A List of the Taxable Property in Captain Duncan's Co. for the year 1797 -- Taken by me- J Isaac Depew

Names	Wh Polls	Bl Polls	Land	Studs
Allison, Ann			145	
Adier, James			100	

1797

Captain Duncan's Co. (cont'd)

Names	Wh Polls	Bl Polls	Land	Studs
Allison, Robart	1	4	702	
Anderson, John	1	1	108	
Bails, Daniel	1		56	
Bails, Isaac	1			
Bails, David	1			
Bails, Jacob	1		295	
Bell, George	1		145	
Berry, John	1	1		
Bails, Jacob, Jr.	1		100	
Blair, Samuel	1	2		
Boman, Elias			118	
Bowman, John	1			
Brison, Samuel	1		75	
Bullington, William	1		99	
Campbill, John	1		196	
Carson, David	1		250	
Carson, David	1		58	
Carson, Robart	1			
Conley, David	1			
Cowin, John	1	1	740	
Charlton, Pointtin	2	1	560	1
Davis, Nathaniel senr	1	1	700	
Duncan, Andrew	1		228	
Duncan, Joseph	1		440	
Epperson, Samuel	1		250	
Ferguson, Alexander	1			
Ferguson, Henry	1			
Ferguson, John			299	
Ferguson, Thomas	1			
Fraker, Michel			327	
Glass, William			384	
Gray, William	1		300	
Henard, Robert	1			
Herrald, Amasa	1			
Herrald, Elisha	1		140	
Herrald, Jonathan	1		156	
Hickman, Henry	1		99	
Hunt, Uriah	1	1	980	
Hunter, James	1			
Jones, Nathaniel	1		90	
Kye, Phillip	1		100	
Likeings, William	1		100	
McAdams, Hugh	1			
McCluar, Hugh	1			
McCord, James			250	
McLin, Robart			200	
McNeet, Anthony			150	
McNeet, John	1			
Montgomery, John	1			
Nelson, Nathan	1			
Patton, John	1			
Phillipps, David	1			
Purseley, William			142	

Captain Duncan's Co. (cont'd)

Names	Wh Polls	Bl Polls	Land	Studs
Rigs, Elias	1			
Rigs, Isiah	1			
Rolston, John	1		55	
Russel, David	1		333	
Shaw, Francis	1		300	
Shaw, Samuel	1	1	182	1
Smith, Abraham	1		395	
Smith, Seth	1		200	
Smith, William	1			
Stewart, Alexander	1		100	
Stewart, David		1	341	
Stewart, David	1		50	
Strain, John	1		100	
Taylor, Leroy	1	2	354	
Tempel, James	1			
Thomson, David	1		100	
Tucker, Joseph	1		385	
Tucker, Nicholis	1		70	
Walker, William	1		184	
Wester, Vulgim	1	1	180	
White, Isaac	1	2	420	

....

Captain Gann's Company - 1797

Names	Wh Polls	Bl Polls	Land	Studs
Adams, Wm	1			
Allison, Francis			200	
Allison, Robert	2	1	280	
Baxter, Francis	1		60	
Blackburn, Archibald	2	1	160	
Bitner, John	1		100	
Brown, Wm	1		155	
Broyles, Adam			270	
Broyles, James	1		200	
Clark, John	1		200	
Clark, William		4	300	
Collons, George	1			
Collons, John	1		200	
Cooper, James	1			
Dickson, John	1			
Ellison, Saml	1			
Gann, Adam Jr.	1			
Gann, Adam Sr.			145	
Gann, Clem			150	
Gann, John	1			1
Gann, Nathan	1		220	
Gann, Thomas	1		50	
Gray, James	1		147	
Greene, Arnold	1			
Greenway, Wm	1		112	
Harbison, Wm.	1			
Harmon, Adam	1		220	

1797

Captain Gann's Company (cont'd)

Names	Wh Polls	Bl Polls	Land	Studs
Hetler, Sebastian		1	300	
Heth, Richard	1	1		
Humphreys, Richard	1		500	
Hunt, Simon			75	
Jurdan, John	1			
Kenedy, David	1		125	
Kenedy, Daniel Sen.			75	
Lamon, Jacob	1			
Lamon, John	1			
Lewis, James	1			
McCloud, John	1			
McGee, George	1			
McGee, John	1		100	
McGee, Wm	1			
McGee, Aller	1		550	
Millar, James	1		100	
Miller, Peter			260	
Millar, Theophilus	1			
Moore, Alexr	1			
Moore, William			368	
Nunn, Whorton	1			
Pain, Reuben			200	
Panther, Adam			300	
Prethorow, Alexr	1		100	
Ramsey, Randolph	1			
Shuffield, George	1			
Smith, Daniel	1			
Smith, Phillip	1			
Vandergriff, Leonora	1			
Waddill, Charles	1			
Waddill, John			533	
Waldrep, James	1			
Wire, Benj.	1			
Wire, George	1			
Woods, Michal		8	640	

Note on back: February Term 1798. Ordered by Court that John Wire, Esq. take in the Taxable Property in the Company for the year 1798.

Test- Jas Sevier, Clk.

....

Captain Hannah's Company - 1797 - Returned by Henry Nelson

Names	Land	Wh Polls	Bl Polls	Studs
Blair, John, Senr	280		2	
Bottles, Henry	125	1		
Bowman, Enoch		1		
Broyle, Abraham	100	1	1	
Broyle, Adam		1		
Broyle, Daniel	110	2	1	
Broyle, Nicholas	130		3	
Broyle, Samuel	240	1		
Broyle, Cyrus	100		2	

Captain Hannah's Company (cont'd)

Names	Land	Wh Polls	Bl Polls	Studs
Click, Lewis	245			
Click, Peter		1		
Crookshanks, George	133	1		
Cunningham, Hugh	150	1		
Cunningham, John Jr.	150	1		
Cunningham, Samuel		1	1	
Denton, Jonathan	100	1		
Doak, Rd Samuel	180	1	2	
Deane, Benjamin		1		
Dunwody, Adam, Ex	350			
Embree, John	200	1		
Embree, Thomas	310	1		
Evans, George	57	1		
Falls, John		1		
Gillespie, George	119	3	11	
Gillespie, Thomas	681	1	3	
Graham, Charles		1		
Graham, James		1		
Greenway, William	112	1		
Hannah, Andrew	320	1		
Harris, John C.		1		
Hatcher, Henry		1		
Helms, John	30	1		
Hervey, James		1		
Holley, John		1		
Hoofman, Jesse		1		
Hoover, Matthias	370	2		
Jordan, Lewis	375	1		
Killgor, Isaac	350	1		
Lott, Gasper		1		
Lowry, Adam	176	2		
McAllister, John Senr	642			
McBath, Robert	250	1		
McBath, William		1		
McEwen, Margaret	365			
McFarran, Andrew	200	1		
McLin, Alexander	200	1		
McNeese, William		1		
Mathes, Alexander	465	2	3	
Mercer, Joseph	225	1		
Miligan, John	225	1		
Murrah, Joshua		1		
Nelson, Henry	394		2	
Nelson, John	200	1	1	
Payne, Jesse Esq.	585	2		
Rush, William		1		
Scott, Robert	100	1		
Scott, Thos.	200		3	1
" "	325 in Greene Co on Cedar Branch			
Shields, Patrick	278			
Slaughter, William		1		
Squip, John	204	1		
Stephenson, Alice	467			

1797

Captain Hannah's Company (cont'd)

Names	Land	Wh Polls	Bl Polls	Studs
Sturgeon, Sympson	240	1		
Wallace, James Senr.			1	
Tilford, Thomas		1		
Willet, Zadock	30	1		
Willhite, Reuben		1		
Willhite, Samuel		1		
Yeager, Solomon	200	1	2	
Yeager, Solomon for Wm Breeding	100			

N.W. Doak was absent on the day of taking in or of my receiving orders and continues to be.

All below was taken in on the best information I could get.

Except Lewis Jordan and S. Cunningham, who gave in on oath.

....

Capt. Longmire's Co. - 1797

Names	Wh Polls	Bl Polls	Land	Studs
Acton, James	1			
Acton, James Sr.			138	
Bowman, Jacob	1		100	
Branham, James	1			
Branham, Thomas	1			
Brown, John	1		250	
Clouse, George Jr.	1			
Clouse, George Sr.	1		100	
Culbertson, Joseph	1		500	
Culbertson, Samuel			1160	
Deakins, James	1		110	
Deakins, John	1		50	
Deakins, Richard			113	
Dillard, Martha		9	200	
Dillard, Thomas	1	2	100	
Doyel, Patrick			109	
Edwards, John	1		200	
Elkins, David	1			
Elkins, Wm	1			
Eavins, Farlow	1			
Eavins, John	1		80	
Eavins, Thomas			45	
Garvis, Alexander			25	
Harrell, John	1			
Hath, Ephraham	1			
Hath, Jacob	1		150	
Haun, Adam	1		130	
Howell, Thomas	1			
Howell, Thomas Sr.			25	
Hutchings, Charles	1			
Lewis, William	1		100	
Longmire, Charles	1		600	
Longmire, John	1			

Capt. Longmire's Co. (cont'd)

Names	Wh Polls	Bl Polls	Land	Studs
Love, Robert	1	5	300	
McCray, Charles	1		274	
McInturff, Gasper	1		100	
Nelson, Berry	1		25	
Nelson, William	1			
Paterson, William	1		100	
Polley, James			109	
Polley, John	1			
Randall, Samuel	1		100	
Reador, William	1			
Sams, John			61	
Seamons, John	1			
Seamons, Joseph	1			
Title, John	1		76	
Wilkels, John	1			
Young, John			100	

....

Capt. Chas. Robertson's Company - 1797

Names	Wh Polls	Bl Polls	Land	Studs
Armstrong, John	1			
Ballenger, Jacob	1			
Ballenger, James	1			
Bartelaben, Arthur D.	1	7	231	
Baylis, George	1			
Baylis, Reubin	1		291	
Bond, Heirs			150	
Boothe, Joseph	1		120	
Boriff, Valtintine	1			
Boyd, Henry	1			
Briant, Josiah	1			
Brown, Benj.	1		300	
Brown, Maj. Jacob	1	2	326	
Brown, John	1		326	
Brown, Ruth		3		
Burket, George			250	
Casner, Jacob			330	
Brown, Thomas	1	1	326	
Cohee, John	1			
Colyer, Stephen	1			
Colyer, Wm	1	2	310	
Embree, Isaac	1		70	
Embree, Jacob	1			
Embree, Margaret			183	
Frinch, Peter			200	
Fukey, John	1			
Goier, Jacob			1024	
Goin, Henry	1			
Hammond, Christopher	1		100	
Hamton, John	1			
Hamton, Mary			200	
Hanley, James	1			

1797

Capt. Chas. Robertson's Company (cont'd)

Names	Wh Polls	Bl Polls	Land	Studs
Henley, John	1		300	
Ingle, Wm			80	
Irwin, Samuel	1			
Jones, Richard	1		112	
Lamon, David			200	
Leach, Wm			100	
Lilburn, Andrew	1		100	
May, Cassimore	1		6	
Neal, George	1		200	
Neal, Henry	1		85	
Neal, Wm			96	
Roberson, Capt. Chas.	1		258	
Rogers, Ezekiel	1			
Rogers, John	1		115	
Rogers, Joseph	1		50	
Sevier, James	1	2	731	
Sevier, John	1	1		
Sevier, Gov. John			300	
Sevier, John Junr	1	2	640	
Shannon, Joseph	2		178	
Shannon, John	1		100	
Sherrell, Samuel	1	7	250	
Templin, William	1			
Tucker, Abraham	1			
Wear, John			100	

....

Captain Nathan Shipley's Company - 1797

Names	Wh Polls	Bl Polls	Land	Studs
Archer, Benjamin	1		100	
Baker, Charles	1		100	
Baker, James	1		176	
Baker, Jonathan	1		200	
Ball, Jacob	1		225	
Barron, John	1			
Barron, Joseph	1		200	
Barron, Thomas	1		125	
Barron, Walker	1		230	
Barron, William	1		100	
Billingsley, Samuel	2	2	200	
Britten, Joseph	1		222	
Britten, William Estate			100	
Brown, James	1		200	
Burch, Richard	1		136	
Chamberlain, James	1	1	160	
Cox, Elija	1			
Crouch, John Jr.	1		760	
Crouch, John Sen.			50	
Denham, Charles	1		125	
Denham, David			163	
Duglas, John	1			
Duncan, Joseph	1		200	

Captain Nathan Shipley's Company (cont'd)

Names	Wh Polls	Bl Polls	Land	Studs
Ellis, John	1		100	
Ellison, Charles	1		397	
Ensor, William	1			
Eppeson, Anthony		1	400	1
Eppeson, Benjamin	1		100	
Eppeson, Peter	1	2	350	
Foard, John	1	1	220	
Ford, Loyd, Jun.	1	1	121	
Ford, Loyd Sen.	0	2	100	
Ford, Mordecai			200	
Ford, Thomas	1	1	100	
Ford, William	1		100	
Fraley, Christopher	1			
Giffert, John	1			
Glascock, Archibald	1	2	501	
Gott, Anthony			583	
Gott, John	1		130	
Gott, Lott	1			
Gray, Roben	1		550	
Grimsley, William	1			
Gristham, Thomas	1	1	84	
Haile, Abednego	1		205	
Haile, George, Junr	1	2	190	
Haile, George, Sen.		1	200	
Haile, John			92	
Haile, Joseph of George	1		100	
Haile, Joseph the older		3	836	
Haile, Joshua	1	1	88	
Haile, Masak	1		100	
Haile, Machash	1		500	
Haile, Nathan	1		200	
Haile, Nicholas, Senr	0	1	272	
Haile, Samuel	1	2	100	
Haile, Shadrach	1		100	
Haile, Thomas	1			
Haile, William of Nicholas	1		200	
Haile, William of Richard	1		75	
Haws, John			430	
Hays, James	1			
Holland, Benjamin	1	4	550	
Holland, Peter	0	1		
Hunt, Jesse	1		422	
Hunt, Samuel	1			
Jackson, George	1		88	
Jackson, William	1		160	
Kincheloe, Charles	1	1	200	
Kincheloe, Enoch	1	2	700	
Kincheloe, George	1	2	300	
Kincheloe, John	0	7	930	
Lane, Samuel	1		100	
Lane, Tidence			238	
Lane, Tilman	1			
McCubbin, Zachariah	0	1	200	

1797

Captain Nathan Shipley's Company (cont'd)

Names	Wh Polls	Bl Polls	Land	Studs
Maden, Andrew	1			
Martin, James	1		120	
Matlock, Moore	1	1	120	
Moore, Samuel	1		180	
Mulkey, Jonathan	1		100	
Murry, Christopher	1			
Murry, Thomas, Senr.	0	0	290	
Murray, Thomas Junr	1			
Murrey, Morgan			205	
Murrey, Shadrach	1		150	
Nolan, George	1	4	858	
Nolan, James	1		150	
Norwood, John	1		739	1
Odeneal, Bartholomy	0	0	100	
Pearce, Joshua	1			
Pipcock, John	1		50	
Porter, Charles	1		64	
Ruston, Jesse	1			
Sander, Frederick	1		50	
Shipley, Benjamin			175	
Shipley, Nathan	1		100	
Shipley, Thomas	1		200	
Shipley, Peter	1		150	
Smith, Anderson			250	
Starkes, Joshua	1			
Van Sickel, ---			100	
Van Vactor, Benjamon	0	1	120	
Whelock, John	2	3	750	
Wheyley, Thomas	1		75	

Returned by me
John Norwood

....

Undated - Captain York's Company - Likely 1797 or 1798

Note: The names are the same order as in Capt. Melvan's Company for 1795 & 1796, but we have no Capt. Melvan's for either 1797 or 1798.

Names	Wh Pole	Bl Pole	Acres	Stud
Bacon, Isaac	0		250	
Baker, John			197	
Bean, Edmon	1	1	0	1
Beard, Robert	1		140	
Capps, Thomas	1		149	
Carney, John	1			
Carney, Thomas, Senr.		1	520	
Carr, John	1		100	
Celsey, Samuel			220	
Cowin, John	1		117	1
Cox, James	1	4	232	1
Crabtree, Barnett	1			
Crouch, Elijah	1		45	

Captain York's Company (cont'd)

Names	Wh Pole	Bl Pole	Acres	Stud
Crouch, Jessey	2			
Crouch, Jos.	1		355	
Dunworth, Charles	1		110	
Elles, William	1	3	725	
Ensor, Thomas	1		250	
Fawbush, Hugh	1			
Gates, Jacob	2		200	
Gates, Richard	1		133	
Gillis, John	1			
Gray, Absolum	1			
Grysham, Fullar	1			
Hagan, Arthur	1		175	
Haill, Abednego	1	1	250	
Hall, Nathaniel	0	2	70	
Hall, Samuel	1		117	
Hall, Thomas	0	0	100	
Hall, William	1			
Hammer, Baltis, Jr.	1		100	
Hammer, Baltis, Sr.	1		136	
Hammer, Baltis, Senr.	1		115	
Hemon, Mikel	1			
Hodges, John Junr	1		190	
Hodges, John Senr.	1	1	330	
Hoss, Jacob	0	1	750	
Hoss, Peter	1			
Hunt, Thomas	1		305	
Jenkins, Gorge, Senr	1		500	1
King, Isaac	1		100	
Low, Andrew	1			
Lyon, Ezekiel			200	
Lyon, John	1		276	
McCloud, James	1			
McCloud, Robert	1			
McCloud, William, Junr	1			
McCloud, William, Senr	0		131	
McRay, Daniel	0		350	
Manes, Isaac			200	
Matlock, Zachariah			150	
Meins, Thomas	1	0	0	
Melvin, Joseph, Elder	2		3003	
Melvin, Joseph Junr	1		160	
Melvin, Samuel			100	
Milburn, Samuel	1			
Owen, James			136	
Pritchert, Charles	0	0	323	
Pritchet, Thomas	1			
Starnes, Peter	2	0	227	
Stone, William			270	
Weathers, John	1			
Weathers, William			137	
White, Archible			300	
Wright, Isaac	2		100	1
York, William	2	0	400	

1797

Captain Joseph Young - 1797

	Wh Polls	Bl Polls	Land	Studs
Arwin, Banjamin	1		200	
Anderson, Frederick	1		143	
Ausmis, Henry	1			
Ausmis, Philip			190	
Baly, Daniel	1			
Baly, John	1		215	
Bayles, Daniel Sr			104	
Bell, John			173	
Bell, Thomas	1			
Boren, Joshua	1			
Borin, Absolom	1		150	
Borin, Chana	1		200	
Borin, Ezekiel			120	
Borin, Nicholis	1		100	
Brooks, Giles	1		300	
Buly, Anthony			200	
Casidy, Robert	1			
Compton, Jeremiah	1			
Couff, Felty	1			
Cresileas, John	1		100	
Fine, John	1		250	
Frances, John	1		104	
Gray, Willis	1			
Green, Richard	1			
Headrick, Charles	1		140	
Heartsel, Hana			60	
Henderson, John	1			
Henderson, Joseph	1		200	
Huffman, David	1		250	
Hunter, Abraham	1		200	
Hunter, Henery	1			
Hunter, Jacob	1		230	1
Inks, George	1			
Jinkins, William	1			
Kerby, Malbea	1			
Leach, William			100	
Lilburn, Andrew	1		143	
More, James	1		261	
Murry, Epheraim	1		255	
North, George	1		100	
Orr, Thomas			208	
Parker, John	1			
Pewet, Joel	1			
Pitner, John	1		200	
Price, Mordeca	1		451	
Rader, Adam	1	1	540	
Roads, Elisha	1			
Rosea, Hosea			320	
Ruble, Jacob	1			
Ruble, John	1		200	
Ruble, Peter			573	
Smith, Edward	1		218	
Starmer, George			218	

Captain Joseph Young (cont'd)

Names	Wh Polls	Bl Polls	Land	Studs
Swanger, John	1			
Taylor, Henery	1		300	
Tipton, Col. John		5	947	2
Walker, Barbary			275	
Watson, John	1			
Watson, Jonathan			300	
Watson, William	1		600	
Witt, Hevis	1			
Witt, James	1			
Young, Capt. Joseph	1	6	915	1
Young, Mary		3	343	
Young, Rebecca			320	

....

1798

Captain Bidelle's Company - 1798 - Taken by me- John Alexander

Names	Wh Polls	Bl Polls	Land	Studs
Alexander, Francis	1		125	
Alexander, John Jnr	1			
Alexander, Jonathan	1		100	
Barcroft, Jonth.	1			
Beise (?), Thomas	1			
Biddle, Thomas	1		500	
Blair, John	1	4	295	
Blair, John (Big)	1		300	
Blair, Richard	1		740	
Blair, Robat	1	1	175	
Blair, Wm	1		215	
Bleckley, Robart			200	
Blerley, Daniel	1		130	
Blesley, John	1		130	
Brown, David			225(?)	
Brown, Wm	1		73	
Campbell, Abraham	1		120	
Campbell, Hugh	1		210	
Campbell, John			100	
Campbell, Robert	1		280	
Carson, Adrone	1		80	
Carson, Moses			424	
Carmichael, John		2	200	
Causon, Rev John	1	1	614	4
Comens, Hugh			200	
Comins, Gilbrel	1			
Craford, John	1			
Davis, Gorg	1		160	
Davis, Samuel	1	1	124	
Gilwort, John	1			
Grastey, Gorg	1			
Humphes, William	1	1	520	
Kelsey, John	1			
Kelsey, William		1	300	
Lackin(?), Robert	1		114	
Lenen, Richard (?)	1		100	
McAll, John	1		250	
McConnal, John	1		200	1
McWhorter, James			150	
Martein, James	1		140	
Mills (?) Henr	1			
Miller, John Blair	1		250	
Patterso(n), James	1		143	
Patten, Antiney	1			
Richards, David	1			
Rogar, Andrew	1			
Rogars, Thomas, senr			500	
Sands, Mickals	1			
Seehorn, James	1		140	
Shanks, William	1		150	
S- et(?) James			27	
Shelds, Joseph	1		230	1
Shelds, Gog	1		180	

Captain Bidelle's Company (cont'd)

Names	Wh Polls	Bl Polls	Land	Studs
Shields, Kennery	1		155	
Slurd(?), Charls	1		153	
Smith, Richard	1		125	
Snitior(?) Peter	1			
Tedlock, Lonas(?)	1	3	300	
Thomson, Andrew		2	350	
Trotter, James	1	1		
Tweedy(?) James	1		100	
Widles, James	1		160	
Williams, John	1		200	

....

List of the Free Taxable Inhabitants in Capt Biddle's Company, 1798

1- Alexander, Francis
2- Allexander, Jonathan
3- Allexander, John
4- Bail, Thomas
5- Berricraft, John
6- Biddle, Thomas
7- Blackley, Daniel
8- Blackley, John
9- Blair, John
10- Blair, Big John
11- Blair, Richard
12- Blair, Robert
13- Blair, William
14- Brown, William
15- Camble, Hugh
16- Camble, Robert
17- Carson, Andrew
18- Christie, Georg
19- Craford, John
20- Cumins, Gabriel
21- Davice, Georg
22- Davice, Samuel
23- Humphreys, William
24- Gilwort, John
25- Imepox(?), Peter
26- Imgrum, Zechicariah
27- Kellee, John
28- Lucas, Robert
29- McCall, John
30- McConnal, John
31- Martain, Joseph
32- Mille(r) Hir (?) (Henry)
33- Miller, John Blair
34- Nelson, Joseph
35- Patten, Antony
36- Patteson, James
37- Richards, David
38- Richards, Luis
39- Rodgers, Andrew
40- Rodgers, Moses
41- Ruston, John
42- Sands, Michel
43- Seehorn, James
44- Shanks, William
45- Sheels, David
46- Sheelds, Henry
47- Sheelds, Joseph
48- Shields, Georg
49- Shira, Charles
50- Smith, Richard
51- Tedlock, Luis
52- Tweedy, James
53- Wenles, James
54- Williams, John

Taken 10th of November 1798 Returned by me-
John Alexander

November Term 1798 the above was returned
Joseph Britten, Cha.

....

Calvert's Company
Taken by John Waddell

"The Worshipful Court of Washington"
May Term 1798- John Waddell

Persons Names	Quantity	Situation	Polls Free	Bl	Town Lots	Scalps	Stud
Allison, Frank	301	on L Stone	1	2	0	50	
Ball, Thos			1				

Calvert's Company (cont'd)

Persons Names	Quantity	Situation	Polls Free	Bl	Town Lots	Scalps	Stud
Bayles, Daneal			1				
Bayles, Samuel	2092¼	on L Stone	1	1			$2.50
Bayles, William			1				
Beard, John			1			25	
Boils, Abraham			1			25	
Brown, Abraham	182	Little L Stone	1				
Brown, Conrad			1				
Brown, Daniel	179	on L Stone	1			22	
Brown, David	80	ditto	1			7	
Brown, Jacob Jr	124¼	Little L Stone	1				
Brown, Jacob Sr	120	ditto					
Brown, John Jr			1				
Brown, John (M)	324	L Stone	1				
Brown, Philip			1			25	
Brown, Solomon			1			25	
Burkhart, George	200	Little L Stone				2	
Cash, James	328	on L Stone		3		75	
Cloyd, William	200	ditto	1			7	
Calvert, William	127	Little L Stone	1	1		50	
Davis, Nathl, Jnr	450	B Creek	1			9	
Deaderick, David	400	K Creek	1	2	7½	75	
also	89	L Stone			& 23 of D.		
Fain, William	800	ditto	1	2		75	
Finch, Colvin	150	Cherokee	1			25	
Gere, Jacob	1412	Little L Stone	1				
Gillespie, Allen	200	L Stone					
Hair, Isaac	172	ditto	1			25	
Harris, Benj	100	Little L Stone					
Harris, John C.			1			25	
Harrison, Michl			1	2	2	23	
Hodgcase, Jerred			1			25	
House, George	200	L Stone	1		3½	25	
Jacobs, Dufty			1		#60,50, 44,14		
Kindle, Barbary	175	Little L Stone					
Kyger, Conrad	96	L Stone	1			25	
McAllister, John Jr			1				
McCormack, William			1			25	
McFarron, Andw	400	L Stone					
McGinness, Jno	430	ditto	1		#1,18	25	
Million, Edward	162	Little L Stone	1				
Moore, Jettha					½	25	
Moore, Robert	400	Little L Stone	1			25	
Agt-Michel Ingle							
Nodding, William	300	ditto		4		10	
Outlaw, Alexr	1360	L Stone					
Salt, Henry			1		part 1-50ft		
Sidner, Martin	175	Little L Stone	1			25	
Robertson, Charles Sr.	490	Cherokee		10		250	
Sliger, Adam			1			25	
Sliger, Gasper	94	Cherokee					
Sliger, John Jr	100	Little L Stone	1			25	

Calvert's Company (cont'd)

Persons Names	Quantity	Situation	Polls Free	Polls Bl	Town Lots	Scalps	Stud
Sliger, John Sn	250	L Stone		1		25	
Sloan, George				1			$3.33 2/
Smith, John	250						
Stormer, John	150	Little L Stone	1			25	
Stuart, James	1984	L Stone	3	8	6		
Vaughn, Jno			1				
Waddell, John			1	1	5	27	
Waller, Peter	85$\frac{1}{4}$	Little L Stone	1	1			
Witt, Burgis			1			25	
Witherspoon, James			1			25	
Wood, James	200	Little L Stone	1			25	
Wood, Samuel Jr	100	ditto	1			14	
Wood, Samuel Sr	300	ditto			1		
Wood, William, by	80	ditto					
Agt-Samuel Wood	100	Cherokee					

Taken by John Waddill, Jr.

This Tax List also listed "Billiard Tables", but there were none in this Company.

....

A List of the Free Male Inhabitants in the District of Captain Calvert's Company Agreeable to Act of Assembly Passed 1797

1- Allin, John, marchant
2- Allison, Francis
3- Ball, Thomas
4- Barneywell, Joseph
5- Bayls, Abraham
6- Baylis, Daniel
7- Baylis, Saml
8- Baylis, Willm
9- Brown, Abraham
10- Brown, Conrad
11- Brown, Daniel
12- Brown, David
13- Brown, Jacob
14- Brown, John
15- Brown, John
16- Brown, Joseph
17- Brown, Philip
18- Brown, Sollomon
19- Brummit, Samuel
20- Calvert, William
21- Cash, John
22- Cash, John
23- Cash, Leonard
24- Cash, Willm
25- Chester, Willm P
26- Cloyd, Willm
27- Coppick, Aaron
28- Dederick, David
29- Dickerd, George
30- Edwards, Eli
31- Faine, John
32- Faine, William
33- Finch, Calvin
34- Finley, Daniel
35- Gordon, James
36- Gyer, Jacob
37- Hair, Isaac
38- Haner, Lewis
39- Harriss, John
40- Harrison, Michael
41- Hodgkiss, Jeremiah
42- House, George
43- Ingle, Michael
44- Jacobs, Dufty
45- Joines, Thomas
46- McCollister, John
47- McGinnis, John
48- Mackin, Edward
49- May, Samuel
50- Million, Edward
51- Million, John
52- Mitchal, Robert
53- Newman, Hugh
54- Newsman, Paul
55- Parks, James
56- Reed, James
57- Roberson, George
58- Salt, Henery
59- Shanon, Willm
60- Sidener, Martin

Free Male Inhabitants in Captain Calvert's Company (cont'd)

61- Sliger, Adam
62- Sliger, John
63- Smith, George
64- Starmer, John
65- Stewart, Thos
66- Stone, George
67- Sullen, Willm
68- Taylor, Abraham
69- Vaun, John
70- Vaun, Sherewood
71- Walter, Peter
72- Weatherspoon, James
73- Witt, Burgiss
74- Wood, Charles
75- Wood, James
76- Wood, Samuel Jr

Certified by me- Samuel Wood, J P

November Term 1798- The above was returned. Joseph Britten, Ch.

....

Captain Duncan's Company - Taken by me- Isaac Depew-For the Year 1798

Names	Wh Polls	Bl Polls	Land	Studs	Town Lots
Adaer, James	0		100		0
Adams, John	1		200		1
Allin, Robart	1		166		
Allison, Ann			145		
Allison, Robert	1	4	702		1
Archer, Benjeman	1		100		
Ashley, Robart	1				
Bails, Daniel	1		56		
Bails, Isaac			130		
Bails, Jacob	1		100		
Bell, George	1		145		
Berry, John	1				
Blair, Hugh	1		300		
Bowman, Elias			118		
Bowman, John	1				
Bruer, Samuel					1
Carson, David	1		58		
Carson, David	1		125		
Carson, Robert	1		125		
Campbill, John	1		195		
Charlton, Pointing	1		510		
Coppock, Aaron	1		20		
Cowin, John	1	1	742	1	
Davis, Nathaneal	1	1	700		
Depew, Isaac	1		164		
Duncan, Andrew	1		229		
Duncan, Joseph	1		418		
Ellaman, John	1				
Firguson, Alexander	1				
Firguson, Henry	1				
Firguson, John			299		
Firguson, Samuel	1				
Firguson, Thomas	1	1			
Frakee, Michel			250		
Glass, Joseph	1				
Glass, William			384		
Harrea, James	1				
Heair, Henry	1				

Captain Duncan's Company (cont'd)

Names	Wh Polls	Bl Polls	Land	Studs	Town Lots
Heavenrig, John	1				
Henard, Robart	1				
Henderson, Joseph	1				
Herrah, Elsha	1				
Hickman, Elisha	1				
Hickman, Henry	1		445		
Highit, Joseph	1				
Hunt, Uriah	1	1	980		
Hunter, James	1				
Johnston, Samuel	1		90	1	
Jones, Nathaneal	1		90		
Key, Phillip	1		120		
McAdams, Hugh	1				
McLin, Robart	1		200		
McNutt, John	1				
Matthis, William	1				
Pattan, John	1				
Phillips, David	1				
Pursley, William			242		
Rice, David					1
Russel, David			332		
Shaw, Francis		1	300		
Shaw, Samuel	1	1	200		
Smith, Abraham	1		395		
Smith, Seth	1		150		
Smith, William	1		2		
Stanfeale, Samuel	1				1
Stewart, Alexander	1		150		
Stewart, David Jr.	1		50		
Strain, John	1		100		
Taylor, Leeroy	1	2	354		
Taylor, William	1				1
Temple, James	1	1	1		
Thomson, David			100		
Tucker, Joseph	1		387		
Tucker, Nicholas	1		70		
Walker, William	1		184		
Wisher, John	1				

\- - - - - - - -

Scrap:

David Conley given in for Taxable Property- 1 white pole for 1798

Ordered that this return be added to Esqr. Depews return for Capt. Duncan's company for 1798.

....

October 25, 1798

A List of the Taxable Inhabitants of Capt. Joseph Duncans Company
Taken by me Isaac Depew J P

- - - complete list given on following page - - -

1798

A List of the Taxable Inhabitants of Capt. Joseph Duncans Company

1- Adair, James
2- Adams, John
3- Allason, Robart
4- Anderson, John
5- Archer, Benjaman
6- Archer, James
7- Archer, Thomas
8- Ashley, Robart
9- Bails, Daniel
10- Bails, Isaac
11- Bails, Jacob Snr
12- Bails, Jacob
13- Bell, George
14- Bowman, Elias
15- Bowman, John
16- Bullington, Benjamin
17- Bullington, William
18- Campbill, Abraham
19- Campbill, John
20- Carson, David
21- Carson, David Sr
22- Carson, John
23- Carson, Robert
24- Charlston, Pointing Jr
25- Charlston, Pointing Sr
26- Clemons, John
27- Conley, David
28- Cowin, John
29- Cunningham, James
30- Davis, Nathaniel
31- Depew, Isaac
32- Duncan, Andrew
33- Duncan, Joseph
34- Firguson, Alexander
35- Firguson, Andrew
36- Firguson, John
37- Firguson, Samuel
38- Firguson, Thomas
39- Fraker, Michel
40- Fuston, John
41- Glass, Joseph
42- Glass, William
43- Graham, John
44- Harrel, James
45- Haire, Henry
46- Henard, Robart
47- Henderson, Joseph
48- Hickman, Henry
49- Highit, Joseph
50- Hunt, Uriah
51- Huntter, James
52- Ingram, Zecheriah
53- Johnson, Francis
54- Johnston, Samuel
55- Jones, Nathaniel
56- Likeings, William
57- McAdams, Hugh
58- McCord, John
59- Mclain, John
60- McCloud, William
61- McLin, Robart
62- McNutt, Anthony
63- McNutt, Bengemen
64- McNutt, John
65- Mark, (Mash) William
66- Mathas, Mr William
67- Mulkey, Jonathan
68- Nelson, Nathan
69- Orr, Thomas
70- Pattan, John
71- Phillips, David
72- Pursley, William
73- Ralston, John
74- Richee, Robart
75- Rigs, Isaiah
76- Rigs, Josiah
77- Robartson, Daniel
78- Robertson, James
79- Russel, David
80- Shanks, Nicholis
81- Shanks, William
82- Shaw, Francis
83- Shaw, Samuel
84- Sheals, Joseph
85- Smith, Abraham
86- Smith, Seth
87- Smith, William
88- Southerland, Isaac
89- Stewart, Alexander
90- Stewart, David Snr
91- Stewart, David
92- Stewart, Robart
93- Strain, John
94- Taylor, Leeroy
95- Taylor, William
96- Thomson, David
97- Tucker, Joseph
98- Walker, William
99- White, Lois
100- Wisher, John
101- Woods, John
102- Woods, William

November term 1798 the within was returned

Joseph Britten Cha.

Capt Gann's Compt - 1798

Names	Wh Polls	Bl Polls	Land	Studs	Scalps
Allison, Robert	2	1	276		50
Baxter, Francis	1		66		
Beys, Edward	1				
Bitner, John	1		100		
Blackburn, Archable	1	2	400		
Broils, Adam			270		
Broils, James	1		200		25
Broils, Sires		2	100		
Brown, James	1	1	140		50
Brown, William	1		152		25
Broyls, Toby	1				
Clark, Jesse	1			1	25
Clark, John	1		200		25
Clark, William	1	4	300		125
Cleck, Luis			245		
Cleck, Peter	1				25
Collems, Jonathan	1		200		25
Collome, George	1				25
Dickson, John	1				25
Gann, Adam	1	1	72		
Gann, Clemon			150		
Gann, Isaac	1				25
Gann, John	1		50		
Gann, Nathan	1		200		25
Gann, Thomas	1		50		
Givens, James	1				
Gray, James	1		104		
Green, Joshua			300		
Greenway, William	1		112		
Harbison, William	1				
Harbison, Samuel	1				
Hermon, Abram	1				
Hermon, Adam	1		220		
Hermon, Joseph	1				
Hetler, Sebastian		1	300		
Hover, Jacob	1				
Hover, Methias	1		370		
Humphreys, Jehue	1				
Humphreys, Richard			400		
Hunt, Simon	1		250		
Jinkins, Wilam	1				25
Jurden, John	1				
Kenneday, David Junier	1		125		
Kenneday, David Seanr			75		
Lemon, Jacob	1				25
Lemon, John	1				25
Luis, James	1				25
Luis, James	1				
McCloud, John	1				
McKee, Alexander	1		450		
Megee, Gorge	1				
Megee, John	1		100		25

1798

Capt Gann's Compt (cont'd)

Names	Wh Polls	Bl Polls	Land	Studs	Scalps
Megee, William	1				
Miller, James	1		100		25
Miller, Peter			360		
Miller, Theophiles	1				25
More, Alexander	1				25
More, William			357		
Nilson, Southy	1		100		25
Pain, Ruban			200		
Penter, Esakel	1				
Pinter, Adam	1		300		
Pritherow, Alexander	1		100		
Rymel, John	1		200		25
Sevier, Governer John		6	275		55
Waddle, Charls	1				
Waddle, John	1		336		25
Waddle, Samuel	1				25
Waddle, Sethq	1		160		
Waldrip, James	1				25
Weir, Benjemin	1				25
Weir, George	1				25
Weir, John		1	514		25
Wilson, Isaac	1		250		25
Woods, Michl		8	640		

....

State of Tennessee

Washington County November 6, 1798 a Lest of the taxabels

White pols in Capt hannahs Company teken by Jesse Payne J P

Aiken, James
Blar, Brice
Bler, Joseph
Botels, Henery
Brabson, Ephrefrem
Broyls, Abraham
Broyls, Adam
Broyls, Nicholas
Broyls, Samuel
Bowman, Anoch
Connanghaham, Hugh
Conningham, John
Conningham, Samuel
Crookshanks, George
Doke, Samuel
Drain, Benjamin
Embree, John
Embree, Thomas
Evens, George
Gelaspee, Allen
Gelaspee, George
Gelaspee, James
McCollom, Jecob
McCutchen, Willam
McLin, Alaxander
McNees, Willam
Mathes, Alaxander
Mathes, Allen
Mecy, Thomas
Meliken, John
Meser, Joseph
Nelson, Henery
Nelson, John
Payne, Jesse
Scott, Robert
Scott, Thomas
Shelds, Patrick
Slaughter, Willam
Squibb, John
Stephenson, Mathew
Sturgen, Simpson
Sympson, James
Thompson, Andraw
Tilford, Thomas

Capt Hannah's Company (cont'd)

Gelaspee, Thomas
Gibins, James
Graham, James
Greham, Charls
Greham, James
Grey, Andrew
Glo, William
Hannah, Andrew
Helms, John
Holley, John
Hus, John
Jorden, Lewes
Lot, Gasper
Lowry, Adam
M'allester, John
McBath, Andrew
McBath, William
Wallace, James
Wallece, Thomas
Walls, James
Wellett, Zadoc
Willhite, Samuel
Willhite, Ruben
Yegar, Solomon

A Lest of
Numeration teken by
Jesse Payne Esquire

November term 1798

the above was returned
Joseph Britten Cha

....

List of the Taxable Inhabitants of Capt Longmires Company - 1798

Claimants Names	Wh Polls	Bl Polls	Quantity of Land	Stud Horses
Brown, John	1		270	
Burrass, Elijah				
Carroll, Williams				
Clouse, George Junr.	1			
Clouse, George Senr.	1		100	
Culberson, Joseph	1		311	
Culbertson, Samuel			1000	
Deakins, James	1		110	
Deakins, John	1		50	
Deakins, Richard			113	
Dillard, Martha		10	200	
Doil, Patrick			106	
Eaton, John	1			
Ecton, James Junr	1			
Ecton, James Sen			138	
Edwards, John	1		200	
Elkins, David	1			
Elkins, William	1			
Evans, Farlar	1			
Evans, Thomas			45	
Evins, John	1		66	
Haun, Adam	1		150	
Herrald, John	1			
Holt, Ephraim	1		50	
Holt, Jacob	1		100	
Holt, Peter	1		130	
Howell, Thomas Junr	1			
Hutchons, Charles	1			
Jarvis, Alexander			47	
Layman, Christopher	1			
Lewis, William	1		100	

Capt Longmires Company (cont'd)

Claimants Names	Wh Polls	Bl Polls	Quantity of Land	Stud Horses
Longmire, John	1			
Longmires, Charles		1	676	
Love, Robert	1	5	400	1
McCray, Charles			160	
McInturff, Gasper	1		200	
McInturff, Israel	1			
McRunnals, Thomas	1		100	
Nelson, Berryman	1			
Patterson, William	1			
Polly, James			100	
Polly, John	1			
Randolph, Samuel Junr	1		100	
Randolph, Samuel Sen				
Reeder, William	1		50	
Rinehart, John	1		100	
Samms, John				
Seamans, Joseph	1			
Tittle, John	1		180	
Winkels, James	1			
Young, John			100	

....

Capt Longmires Company of Free Taxable Inhabitants
By order of three justices taken by Samuel Wood 1798

Brown, John	1	Holt, Peter	25
Burgiss, Elijah	2	Howel, Thos junr	26
Carrold, James	3	Hutches, Charles	27
Clouse, George Jur	4	Jarvis, Alexr	28
Clouse, George Senr	5	Kredil, Willm	29
Culverson, Joseph	6	Laymon, Chris	30
Culverson, Saml	7	Lewis, Wm	31
Deacons, James	8	Longmires, Chas	32
Deacons, John	9	Longmirse, John	33
Deacons, Richard	10	Love, Robert	34
Doyle, Patrick	11	Mcinturff, Gasper	35
Ecton, James junr	12	Mcinturff, Israel	36
Ecton, Jas Senr	13	Mcrenolds, Thos	37
Ecton, John	14	Nellon, Berryman	38
Edwards, John	15	Paterson, Willm	39
Elkins, David	16	Polley, Jas	40
Elkins, Wilm	17	Randolph, Saml J(r)	41
Evins, Farler	18	Randolph, Saml Sr	42
Evins, John	19	Rineheart, John	43
Evins, Thos	20	Simmons, Joseph	44
Harrold, John	21	Simms, John	45
Haun, Adam	22	Tittle, John	46
Holt, Ephraim	23	Wilmbles, James	47
Holt, Jacob	24		

List of Capt Longmires Company of taxable free male inhabitants taken by order of three justices- Taken by No. 46- Saml Wood J P

November term 1798- the above was returned- Joseph Britten Cha

Captain Morrison's Company - #1

Names	Wh Poll	Bl	Land	Studs	Scalps	Situation
Ball, Amos	2	1	307		40	Lying on Sinking Cr.
Barnes, William	2				28	
Boid, Joseph	1				Dbr	
Boring, William	1		176 3/4		Dbr	
Brown, Samuel	1				Dbr	
Carether, Jonathan	1		240		25	
Carr, John		2	232		50	
Carter, John	1				25	
Cobb, William	1				25	
Collins, Joseph	1		100			
Cople, Nicholas	1				Dbr	
Crouch, James	1		100		Dbr	
Daniel, William			260			
Danil, John	1		30		25	
Denton, James	2				50	
Denton, Joseph			185			
Denton, Samuel	1		402			
Duncan, Charles	2		460		50	
Dungans, Jeremiah		3	1000		75	
Duran, William	1				25	
Eagen, Barnebe		1	200		Dbr	
Eagan, James	1				25	
Edwards, Jonathan	1				1	
Foard, Horatio	1		100		Dbr	
Gibs, Thomas	1				25	
Gibson, Thomas			117½			
Hammer, Isaac	1		250		25	
Hammer, Jacob	1		100		25	
Hammer, John Jr.	1	1	240			
Hammer, John Sr.			265			
Hammer, Jonathan	1				25	
Hamock, John	1				Dbr	
Harris, Joshua	1				25	
Hog, Ruben	2				Dbr	
Humphres, George	1				25	
Huston, John	1	1			25	
Job, David	4		280	1	63	Lying on Sinking Cr.
Jones, Darling	1		195		24	
Keley, Kinchen			200			
King, Henry	1		170		25	Lying on waters of Nob Cr.
King, Thomas		1	1480		25	
King, William	1	1			42	Sinking Creek ?
Litte, Jonah			300			
Lucas, George	1				25	
Maples, James	1				25	
Maples, John	1				Dbr	
Masengill, Henry	1	4	1775		125	
Melvin, Joseph			250			
Millar, Peter	1		458		25	
Miller, John	1		222		25	
Mitchell, Adam	1		280		25	
			460 acres of land Samuel Fain Heirs			

Captain Morrison's Company (cont'd)

Names	Wh Poll	Bl	Land	Studs	Scalps	Situation
Mitchell, John	1				25	
More, Ruben	2		386		Dbr	
Morrison, James	1		50		25	
Morrison, Joseph	1		200		25	
Nelson, George	1				25	
Nelson, Jane		3	100		75	
Nelson, William Jr.	1				25	
Nelson, William Sr.		2	500		50	
Paten, Alex	1				25	
Range, Peter	1		553		Dbr	
Smith, Zebulen	1				25	
Stevens, Henry	1	1	430		50	
Stockly, Jehu	1				Dbr	
Tipton, Jonathan	1					
Tipton, Joshua	1				25	
Tipton, Reseboing	1				25	
Tullis, Jonathan	1		399		25	
Ward, William			250			
Wood, William	1		177		Dbr	
Young, John		2	252		50	
Young, Robert	2	1	640		75	
Young, William	1		100		25	

John Bean, William Bean, Isaac Denton, Jeremiah Denton has not given their taxes to William Nelson. May 11th. 1798.

....

Captain Morrisson's Company - #2

Names	Wh Polls	Bl Polls	Land	Studs
Agens, Barnabas		1	200	
Ball, Ames	1		407	1
Barnes, William	1			
Bean, John				
Bogart, Henry			460	
Boring, Absolum			91	
Boring, Elijah	1			
Boreing, William			176 3/4	
Breden, James	1			
Carr, John		3	232	
Collens, Joseph	1		100	
Corethers, Jonathan	1		240	
Daniel, William			260	
Danil, John	1		30	
Denton, Iseec	1			
Denton, Jeremiah	1		60	
Denton, Joseph	1		185	
Denton, Samuel	1		402	
Duncan, Charles	2		460	
Dungen, Jeremiah		3	1000	
Edwards, Henry	1			
Edwards, Jonathan	1			
Engle, John	1		200	

Captain Morrisson's Company (cont'd)

Names	Wh Polls	Bl Polls	Land	Studs
Ford, Horash	1		100	
Gibbs, Thomas				
Gibson, Thomas			117 2/4	
Grate, David	1		100	
Hammer, Iseec	1			
Hammer, Jacob	1			
Hammer, John Jr	1	1	240	
Hammer, John Sr.			349	
Haress, Joshua	1			
Humphries, George	1			
Humphres, John			100	
Huston, John	1			
Job, David		5	280	
Jones, Darling	1		195	
Kelley, Kinchen			200	
King, Henry	1		170	
King, Thomas		1	1480	
King, William	1			
Little, John	1			
Little, Jonah			320	
Luces, George	1			
McMahen, John Br	1	1	627	
Mapel, James	1			
Maples, John	1			
Masengill, Henry	1	4	1430	
Melvin, Joseph			250	
Miller, John	1		222	
Mitchell, Adam	1		280	
Mitchell, John	1			
Morison, James	1		50	
Nelson, George	1			
Nelson, Jane		2	100	
Nelson, William		2	500	
Range, Peter	1		553	
Ryens, James	1		258	
Smith, Zebulon	1			
Stevens, Henry	1	1	430	
Tipton, Rees	1			
Tulles, Jonathan	1		399	
Ward, William			250	
Wood, William			177	
Young, John		2	252 2/4	
Young, Robert	1	1	640	
Young, William	1			

....

A List of the Free Taxable Inhabitants of Capt Joseph Morrisons District Washington County State of Tennessee Takeing in by me William Nelson J P
October 20th 1798

- - - complete list given on following page - - -

1798

List of Free Taxable Inhabitants of Capt Joseph Morrisons District

Ball, Amos
Bean, William
Bogart, Abraham
Boid, Joseph
Boreing, James
Boreing, Joshua
Boreing, William
Brown, Samuel
Byolee, Michel
Carreathers, Jonathan
Collins, Joshua
Copeck, Nicholas
Crouch, Jeams
Daniel, John
Davis, George
Deonton, James
Dugan, William
Duncan, Marshall
Eagan, James
Edwards, Janathan
Edwards, Joshua
Engill, John
Engill, Michal
Ford, Horatio
Gibbs, Thomas
Hammer, Isaac
Hammer, Jacob
Hammer, Jacob, Jur
Hammer, John, Jur
Hammer, Jonathan
Hammer, Joseph
Hammock, John
Harris, Joshua
Hog, Archable
Hog, Rubin
Hose, William
Humphris, George
Huston, John
Jester, Isaac
Job, Abraham
Jones, Darling
King, Henry
King, William
Lucas, George
Maples, John
Maples, William
Martian, Hugh
Martian, James
Millar, John
Millar, Peter
Mitchell, Adam jnr
Mitchell, John
More, James
More, Ruben
Morrison, James
Morrison, Joseph
Nelson, James
Nelson, William Junr
Reives, Edward
Right, Isaac
Smith, Zebulon
Stevens, Henry
Stokely, Jehue
Tipton, Joshua
Tipton, Rees
Tullis, Jonathan
Wissom, Frances
Young, James
Young, Robert
Young, William

November term 1798
the above was returned
Joseph Britten-Cha

....

A true Number of the district by Joseph Crouch - 1798

Note: Most likely Capt John Norwood's Co as Joseph Crouch took this Co in 1799. MHMcC.

Male Inhabitants

November Term 1798 the above was returned
Joseph Britten Ch

Baken, Jeremiah
Bean, Edmon
Beart, Robard
Braden, James
Chapman, Benjamin
Cowen, John
Cox, James
Crabtree, William
Crabtreet, Barnet
Crouch, Elijah
Crouch, John
Dungworth, Charles

A true Number of the district by Joseph Crouch (cont'd)

Ellis, James
Ellis, William
Fawbush, David
Fawbush, Hugh
Garner, Brice
Gates, Jacob
Gates, John
Gates, Richard
Genkins, George
Gillis, John
Gray, Absolom
Grysham, Fuller
Hagan, Arther
Haill, Abednigo
Hall, James
Hall, Samuel
Hall, William
Hammor, Baltis
Harmon, Mikel
Hoass, Jacob
Hoass, Peter
Hodges, John
Hodges, Roland
Hunt, Samuel
Hunt, Thomas
Low, Andrew
Lyon, John
McCloud, James
McCloud, Robart
McCloud, William
Mcdannel, James
Meins, David
Melven, John
Melven, Joseph
Melven, Joseph
Milburn, Samuel
Norward, John
Paten, Charles
Pritchet, Charles
Starnes, Peter
Weathers, John
Wilborn, John
Wright, Isaac
York, William

....

Capt. Robersons Company

Undated - but conforms to List of Free Taxable Males for 1798

	WP	BP	Land	StH.	Squirrels
Armstrong, John	1				
Bailey, George	1				
Barret, James	1				
Ballenger, James	1				
Booth, Joseph	1		120		25
Borouff, Vallentine	1				
Boyd, Henry	1				
Brown, Benjamin	1				14
Brown, Jacob	1	2	300		
Brown, John	1		200		
Brown, Ruth		3	326		75
Brown, Thomas	1		326		
Briant, Ambrose	1				25
Burget, George			250		
Casner, Jacob			250		
Cohe(e), John	1				
Colyar, Wm	1	3	310		100
Frinch, Peter			200		
Embree, Isaac	1		70		
Embree, Jacob			135		25
Gyer, Henry	1				
Gyer, Jacob			1000		
Hammond, Christopher			100		
Hampton, John	1				
Hampton, Mary			200		
Henly, James	1	1	100		

Capt. Robersons Company (cont'd)

	WP	BP	Land	StH.	Squirrels
Henly, John	1	1	200		
Hyfman, David	1		236		
Ingle, Wm			80		
Jones, Richard	1		112		25
Layman, David			200		
Leach, William			100		
Lilburn, Andrew	1		101½		
May, Cassimore	1		56		
Nail, Henry	1		85		
Neal, George	1		286		
Neal, Wm			96½		
Regan, Benjamin	1				
North, George	1		100		
Rogers, Joseph	1		50		
Roggers, John	1		116		
Robertson, Charles, Junr	1		237		
Sevier, James	1	2	950		
Sevier, John, Junr.	1	2	640		75
Shannon, Elijah	1		178		
Shannon, Joseph	1				
Shannon, John	1		150		
Sliger, Henry	1		114½		
Spring, Nicholas	1				
Sherril, Samuel	1	7	250		100
Stout, Charles	1		199		13
Tenplin, William	1				
Tucker, Abraham			100		
Wear, John			100		
Witt, Jesse	1				
Witt, Rutherford	1				

....

A List of the Free Poles in Capt. Robersons District

Armstrong, John	1	Hammond, Christopher	21
Ballanger, James	2	Hamton, John	22
Barret, James	3	Hanly, James	23
Baylis, George	4	Hanly, John	24
Baylis, Rheuben	5	Ingle, Adam	25
Booth, David	6	-------, Jonathan	26
Booth, Joseph	7	Jones, Richard	27
Boruff, Valentine	8	May, Cassimore	28
Boyd, Henry	9	Neal, George	29
Briant, Ambus	10	Neal, Henry	30
Brown, Ben.	11	Neal, William	31
Brown, Jacob	12	Ragan, Benja	32
Brown, John	13	Ragan, Daniel	33
Brown, Thomas	14	Roberson, CaptCharles	34
Cline, Daniel	15	Rogers, John	35
Cohee, John	16	Rogers, Joseph	36
Colyar, William	17	Sevier, Charles	37
Embree, Isaac	18	Shannon, Elijah	38
Embree, Jacob	19	Shannon, John	39
Gyre, Henry	20	Shannon, Joseph	40

Free Poles in Capt. Robersons District (cont'd)

Sherrill, William	41	Templin, William	47
Sivier, James	42	Toppin, James	48
Sivier, John juner	43	Tuckker, Abraham	49
Sliger, Henry	44	Witt, Jesse	50
Spring, Nicholus	45	Witt, Rutherford	51
Stoutt, Peter	46		

I do cirtify that the with list is a true account of the Taxable Inhabitants of Capt. Robersons Company taken this firs day of September 1798

Joseph Brown

November term 1798
The within was returned
Joseph Britten Cha.

....

Captain Shipley's Company - 1798

Names	Wh Polls	Bl	Land	Studs	Scalps
Archer, Benjamin	1		100		
Bacon, Charles	1		180		25
Bacon, James	1		176		
Bacon, Jonathan	1		200		25
B - llet, William	1		199		25
Barron, Joseph	1		200		25
Barron, Thomas	1		125		25
Barron, Walter	1		230		25
Barron, William	1		100		25
Berch, Richard	1		136		25
Billingsley, Samuel	1	2	200		
Britain, Joseph	1		222		25
Britain, William, his estate			100		
Brown, James	1		200		25
Capp, Thomas	1		122		25
Carr, John	1		100		25
Chamberlain, James	1	1	160		
Chinewth, Nicholas	1		49		25
Cocks, Elijah	1				
Conner, Lewis			150		
Dunham, Charles	1		125		25
Ellis, John	1		100		20
Ellis, Tilmon	1				25
Ellison, Charles	1		397		25
Epperson, Anthony		1	400		25
Epperson, Peter	1	2	250		75
Epperson, Samuel	1		250		25
Finley, Christian	1		65		25
Ford, James	1				
Ford, John	1	1	220		50
Ford, Loid		2	100		18
Ford, Loid Juner		1	120		25
Ford, Mordecai			200		
Ford, Thomas	1	1	100		
Ford, William	1		100		25
Gaught, Dott	1				

Captain Shipley's Company (cont'd)

Names	Wh Polls	Bl	Land	Studs	Scalps
Gifford, John	1		100		
Glakock, Archable	1	2	500		75
Gott, Anthony			594		
Gott, John	1		130		7
Gray, Robert	1	2	550	1	75
Grimsley, Loftin	1				
Grimsley, William	1				25
Hail, Abednego	1		495		
Hail, Abednego Sr.	1	1	200		
Hail, Amon	1				
Hail, George		1	200		25
Hail, George Junir	1	2	200		75
Hail, Henry son of John	1		100		15
Hail, John			84		
Hail, Joseph	1		100		25
Hail, Joseph Elder		3	836		
Hail, Meashack	1		650		
Hail, Mesheck son of Shadrack	1		100		25
Hail, Joshua	1		88		25
Hail, Nathan	1		200		
Hail, Nicholas Senior		1	272		23
Hail, Sharack	1		170		25
Hail, Samuel	1	1	100		
Hail, William	1		200		25
Harril, Jonathan	1		156		25
Haws, John	1				25
Hoas, John Senr			930		
Holland, Benjamin	1	5	550		150
Horten, Daniel	1				
Hunt, Jesse	1		422		~~25~~
Jackson, George	1		88		25
Jackson, William	1		160		50
Kincheloe, Enoch	1	2	700		75
Kincheloe, George	1	2	363		75
Kincheloe, John		6	140		150
Kincheloe, Lijah	1		150		25
Lain, Samuel	1		124		25
Lain, Tidance	1	1	244		
McCubbin, Zachariah		1	200		25
Maiden, Andrew	1				
Martin, James	1		125		25
Meadlock, More Jr.	1	1	187		50
More, Peter	1		112		25
More, Samuel	2		180		
Murray, Christopher	1				25
Murray, Morgan			205		
Murray, Shadrack	1		150		25
Murray, Thomas			145		
Murray, Thomas Jr.	1		145		25
Noland, James	1	1	150		50
Nolang, George	1	9	900	1	125
Odineal, Bartholom			190		
Pain, John	1				

Captain Shipley's Company (cont'd)

Names	Wh Polls	Bl	Land	Studs	Scalps
Pitcock, John	1		100		
Pratt, John	1		100		
Rustin, Jesse	1		50		25
Sanders, Frederick			50		
Shipley, James	1		245		
Shipley, Nathan	1		170		25
Shipley, Peter	1		150		
Shipley, Thomas	1		200		
Smith, Anderson			300		
Smith, Edward	1				
Tiffin, Henry	1	1	450		50
Turner, William	1				
Vasickle, Vardenan			50		
Westen, Fulgham	1	1	95		
Whelock, John Sr.	2	3	750		125
White, Isaac	1	2	420		75
Wiley, Thomas	1		75		25

....

List of free Taxable Inhabitants of Capt. Shipleys Dist.

1 Allin, (first name not known)
2 Allison, Charles
3 Alsop, Thomas
4 Archer, Benjamin
5 Baken, Charles
6 Baken, James
7 Baken, Jonathan
8 Barron, Joseph
9 Barron, Thomas
10 Barron, Walker
11 Barron, William
12 Billingsley, James
13 Billingsley, John
14 Billingsley, Samuel
15 Britten, Joseph
16 Brown, James
17 Bull, Jacob
18 Bull, John
19 Burch, Richard
20 Capps, Thomas
21 Carr, John Junr
22 Chamberlain, James
23 Chapman, John
24 Chinueth, Nicholus
25 Chinueth, Permenes
26 Conner, Luis
27 Cox, Elijah
28 Denham, Charles
29 Dorman, Isaac
30 Duglass,(first name not known)
31 Duncan, Jesse
32 Duncan, Joseph
33 Duncan, Rice
34 Duncan, Robert
35 Dyer, David
36 Ellis, John
37 Ensor, William
38 Eppeson, Peter
39 Eppeson, Samuel
40 Faley, Christian
41 Ford, James
42 Ford, John of Wm
43 Ford, Lloyd Junr.
44 Ford, Mordecai
45 Ford, Thomas
46 Ford, William
47 Giffort, John
48 Glascock, Archabald
49 Gott, Lott
50 Gott, John
51 Gray, Robert
52 Grille, Richard
53 Grimsley, Loften
54 Grimsley, William
55 Haile, Abednego the younger
56 Haile, Amon
57 Haile, George Junr
58 Haile, Henry
59 Haile, John
60 Haile, Joshua
61 Haile, Nathan
62 Haile, Mashack the older
63 Haile, Meshack the younger
64 Haile, Samuel

Free Taxable Inhabitants of Capt. Shipleys Dist. (cont'd)

65 Haile, Shadrack
66 Haile, William the older
67 Haile, William the younger
68 Hammer, Richard
69 Hanol, Jonathan
70 Hays, John
71 Holland, Benjamin
72 Horton, Daniel
73 Hunt, Jesse
74 Jackson, George
75 Jackson, Peter
76 Jackson, William
77 Kincheloe, Elijah
78 Kincheloe, Enoch
79 Kincheloe, George
80 Lane, Samuel
81 Lane, Tidance
82 Lane, Tilmon
83 McCubbin, Zachariah
84 Maden, Andrew
85 Martin, James
86 Messer, Edward
87 Moore, Peter
88 Moore, Samuel
89 Murrey, Christopher
90 Murrey, Morgan
91 Murrey, Sharack
92 Murrey, Thomas
93 Nolan, George
94 Nolan, James
95 Ozborn, Richard
96 Pain, John
97 Pitcock, John Junr
98 Pratt, John
99 Rustin, Jesse
100 Shipley, James
101 Shipley, Nathan
102 Shipley, Peter
103 Shipley, Thomas
104 Stevenson, Nicholas
105 Stevenson, William
106 Surrer, William
107 Tiffin, Henry
108 Western, Fulgan
109 Wheelock, John
110 Whiley, Thomas
111 White, Isaac

Taken November 9, 1798
Returned by me Joseph Britten

November term 1798
the above was returned
Joseph Britten Cha

....

List of the White Poles in my District Joseph Young J.P. 1798

1 Anderson, Frederick
2 Bayles, Daniel
3 Boring, Absolem
4 Boring, Chane
5 Boring, Joshua
6 Boring, Nicholes
7 Boman, Peter
8 Brooks, Giles
9 Casaday, John
10 Cashaday, Robert
11 Chrisselles, John
12 Erwene, Benjamin
13 Erwene, Robert
14 Fine, John
15 Fitzgerald, George
16 Frances, John
17 Grate, David
18 Gray, Willias
19 Hartsell, Abraham
20 Headrick, Charles
21 Huffman, David
22 Hunt, Abraham (?)
23 Hunter, Jacob
24 Kerby, Malicai
25 Miers, Frederick
26 Moor, James
27 Murry, Ephraim
28 North, George
29 Osimas, Henery
30 Parker, John
31 Pewet, Joel
32 Pitner, John
33 Pitner, Michael
34 Price, Mordecai
35 Rader, Adam
36 Roads, Elisha
37 Ruble, Jacob
38 Ruble, John
39 Smith, Edward
40 Swangor, John
41 Taylor, Henery
42 Wiett, Ares
43 Wiett, James
44 Young, Joseph

This I Certify to bee a just and True List of the White Poles
In my Destrict. Joseph Young J.P.

November turm 1798 the above was returned- Joseph Britten Cha.

Persons that have not given in their taxes - 1798

Allen, John	1 town lot		
Chester, Wm.	2 town lots	1 pole	
Davis, John		1 pole	
Fuston, John		1 pole	
Gilesspie, George			
Gray, Wm.			250 acres of land
Hathorn, Noah		1 pole	
Hinds, Saml.		1 pole	
Ingram, Zechariah		1 pole	
Larkkins,		1 pole	100 acres
May, Cassimore			100 acres of land
May, Saml Junr.		1 pole	
May, Saml Senr.	2 town lots		
Meenon, John		1 pole	
Moing, Edward	1 town lot	1 pole	
Nash,		1 pole	250 acres
Nelson, Joseph		1 pole	
Reed, James	2 town lots		
Rhea, John	2 town lots		
Robertson, George		1 pole	
Robertson, James		1 pole	
Swinor, Jacob		1 pole	120
Taylor, Abraham		1 pole	
Taylor, Chris			

....

County Taxes for the Court House - 1798

On each hundred acres of land	.21½
Each town lot	.25
Each stud horse kept for covering mares	.25
Each Black pole	.43
Each white pole	.21½
Each Billiard table	$10.00

For the purpose of building, and repairing the courthouse, prison and stocks in the county to be laid by the Court on the returns of the property for the year 1798-

For the poor tax:

on white poles	.01½
on black poles	.03
on each hundred acres	.03

....

1799

Justices to take in Taxable Property for Year 1799

Ordered that John Weire Esq. take in the Taxable property in Capt Moors Company

Henry Nelson Esqr take in Capt Hanahs Co.
Jacob Brown Esqr in Capt Robesons Co.
Robert Love Esqr in Capt Longmires Co.
John Balis Esqr in Capt Youngs Co.
John Hammer Esqr in Capt Morrisons Co.
Joseph Crouch Esqr in Capt Norwoods Co.
Joseph Britten Esqr in Capt Shipleys Co.
John Adams Esqr in Capt Duncans Co.
Robert Blair Esqr in Capt Biddles Co.
James Stuart Esqr in Capt Calvert Co.

for the year 1799.

....

Amount of Taxes for the year 1799

	State	Coy.	Poore
Norwoods cpy.	D 13.13	13.13	5.27
Shipley Do	59.89	54.92	20.19
Hannah Do	34.43-1/2	29.82-3/4	6.27-1/2
Robinson Ditto	22.23-1/2	22.23-1/2	8.8
Longmires Ditto	17.59-3/4	17.59-3/4	5.87-1/4
Gann Ditto	22.10	19.85	4.7 -1/2
Taylor	27.58	27.58	10.21
Morrison	27.98	27.98	10.50
Town Lotts	8.62-1/2	8.62-1/2	----
Calverts Company	38.51-1/2	36.30-1/2	12.25
Town Lotts Certified Copy	14.55-1/2	14.55-1/2	

....

Capt. William Calvert's Tax List - 1799

Mens Names	Land	Wh Poles	Bl	Town Lots	Stud Horses	Billiard
Allen, John		1				
Allen, Robert		1				
Allison, Frank	360	1	1			
Ball, Thomas		1				
Baylis, Daniel		1				
Baylis, Samuel	2218	1			1 12/	
Baylis, William	100	1				
Belfore, Andrew of North Carolina				3		
Boils, Abraham	12	1				
Boyd, Benjn.		1				
Brabston, Thomas	119					
Brandon, Joshua		1				
Brown, Abraham	180	1				
Brown, Conred		1				
Brown, Daniel		1				
Brown, David	80	1				

Capt. William Calvert's Tax List (cont'd)

Mens Names	Land	Wh Poles	Bl	Town Lots	Stud Horses	Billiard
Brown, Jacob Junr	124	1				
Brown, Jacob Senr	118	1				
Brown, John	324	1				
Brown, John		1				
Brown, Josep	190	1	1	1		
Brown, Phillip		1				
Brown, Solomon		1				
Brummitt, Danuel	50	1				
Calvert, Wm.	277	1	1			
Cash, James	328		3			
Cash, John		1				
Cash, Wm.		1		½		
Chester, John	502	1		1		
Chester, Wm P.	25	1		8		
Chism, Geo.		1				
Cursealus, John		1				
Davis, Nathaniel Junr	450	1				
Deaderick, David	689	1	2	7½ & 23 foot front of another		
Fain, John		1		1		
Fain, Wm.	640	1	1			
Finley, Daniel		1				
Gordin, James		1				
Hair, Isaac	172	1				
Hammell, Geo.		1				
Hammell, Peter		1				
Hanger, John		1				
Harrison, Benjamin	100					
Haymon, Lewis		1				
Hinds, Samuel		1				
Hodgcase, Jarred		1				
Holsinger, John		1				
House, Geo.	680	1		3½		
Ingle, Michael	100	1				
Jacobs, Dufty		1		3 & 60 foot front of 2 lots		
Kennedy, John		1				
Kiger, Conrad	146	1				
Kindle, Barbery	175					
McAlister, John		1				
McCrakin, John Junr		1				
McGiniss, John	430	1				
Macey, Edward		1				
Makin, Edward		1		1		
Miller, Wm.		1				
Million, Edward	162	1				
Mitchell, Robert	395	1	2	9		
Murr, John		1				
Nace, Jesse	100					
Noding, Wm.	300		4			
Norman, Hugh		1				
Parker, James	100	1				

1799

Capt. William Calvert's Tax List (cont'd)

Mens Names	Land	Wh Poles	Bl	Town Lots	Stud Horses	Billiard
Payne, Rubin	200					
Reid, James	100	1		2		
Rhea, John				2		
The Executors of Charles Robert Deceased			5			
Salts, Henry		1				
Seveir, Govinor	250		6			
Shannon, Wm.	160	1				
Shields, David		1				
Sidner, Martin	175	1				
Sligar, Adam		1				
Sligar, Gasper	94	1				
Sligar, John, Junr	100	1				
Sligar, John Senr	250		1			
Smith, Geo.		1		½		
Smith, John Junr		1				
Smith, John Senr	250					
Starmer, John	150	1				
Stone, Geo.		1				
Stuart, Thomas						
Sullings, Wm.		1				
Taylor, Christofor	305		3			
Taylor, Nathaniel				1		
Temple, James				3 Leesburg		
Vance, David		1				
Vaughn, John		1				
Vaughn, Sharrad		1				
Walters, Peter	84	1		1 Leesburg		
Witt, Burgiss		1				
Wood, Samuel	400			1		

A List of James Stuarts taxable property for the yeare 1799

1 tract of land on nolichukey 424
1 Do Do joining 400
1 Do Do near to above 160
1 joining the town land 150
1 Do Do joining 150
1 near Jonesboro 400
1 on the watters of big limestone 300
1 Ditto on Cherekee 225
L 2209

1 White Pole
9 Black Poles
3½ town Lotts

Signed: James Stuart

....

List of Taxables for the Year 1799

Note: This list was evidently taken by James Stuart as it is in same writing as his own list signed at end of total list. It is identical with the list of Captain William Calvert, 1799, signed James Stuart. MHMcC.

List of Taxables for the Year 1799 (cont'd)

Mans name	Land	wh Poles	Bl	Town Lots	Studs	Billiard Table
Allen, John		1				
Allen, Robert		1				
Allison, Frank	360	1	1			
Ball, Thomas		1				
Baylis, Daniel		1				
Baylis, Samuel	2218	1			1 12/	
Baylis, Wm	100	1				
(B)elfor, Andrew M of North Carolina			3			
Boils, Abraham	12	1				
Brabston, Thomas	119					
Brandon, James		1				
Brown, Abraham	180	1				
Brown, Conrad		1				
Brown, Daniel		1				
Brown, David	80	1				
Brown, Jacob Jn.	124	1				
Brown, Jacob Snr.	118					
Brown, John	324	1				
Brown, John		1				
Brown, Joseph	190	1	1	1		
Brown, Philip		1				
Brown, Solomon		1				
Brummitt, Danuel	50	1				
Calvert, Wm	277	1	1			
Cash, James	328		3			
Cash, John		1				
Cash, William		1		½		
Chester, John	502	1		1		
Chester, Wm P.	25	1	8	8		
Chism, Geo		1				
Cursealous, John		1				
Davis, Nathaniel Junr	450	1				
Deadrick, David	689	1	2	7½ & 23 foot front of another one		
Fain, John				1		
Fain, Wm	640	1	1			
Finley, Daniel		1				
Gordin, James		1				
Hair, Isaac	172	1				
Hammell, Geo.		1				
Hammell, Peter		1				
Hanger, John		1				
Harrison, Benjamin	100					
Haynon, Lewis		1				
Hinds, Samuel		1				
Hodgesse, Jurred		1				
Holsinger, John		1				
House, Geo.	680	1		3½		
Ingle, Michael	100	1				
Jacobs, Dufty		1		3 & 60 foot front of 2 lots		
Kennedy, John		1				

List of Taxables for the Year 1799 (cont'd)

Mans name	Land	wh Poles	Bl	Town Lots	Studs	Billiard Tables
Kiger, Conrad	146	1				
Kindle, Barbary	175					
McAlister, John		1				
McCraken, John Junr.		1				
McGiniss, John	430	1				
Macey, Edward		1				
Mekin, Edward		1		1		
Miller, Wm.		1				
Million, Edward	162	1				
Mitchell, Robert	395	1	2	9		
Murr, John		1				
Nace, Jesse	100					
Noding, Wm	300		4			
Nurman(?), Hugh		1				
Parker, James	100	1				
Payne, Rubin	200					
Reid, James	100	1		2		
Rhea, John				2		
Robert, Charles Dec.			5			
Salts, Henry		1				
Sevier, Govinor	250		6			
Shannon, Wm	160	1				
Shields, David		1				
Sidner, Martin	175	1				
Slegar, Adam		1				
Slegar, John Junr	100	1				
Slegar, John Snr	250		1			
Stigar(?), Gasper	94	1				
Smith, Geo		1		½		
Smith, John Junr		1				
Smith, John Snr	250					
Stone, Geo.		1				
Stormer, John	150	1				
Stuart, Thomas						
Sullings, Wm		1				
Taylor, Christopher	305		3			
Taylor, Nathaniel				1		
Temple, James				3 in Leesburg		
Vance, David		1				
Vaughn, John		1				
Vaughn, Sharred		1				
Walters, Peter	84	1		1 in Leesburg		
Witt, Burgiss		1				
Wood, Samuel	400			1		

A list of James Stuarts Taxable Property for the year 1799

1 White Poll
9 Black Polls
3½ Town Lots

1 tract of land on Nolichukey			424
1 Do	Do	joining	400
1 Do	Do	near to above	160

List of Taxables for the Year 1799 (cont'd)

1 Joining the Town land	150
1 Do Do joining	150
1 near the Jonesboro	400
1 on the waters of big limestone	300
1 Do on Cherokee	225
T	2209

James Stuart

....

A List of ye Taxable property as returned in Captain Duncan's Company

May 7th 1799

Names	Wh Polls	Bl	Land	Studs	Lots
Adair, James			100		
Adams, Alexander			116		
Adams, John	1		50		1½
Allison, Ann			145		
Allison, Charles	1		397		
Allison, Robert	1	4	702		1
Anderson, John	1	1			
Anderson, Wm			100		
Bails, Isaac			90		
Bailes, Jacob Snr			289		
Bailes, Jacob	1		100		
Bailes, Samel	1		56		
Bailes, Solomon	1				
Bell, George	1		145		
Blair, Bruce	1		107½		½
Blair, Robt	1	1	175		
Bowman, Elias			118		1
Bowman, John	1				1
Brewer, Samuel					1
Bullington, Benjamin	1				
Bullington, Wm	1		149		
Campbell, Abraham	1		112		
Campbell, John	1		13 (8)0		3 or 2
Carson, David	1		125		
Carson, Robert	1		125		
Charlton, Pointon	1		510		
Clun (?), Wm	1		100		
Cowin, John	1	2	740	1 2/D	3
Cristy, Israel			100		
Davis, Nathaniel	1	1	600		
Depue, Isaac Esq.	1		230		
Duncan, Andrew			229		
Duncan, Joseph	1		417		
Fargisson, Alexander	1				
Fargusson, Henry	1				
(F)argusson, John T	1		299		
Fargisson, Thomas		1			
Fraker, Michael			250		1½
Fuston, John	1				
Glass, Joseph	1				
Glass, Wm	1				

Captain Duncan's Company (cont'd)

Names	Wh Polls	Bl	Land	Studs	Lots
Glass, Wm Senr			384		
Gray, Wm	1	1	300		
Grayham, Wm	1				
Gwin, Thomas			100		
Hair, Henry	1		6		1
Harold, Elisha	1				
Harold, Johnathin	1		106	1 6/D	
Hart, Thomas	1				
Havenridge, John Sr.	1				
Havenridge, John	1				
(H)ees, Philip	1		100		
Hickman, Henry	1		445		
Hunt, Uriah	1	1	910		
Hunter, James	1				
Johnston, Samuel	1		90		
Jones, Nathaniel	1		90		
Lackins, Wm	1		100		
McAdams, Hugh	1				
McCord, James			141-3/4		
McCraken, John	1		150		
McLin, John	1				
McLin, Robert			200		
McNut, Anthony	1		150		
McNutt, John	1				
Mash, Henry	1		238		
Mathes, James	1				
Mathews, Wm	1				
Nelson, Nathan	1				1
Our, Thomas			70		
Patton, John					1
Patton, Robt	1				1
Purcley, Wm			242		
Rice, David					1
Richard, Luis	1		200		
Rigs, Elias	1				
Rigs, Iseah	1				
Robesson, Daniel	1		245		
Roulston, John	1		184		
Rusle, David			330		
Shaw, Francis			200		
Shaw, Samuel			200	1 4/Dol.	
Shields, Joseph	1		230		1
Simpson, James	1				
Simpson, John	1				
Slaughter, Wm	1				
Smith, Abraham	1		350		
Smith, Seath	1		150		
Smith, Wm	1		2		8
Sprouse, Jessee	1				
Stanfield, Samuel	1				1
Strain, John	1		100		1
Stuart, Alex	1		155		

Captain Duncan's Company (cont'd)

Names	Wh Polls	Bl	Land	Studs	Lots
Stuart, David	1	1	398		
Suman (?), Jacob	1		122		
Taylor, Leroy	1	2	354		
Taylor, Wm	1				1½
Thompson, David			100		1
Tucker, Joseph	1		400		1½
Tucker, Nicholas	1		70		1
Walker, Wm	1		184		
Weathers, John	1				
Webb, John	1		59		
Wester, Fulgim	2	1	335		
Woods, Wm	1		155		

....

A List of the Taxable Property in Capt. Gann's Compy
Taken in by me John Weir

	Land	Wh Poles	Bl	Stud Horses
Allison, Robert	276	1		
Baxter, Frances	65	1		
Bitner, John	100	1		
Blakburn, Archeble	300	1	2	
Broils, James	252	1		
Brown, James	140	1	1	
Brown, William	252	1		
Clark, Jesse		1		1 15
Clark, John	200	1		
Clark, William		1		
Clark, Willam	300		7	
Cleeck, Petter		1		
Click, Luis	245			
Colloms, Gorge	1	1		
Colloms, Jonathan	200	1		
Cooper, James		1		
Gann, Adam	72	1	1	
Gann, Jacob		1		
Gann, John	70	1		
Gann, Nathan	200	1		
Gann, Thomas		1		
Givens, James	100	1		
Gray, James	106	1	2	
Green, Jassey	312			
Greenway, William	112	1		
Hadler, Sibboston	200		1	
Harmon, Abram		1		
Harmon, Adam	220	1		
Harrison, William		1		
Humphyes, Moses		1		
Humphrys, Richard	300			
Hunt, Simmon	250	1		
Jikans, Willam		1		
Jonsten, James		1		

1799

A List of the Taxable Property in Capt. Gann's Compy (cont'd)

	Land	Wh Poles	Bl	Stud Horses
Kennedy, David	200	1		
Lewis, Obediah		1		
McCubbins (?), Wm		1		1
McGee, John	1	1		
McGee, Solomen		1		
McGee, Willam		1		
McKee, Alexander	550	1		
Miller, James	100	1		
Moore, Alaxander	357	1		
More, Danial	300	1		
Penter, Adam	300			
Prothero, Alaxander	100	1		
Rimel, Jacob		1		
Rimel, John	200	1		
Sheffeild, Gorge		1		
Vandegrif, Lanerd		1		
Wadle, Charls		1		
Wadle, John	336	1		
Wadle, John	200	(lying between James Brown and Clecks)		
Wadle, Seth		1		
Waldrip, James		1		
Weir, Benjamin		1		
Weir, Gorge		1		
Weir, John	514		1	
Wilson, Jassae	350	1		
Woods, Mickal	640	1	6	

(This list similar to Capt Moore's)   Taken by me John Weir

....

Tax List in Capt Andrew Hannahs Company or district - 1799

Name	Land	Wh Poles	Town Lots	Bl Poles	Studs
Bottles, Henry	125				1 stand at $2.
Bowman, Enoch		1			
Broyle, Adam	95	1			
Broyle, Cyrus	100			2	
Broyle, Daniel	113	1			
Broyle, Ebram	100	1		1	
Broyle, Nicholas	130			3	
Broyle, Samuel	145	1			
Broyle, Tobias		1			
Click, Lewis	245				
Click, Peter		1			
Crookshank, George	133				
Cunningham, Hugh	160	1			
Cunningham, Jno Junr	150	1			
Denton, Johnathan	100	1		1	
Dinwiddie, Adam (estate)	350				
Doak, Revd. Saml	180	1		2	
Embree, John	200	1	½		

Capt Andrew Hannahs Company (cont'd)

Name	Land	Wh Poles	Town Lots	Bl Poles	Studs
Embree, Thos	340	1	1		
Evans, George		1			
Gillespie, Thos	?81	1		7	1 stand at three dollars
Graham, Charles	540	1			
Graham, James		1			
Hannah, Andrew	320	2			
Harris, John C.		1			
Helm, John	62	1			
Holly, John		1			
Hoover, Matthias	320	2			
Iles, Willis	99				
Jester, Thos.		1			
Jordan, Lewis	376	1			
Kellsay, Saml, estate	240				
Long, Nicholas		1			
Lott, Gasper		1			
Lowry, Adam	176	1			
McAllister, John	970				
McCardel, Philip		1			
McCrakken, John	150	1			
McEwen, Margaret	365				
McLinn, Alexr	200	1			
McNeess, William		1			
Macey, Thos.	100	1			
Mathes, Alexr	465	1		3	
Mercer, Joseph	225	1			
Mills, Hurr		1			
Moore, Jepthah		1			
Nelson, Henry	394			2	
Nelson, John	200	1		1	
Payne, Jessee Esqr.	585	2		2	
Rush, William		1			
Scott, Thos.	200			3	1 stand at three dollars
Sheilds, Patrick	278	1			
Squibb, John	371	1			
Stephenson, Alice	467				
Sturgeon, Sympson	240	1		1	
Telford, Thos	200	1			
Thompson, Andrew		1			
Thornberry, Thomas		1			
Wilhite, Saml		1			
Willett, Francis		1			
Willett, Zadoc	300	1			
Wilson, Isaac	350	1			
Yager, Solomon	300	1		2	

....

Captain Longmires company Undated Likely 1799

- - - complete list given on following page - - -

1799

Captain Longmires company

(Undated, but could be 1799 or afterwards, as estate of Saml. Culbertson is listed, and Culbertson died 1799, or late 1798. His will was probated Feb. Session 1799. There is a Capt. Longmire Listed for 1799 in Court Minutes for Taxables in 1799.)

Persons names	Quantity land in each separate tract	Situation or place where each tract lies	Free Poles	Black Poles	Town Lots	Billiard Tables	Amt
Acton, James Junr			1				.12½
Acton, James Senr	776	Greasy Cove					.14½
Acton, Samuel			1				.12½
Arvin, Samuel	100	do	1				.25
Barns, Joseph			1				.12½
Brown, John	270	do	1				.46¼
Burrass, Elijah			1				.12½
Carroll, William			1				.12½
Clouse, Elijah			1				.12½
Clouse, George	100	do	1				.25
Clouse, John			1				.12½
Collier, Charles	102-3/4	do					.12-3/4
Culbertson, Joseph	220	do	1				.40
Culbertson, Saml dec Est.	1000	do					1.25
Deakens, James	110	do	1				.26¼
Deakens, John	50	do	1				.18-3/4
Deakens, Richard	113	do					.14¼
Dillard, Martha	200	do		9			$2.50
Doyle, Patrick	105	do					.13
Edwards, Abell	101	do					.12½
Edwards, John	50	do	1				.18-3/4
Edwards, Thomas	50	do	1				.18-3/4
Elkins, David			1				.12½
Elkins, William			1				.12½
Evans, Edmund			1				.12½
Evans, Farler			1				.12½
Evans, John	66	do	1				.20-3/4
Evans, Thomas	45	do					.05-3/4
Haun, Adam	150	do	1				.31¼
Herrald, John			1				.12½
Holt, Ephraim	50	do	1				.18-3/4
Holt, Jacob	100	do	1				.25
Holt, Peter, John Swingle in trust	130	do					.16
Howell, Thomas Junr			1				.12½
Hutchins, Charles			1				.12½
Jarvis, Alexander	47	do					6
Jarvis, William			1				.12½
Lemmon, Christopher			1				.12½
Lewis, William Junr			1				.12½
Lewis, William	100	do	1				.25
Longmire, Charles	476	do		1			.84½
Longmire, John	200	do	1				.37½

Captain Longmires company (cont'd)

Persons names	Quantity land in each separate tract	Situation or place where each tract lies	Free Poles	Black Poles	Town Lots	Billiard Tables	Amt
Longmire, Joseph			1				.12½
Love, Robert	531-3/4		1	5			2.03
McAfee, James	281	Greasy Cove					.35
Joseph Culbertson in trust							
McInturrf, Gasper	100	do	1				.25
McRunnelds, Thomas	100	do	1				.25
Nelson, Berryman			1				.12½
Paterson, William Jr			1				.12½
Paterson, William			1				.12½
Polly, James	110	do					.13-3/4
Polly, John			1				.12½
Randolph, Saml. Junr	60	do	1				.20
Reeder, William			1				.12½
Rinehart, Jno	100	do					.12½
Simmons, Joseph			1				.12½
Taylor, Nathl	300	do					.37½
Tinker, William			1				.12½
Tittle, John	180	do	1				.35
Winkles, James			1				.12½
Witt, Jesse	96	do	1				.24½
Young, John	100	do					.12½

....

Capt. Moore's Co. - Taken by John Were - 1799

Names	Wh Poles	Bl	Land	Studs	Lot
Allison, Robert	2	1	276		
Baxtor, Francis	1		66		
Beys, Edward	1				
Bitner, John	1		100		
Blackburn, Archl	1	2	400		
Brown, James	1	1	140		
Brown, Wm	1		155		
Broyles, Addam			270		
Broyles, Cyrus		2	100		
Broyles, James	1		200		
Broyles, Toby	1				
Clark, Jessee	1			1	
Clark, John	1		200		
Clark, Wm.	1	4	300		
Cleck, Lewis			255		
Cleck, Peter	1				
Collom, George	1				
Collom, Jonathan	1		200		
Dickson, John	1				
Gann, Adam	1	1	72		
Gann, Clem			150		
Gann, Isaac	1				
Gann, John	1		50	1	

Capt. Moore's Co. (cont'd)

Names	Wh Poles	Bl	Land	Studs	Lot
Gann, Nathan	1		200		
Gann, Thos	1		50		
Gibbens, James	1				
Gray, James	1		104		
Green, Joshua			300		
Greenway, Wm.	1		112		
Harbison, Saml.	1				
Harbison, Wm.	1				
Harmon, Adam	1		220		
Harmon, Jos.	1				
Harmon, Sha.	1				
Hedler, Sebastian		1	300		
Hoover, Jacob	1				
Hoover, Mathas.	1		370		
Hunt, Simon	1		250		
Humphry, Richd.			400		
Humphrys, Jehue	1				
Jenkins, Wm.	1				
Jordan, John	1				
Kennedy, David	1		125		
Kennedy, David Ser.			70		
Lemmon, Jacob	1				
Lemmon, John	1				
Lewis, James	1				
Lewis, James	1				
Lewis, John Senr.		6	275		
McCloud, John	1				
McGee, George	1				
McGee, John	1		100		
McGee, Wm.	1				
McKee, Alexr	1		450		
Millar, James	1		100		
Millar, Peter			360		
Millar, Theophilus	1				
Moore, Alexr	1				
Moore, Wm.			377		
Nelson, Southy	1		100		
Pain, Rueben			200		
Painter, Adam			300		
Panther, Ezekiel	1				
Prethero, Alex.	1		100		
Rymal, John	1		200		
Wadell, Seth	1		150		
Waddill, Charles	1				
Waddill, John	1		336		
Waddill, Saml.	1				
Waldrip, James	1				
Were, Benja.	1				
Were, George	1				
Were, John		1	504		
Willson, Isaac	1		350		
Woods, Michl			640		

February Sesso.1799 - ordered that John Were Esqr. take in the taxable property in this Company - Jas. Sevier, Clk.

Capt. Morrison's Company - Undated

Note: Most likely 1799 as it fits the County Minutes. MHMcC

Names	Wh Polls	Bl	Land	Stud
Ball, Amos	1	1	312	
Boren, Absolom			91	
Boren, James	1			
Boren, John	1			
Boren, Joshua	1			
Boren, William			176-3/4	
Carr, John		2	232	
Carrathers, Jonathan	1		240	
Cavehaver, Nickolous	1			
Collins, Joseph			100	
Crouch, James	1		107	
Daniel, John	1			
Daniel, William			260	
Denton, Joseph			185	
Denvold, Gaberel (Devault)	1		640	
Dunken, Charls	1		460	
Dungen, Jariha		4	1000	1
Dunken, Marchel	1			
Eagen, Barnbus		1	200	
Eagen, Hugh	1			
Eagen, James	1			
Edwards, Jonathan	1			
Engle, John			200	
Fain, Samuel-estate			460	
Ford, Horatio	1		100	
Gibbs, Thomas	1			
Gibson, Thomas			117-2/4	
Hammer, Isaac	1		310	
Hammer, John Jn.	1		240	
Hammer, John Sr.		1	265	
Hammer, Johnathan	1			
Hammer, Joseph	1			
Harris, Joshua	1			
Humphary, George	1			
Huston, John	1	1		
Jobb, David	1	5	280	
Jones, Darling	1		195	
Kelley, Kinchen			200	
King, Henry	1		370	
King, Thomas		1	1080	
King, William	1	1		
Luckes, George	1			
Melven, Joseph			280	
Michel, Adam	1		280	
Miller, John	1		222	
Miller, Peter	1		458	
Mitchell, John	1			
More, Ruben	1		386	
Morrison, James	1		50	
Morrison, Joseph	1		200	
Nelson, Jane		3	100	

1799

Capt. Morrison's Company (cont'd)

Names	Wh Polls	Bl	Land	Stud
Nelson, William		2	500	
Nelson, William	1			
Range, Peter	1		533	
Reeves, Edward	1			
Smith, Zebulon	1			
Starns, Peter	1		225	
Stevens, Henry	1	1	440	
Tipton, Recae Boring	1			
Tullis, Jonathan	1		399	
Tussan, William	1			
White, Ann			340	
Wood, William	1		177	
Wydom, Frances	1			
Young, John		2	252	

Taken in by me John Hammer

....

Capt. Norwood Compy

Note: This List was undated but court minutes date it 1799. MHMcC.

Names	Wh Poles	Bl	Land	Stud
Baken, Isaac		1	300	
Baken, Jerimiah	1			
Baken, John			197	
Bean, Edmon	1	1		
Beard, Robart	1		140	
Booman, John	1		190	
Carney, John	1			
Carney, Mary			45	
Carney, Thomas		1	500	
Chapman, Benjamin	1			
Crabtree, James	1			
Crabtree, John			103	
Crabtree, William	1			
Cox, James	1	2	70	
Cowen, John	1	1	117	
Crouch, Elijah	1			
Crouch, Jesse	1		200	
Crouch, John	1		320	
Crouch, Joseph	1		367	
Dungworth, Charles	1		500	
Ellis, James	1			
Ellis, William		2	325	
Ensor, Thomas			200	
Fawbush, Hugh	1			
Fraley, Christian	1			
Gates, Jacob	1			
Gates, Jacob Senr			200	
Gates, John	1		128	
Gates, Richard	1		111	
Garner, Brice	1			

Capt. Norwood Compy (cont'd)

Names	Wh Poles	Bl	Land	Stud
Genkins, George Ser			500	1
Gesham, Fullon	1		168	
Gesham, Thomas	1		189	
Gillis, John	1			
Haill, Abed	1	6	492	
Hall, James	1			1
Hall, Nathaniel	1		291	
Hall, Samuel	1		117	
Hall, William	1			
Hammor, Baltes	1		36	
Hammor, Baltes Sr	1		115	
Hammor, Richard	1		100	
Hodges, John	1		190	
Hodges, John Ser.	1	1	330	
Hoas, Jacob		1	559	1
Hoas, Peter	1		200	
Hunt, Samuel	1			
Hunt, Thomas	1		460	
King, Isaac			100	
Kite, Isaac	2		100	
Lyon, Ezekel			200	
Lyon, John				
McCloud, James	1			
McCloud, Robart	1			
McCloud, Wm.			131	
McCloud, William Ju.	1			
McCray, Daniel			350	
Matlock, Zachariah			126	
Melven, John	1	1	150	
Melven, Joseph	1		335	
Melven, Joseph Elder	1		303	
Melvin, Samuel			100	
Mienes, Isaac				
Milburn, Samuel	1			
Mille, Robart			400	
Norwood, John	1	1	300	
Owen, James	1		136	
Porter, Charles	1		69	
Poter, Charles	1		69	
Pritchett, Charles	1		320	
Pritchet, Thomas	1		220	
Smith, Abram	1			
White, Archable				
Whittacor, Mark	1			
Wiley, Thomas	1		82	
York, William	1			

Taken by Joseph Crouch

Captain Robertson's Company - 1799

- - - complete list given on following page - - -

1799

Captain Robertson's Company

Names	Wh Polls	Bl	Land	Studs
Armstrong, John	1			
Ballanger, Jacob	1			
Barret, James	1			
Bayles, George	1			
Bayles, Reubin	1		416	
Borefe, Vallentine	1			
Booth, David	1			
Booth, Joseph	1		220	
Briant, Ambus	1			
Brown, Ben.	1		200	
Brown, Jacob	1	2	526	
Brown, Jeremiah	1			
Brown, John	1		326	
Brown, Ruth		3		
Brown, Thos.	1		326	
Burget, George			200	
Casner, Jacob			310	
Colyar, William	1	3	310	
Embree, Isaac	2		70	
Embree, Jacob	1		135	
Embree, Margret	1		50	
Frinch, Peter	1		200	
Goforth, Absolum	1			
Gyre, Henry	1			
Gyre, Jacob	1			
Jacob & Henry Gyre adm. Jacob Gyre dec.			1000	
Heirs of James Halley			100	
Hammond, Christopher			110	
Hamton, John	1			
Hamton, Mary	1		200	
Henley, John	1		200	
Ingle, Adam	1			
Ingle, Wm.			80	
Jones, Richard	1		112	
Lamon, David	1		200	
May, Cassimore	1		56	
Neal, George	1		86	
Neal, Henry	1		85	
Neal, Wm	1		96½	
Pane, John	1			
Pirvis, James	1			
Ragan, Benjamin	1			
Ragan, Jeremiah			276	
Roberson, Charle	1		237	
Roberson, Charles-executor Charles Roberson dec.		3	180	
Rogers, John	1		115	
Rogers, Joseph	1		50	
Rogers, William	1			
Sevier, Charles	1			
Sevier, James	1	2	950	

Captain Robertson's Company (cont'd)

Names	Wh Polls	Bl	Land	Studs
Sevier, John Juner	1	2	640	
Shannon, Elijah	1		178	
Shannon, John	1		153	
Shannon, Joseph	1			
Sherrel, Samuel	1	6	250	
Slyger, Henry	1		114½	
Spring, Nicholus	1			
Templin, Wm	1			
Toppin, James	1			
Tucker, Abraham	1		100	
Wear, John			100	

Outside cover: Captain Robertson Company
made out
-1799-

....

Scraps - 1799

Michael Harrison, Dr. to Brice Blair, for Taxes for the year

year	wh	bl	land	T.Lots
1799	1 wh	1 bl	200 land	0 T.Lots
1800	1	3	0	2
1801	1	5	0	2

	County	State	add.	poor
1799	63-	63		22
1800	1.37½	1.37½	1.37½	21
1801	187½	1.87½	1.87½	33
	3.88	3.88	3.25	76

50 per yr for the Sheriff--------
To be sold on Saterday the 19th of October 1805.

....

1799-----

Rec'd of Cheney Boren the Taxes in full for the lands of Mordecai (Rachel) Price for the years 1799-1800 & 1801 by B Blair
8 dollars 36½ cents and 4 dollars of the above paid by Burgis Zitt the receipt to witt (torn---------------)

....

County Tax for the Year 1800

each white pole $12\frac{1}{2}$ cents

do black 25 do.

do hundred acres Land $12\frac{1}{2}$ cents

for the additional Tax for the year 1800 and also the County Tax

Billard Tables 10 dollars

1 Dollar on each stud horse as additional tax

Stud Horse County Tax 25 cents

each Town Lott 25 cents additionel

and 25 cents County Tax

....

Poor Tax Year 1800

Ordrd. by Cort that the poore Tax for the Yeare 1800 Be for each white poole 3 cents on each Black 6 cents and each hundred acres Land 6 cents

....

Amount of Tax fees from October 99 to Octbr 1800

Taxes recd - on deeds Law proceedings and Tavern License from the 1st of October 99 untill the first of Octbr 1800

To the Amount recd on deeds	$16.19
Tavern License	15
Taxes on Law proceeding	28.74
	$59.93

....

Note: The Lists of Taxables for the various companies for the year 1800 were not found. All of the Captains for 1800 were appointed for 1801, and these Lists were found and follow.

Amount of Taxes for the Year 1800

		S Taxes	County Tax		Poor Tax
		D C	D C	D C	D C
Capt. Calverts	Compy	39 93 r	40 18	40 93	14 45½
Wm Taylors	Do.	33 64½	34 39	36 64½	10 12½
J. Morrisons	Do.	36 44	32 44	33 19½	12 28
Biddle's	Do.	18 53	18 53	18 53	6 83
Longmires	Do.	16 64½	16 64½	16 64½	5 77½
Robertsons	Do.	25 97	26 36	26 72½	10 56½
Shipleys	Do.	26 96¼	26 96¼	26 96¼	9 71½
Squibbs	Do.	44 12	35 45	35 45	11 85
Norwoods	Do.	28 65	28 90	29 65	10 28
H Taylors	Do.	24 81	24 81	24 81	9 48½
Town Lotts		13 183/4	13 183/4	13 183/4	———
Glasscockes Cpy		29 13½	29 33½	29 33½	11 67
Gann Comp		25 79	25 79	25 79	8 52½

1801

Justices to Take in the Taxable Property for the Year 1801

Ordered by the Court that John Hammer be appointed to take in the Taxable property in Morrisons Company

Robt Love for Longmires Co.

Joseph Crouch for Norwoods Co.

John Strain for Wm. Taylors Co.

Isaac White for Glascocks Co.

John Baylis for Henry Taylors Co.

Thos. Brown for Robertsons Co.

James Gordon for Aikens Co.

Jacob Brown for Calverts Co.

James Stewart for Ganns Co.

John Adams for Squibbs Co.

John Alexander for Biddles Co.

Nathan Shipley for Shipleys Co.

Note: Every one of the above tax lists is extant with the exception of Shipley's, and Captain Lane's was found for that district. MHMcC.

February term 1801 ordered that the County Tax for the year 1801 be

on each free pole - - - - - - - - - - - - - - - - - - - $12\frac{1}{2}$ cents

on each Slave - 25

on each 100 acres of Land - - - - - - - - - - - - - - $12\frac{1}{2}$

on each town Lot - - - - 25 cents or $12\frac{1}{2}$ if the law will admit

on each Stud horse - - - as high as the law will admit

on each Billiard table - - - - - - - - - - - - - - - 10 dollars

and the additional tax for the Court house Prison, stokes be for said year

on each free pole - - - - - - - - - - - - - - - - - - $12\frac{1}{2}$ cents

on each Slave - 25

on each 100 acres of Land - - - - - - - - - - - - - $12\frac{1}{2}$

on each town lot - - - - - - - - - - - - - - - - - - 25

on each Stud horse - - - - - - - - - - - - - - - - - 1 dollar

on each Billiard Table - - - - - - - - - - - - - - - 10 dollars

....

May term 1801 Poor Tax

Ordered that the poor tax for the year 1801 be on each pole & 100 acres of land be as much as the Law will admit.

And that James Deakins be allowed forty dollars for the maintainance of Elizabeth Dillin for the present year as a poor woman.

....

1801

Capt. Mathew Aikens Company - 1801

Names		Town Lots	Poles White	Poles Black
Aiken, Mathew		½	1	
Allen, John			1	
Allen, Robert		1		
Bean, Russell			1	1
Brandon, Joshua			1	
Brown, John	324 acres land		1	1
Brown, Joseph		1	1	1
Brown, J?uphor			1	
Chester, John		½		
Chester, William P.		6½	1	
Cox, Elijah			1	
Deaderick, David		6 3/4	1	7
Ervin, John	150 acres	1/3	1	
Fain, John		1	1	
Freind, Jacob	1 Stud horse $2.50 season	1	1	
Gordon, Jas.			1	
Harrison, Michl		1½	1	3
Jacobs, Dufty		3½	2	
Jacobs, John			1	
Kennedy, John		3		
McAlister, John		1	1	1
Mackin, Edward		1	1	
Miller, Henry			1	
Rawlings, Moses			1	
Rhea, John		1		
Roberson, Chas. decd. execut.		5		
Roberson, Susana				2
Stone, George			1	
Stuart, James		4		
Stuart, Thomas			1	
Templin, Samuel			1	
Tipton, John Sr.		1		
Troy, John		3	1	
Vance, David		1	1	
Whitlock, John		½	1	

....

Captain Biddle's Company, Year 1801

Names	Poles White	Poles Black	Studs	Land	town lots
Alexander, Francis	1			112	
Alexander, John Jr.	1				
Alexander, John Sr.				138	
Alexander, Jonathan	1			100	
Allen, Robert	1			166	
Barecroft, Jonathan	1				2
Biddle, Thomas				500	
Blackley, Daniel	1			130	
Blackley, John	1			200	
Blackley, Robert				130	

Captain Biddle's Company (cont'd)

Names	Poles White	Poles Black	Studs	Land	town lots
Blackley, William				267	
Blair, Brice	1			270	1
Blair, Big John B.				300	
Blair, Richard	1			70	
Blair, Robert	1	1		175	
Blair, William	1			270	
Brown, David				252	
Brown, John	1				
Brown, William	1			72	
Campble, Hugh	1			210	
Carmicle, Isbell		3		202	
Carson, Andrew	1			80	
Carson, Moses				220	
Conk ? om, Enoch	1			100	
Cosen, Rev. John		1		496	4
Crafford, John	1				
Cumins, Hugh Jr.	1				
Cumins, Hugh Sr.				100	
Davis, George	1			150	
Davis, Samuel	1			100	
Dilson, David	1	1		261	
Eachries ?, Robert	1	1			
Forguson, Cumberland	1				
Gilworth, John	1			100	
Green, Thomas	1				
Hart, Thomas	1				
Iles, William				99	
Kelsay, John	1				
Kelsay, William		1		300	
McLin, Alexd.	1			240	
McLin, William	1				
McRay, John Thomas	1				
McWhorter, James				150	
Martin, Joseph				140	
Mills, Hur	1				
Mitchell, David	1				
Patterson, James	1			143	
Patton, John	1			155	
Philips, Dyer	1			100	
Rhea, John Esq.				100	
Rodgers, Andrew	1				
Rodgers, James	1			100	
Rodgers, Thomas	1			135	
Rodgers, Estate of Thomas, Deceased				380	
Sands, Benjamin				250	
Sands, Michall	1				
Seehorn, James	1			142	
Shanks, William	1			150	
Shields, David	1			250	
Shields, Henry	1			206	
Shields, Joseph	1			350	

1801

Captain Biddle's Company (cont'd)

Names	Poles White	Poles Black	Studs	Land	town lots
Smith, Richard	1			125	
Smitser, Peter	1				
Steel, William	1				
Stuart, John	1				
Tedlock, Lewis	1	1		220	
Thompson, Andrew				514	
Twedy, James	1			100	

This return made by me, John Alexander Esq.

....

Captain Calvert's Co. - 1801

Names	Poles Wh.	Poles Bl.	Studs	Land
Allison, Francis	1	1		330
Ball, Thomas	1			
Bayles, Samuel		1		2070
Bayles, William	1			150
Boiles, Abraham	1			
Boyd, Ben	1			5
Brown, Abraham	1			180
Brown, Daniel	1			130
Brown, David	1			80
Brown, George	1			
Brown, Jacob Sr.				105
Brown, Jacob Jr.				124
Brown, John	1			
Brown, Koonrad (?)	1			
Brown, Phillup	1			
Broyles, Daniel	1			150
Brummet, Samuel	1			50
Calvert, William (Capt.)	1	2		352
Cash, James		3		328
Cash, John	1			
Cloyde, William	1			210
Crezelous, John	1			
Cash, William	1			
Elimon, John	1			
Fain, William	1	1		640
Finch, Calvin	1			150
Grean, Arnel	1			200
Hair, Issac	1			172
Haner, Lewis	1			106
Harris, Benjamin				100
Ingle, Adam	1			
Ingli, Michel	1			100
Keicher, John	1			
Keicher, Koonrod				146
Kindle, Barbara				175
McCray, Daniel		1		542
Mageness, John Jr.	1			

Captain Calvert's Co. (cont'd)

Names	Poles Wh.	Poles Bl.	Studs	Land	
Maganess, John Sr.	1			430	
Miller, William	1				
Million, Edward	1			160	
Million, John	1				
Mitchel, Robert	1	2		395	9 town Lots
Moor, Robert				470	1 town lot
Morr, John	1			50	
Neal, Jesse	1			100	
Parker, James	1			100	
Saults, Henry	1			2	
Sidener, Martain	1			275	
Sliger, Adam	1			80½	
Sliger, John Jr.	1			215	
Sliger, John Sr.	1			100	
Smith, John Jr.	1			100	
Starmer, John	1		1	160	$2.00
Starnes, Jacob	1				
Taylor, Christopher		4		400	
Voughn, John	1				
Walter, Peter	1			115	1 town lot
Wood, Abraham executer				400	1 town lot
Wood, Thomas	1				

....

A list of the taxable property of Capt. Nathan Gann's Co. for 1801

Names	White Poles	Black Poles	Land
Allison, (Mr.) a forriner	———		100
Allbright, John	1		
Baster, Francis			65
Bays, Edward	1		
Bays, John	1		
Bitner, John	1		100
Blackburn, Archibald		2	325
Broyles, Aron South Carolina land joining Mr. McKee			100
Brown, James	1	1	150
Brown, William	1		160
Broyls, Cyrus		2	100
Broyls, Daniel	1		100
Broyls, Obediah	1		
Clark, John	1	2	200
Clark, William Jr.	1	3	300
Cleck, George	1		
Cleck, Lewis			245
Cleck, Peter	1		60
Collam, Jonathan	1		200
Cooper, James	1		
Cooper, Robert	1		2
Cullam, George	1		
Gann, Adam Jr.	1	1	75
Gann, Adam Sr.			75

1801

Capt. Nathan Gann's Co. (cont'd)

Names	White Poles	Black Poles	Land
Gann, Clem			150
Gan, Daniel	1		
Gann, Jacob	1		
Gann, Nathan	1	1	220
Gann, Thomas	1		
Gann, William	1		
Gray, John	1		
Green, Ira	1		
Green, Joshua			13
Grenaway, William	1	1	150
Harbison, William	1		
Harmon, Abraham	1		
Harmon, Adam	1		222
Hedler, Sebastin		1	130
Humphriss, Richard			400
Hunt, Simon			250
Kennady, David	1		200
Layman, Jacob	1		
Layman, John	1		
Lewis, Obidiah	1		
McCullam, David	1		
McGee, John	1		100
McGee, William	1		
McKee, Alexander	1		350
Miller, James			100
Miller, Peter			248
Miller, Theoflis	1		
Mitchell, Wm.	1		
Mock, John	1		400
Moore, Daniel	1		200
Nale, Fredrick	1		
Nelson, Suthey			100
Painter, Adam			300
Painter, Ezekiel	1		
Penney, James	1		
Plum, Fredrick	1		
Prethero, Alexander	1		
Rimall, Jacob	1		
Rimall, John	1		200
Snapp, Jacob			360
Stuart, Thomas	1		
Waddill, James	1		
Waddill, John Sr.			536
Waddle, Charles	1		
Waddle, Samuel	1		
Waddle, Seth	1		
Waggoner, Phillip	1		
Wear, Agness		1	177
Wear, Benjamin	1		168
Wear, George	1		168
Willet, Francis	1		

Capt. Nathan Gann's Co. (cont'd)

Names	White Poles	Black Poles	Land
Wilson, Isaac	1		350
Woods, William	1		
Woods, Michael		6	640

Taken by James Stuart

List of my property for the yeare 1801

1	track	Maner Plantation		424
1	"	Joining "		400
1	"	"	James Miller	160
1	"	"	Moses Carson	300
1	"	"	Town land	150
1	"	"	"	150
1	"	"	Nathaniel Davis	400
1	"	"	Chereke	250
				2234

7 black poles
4½ town lots in Jonesbore

James Stuart

....

Capt. Glasscock's Company - 1801

Names	Poles white	Poles black	Stud	Land
Archer, Benj.	1			100
Bacon, Charles	1	1		180
Bacon, James	1			176
Bacon, Jonathan	1			300
Bails, Jacob	1			100
Bails, Solamon	1			
Barren, John	1			50
Barren, William	1			100
Barron, Joseph	1			200
Bowzer, John	1			60
Brown, James				200
Cade, Hews	1			
Conkin, John	1			60
Conner, John	1			
Crawford, Samuel	1			100
Crowford, William	1			200
Daniel, Richard				200
Elleson, Charles	1			397
English, John	1			200
English, Thomas	1			100
Epperson, Peter	1	1		417
Ford, John	1	1		220
Ford, William	1			80
Fulkirson, John	1			283
Galemoor, Abraham	1			100
Gallaway, Thomas	1			116
Gibson, Billinsley	1			200
Glasscock, Archd	1	2		513

1801

Capt. Glasscock's Company (cont'd)

Names	Poles white	Poles black	Stud	Land
Grimsley, Loften	1			147
Grimsley, William	1			150
Hail, Abednego	1			300
Hail, Shadrick	1			170
Haws, John				300
Haws, John Jr.	1			100
Hedrick, John	1			
Holland, Benjamin	1	3	1	550
Horton, Daniel	1			160
Jackson, Gorge	1	1		88
Jackson, William	1	1		114
Jackson, Peter				155
Jobe, Enuch	1			
Jobe, Nathan				120
Jolley, Dudley		1		108
Jolley, Dudley Jr.	1			
Jolley, Henery				100
Tolly, John				200
Keebler, Jacob	1			250
Kincheloe, Elijah	1	2		233
Kincheloe, George	1	2		113
Kincheloe, John		3		140
Marcer, Edward	1			200
Morgan, Charles	1			137
Morgan, Curnelous	1			
Mullin, Jesse	1			160
Nolen, James				150
Odeneel, Bartholomew				126
Odeneel, William	1			
Porters, Anne				200
Porter, Henery	1			
Pratt, John	1			70
Reed, Andrew				580
Robertson, Jacob	1			125
Rustin, Jesse	1			43
Shiply, Thomas	1			200
Simpson, Nathaniel	1			
Stevenson, William	1	3	1	327
Tiffen, Henery	1	1		538
Turner, Wm.	1			
Vansickle, Vardanan				50
Wheelock, John	1	3		750
Wheelor, Isaac	1			100
White, David	1			
White, Isaac	1	2		400
Whitlock, Alex	1			269

Isaac White, J.P.

Enoch Kincheloe	1	4		870
George Conch				100
Enthony Eperson		1		400

....

Capt. Lane's Company - 1801

Names	Poles white	Poles black	Stud	Land
Billingsley, James	1			165
Billingsley, Samuel	1	2		200
Billingsley, William	1			
Brannon, William	1			70
Britten, Joseph	1			222
Britten, William Estate				100
Bull, Jacob				255
Bull, John	1			
Burch, Richard	1			136
Carr, John	1			100
Chamberlain, James	1	1		160
Chapman, Benjamin	1			58
Chapman, John				100
Chinouth, Nicholas	1			149½
Crouch, Elijah	1			90
Duncan, Jessee	1			300
Duncan, Joseph	1			
Duncan, Rice	1			
Duncan, Robert	1			
Ellis, John	1			200
Epperson, Anthony		1		400
Epperson, Jesse	1			
Epperson, Samuel	1			320
Ford, James	1			
Ford, John	1			
Ford, Loyd		1		200
Ford, Loyd Jr.	1	1		125
Ford, Mordica			15/	150
Ford, Thomas	1	1		100
Fraker, John	1			445
Gifford, John	1			100
Gott, Anthony				314
Gott, Jesse	1			
Gott, John	1			130
Gott, Lott	1			
Gray, Robert	1	1		516
Grisham, Fuller	1	2		200
Grisham, John	1			164
Grisham, Thomas		1		132
Haile, George				200
Haile, George	1			84
Haile, George Jr.	1	2		200
Haile, Joseph Jr.	1			100
Haile, Joseph (Elder)		4	15/	700
Haile, Joshua	1			
Haile, Nathan	1			200
Haile, Nicholas		1		200
Haile, Richard				300
Haile, Samuel	1	2		170
Haile, Thomas	1			
Haile, William	1			200
Hennard, Robert	1			

Capt. Lane's Company (cont'd)

Names	Poles white	Poles black	Stud	Land
Hunt, Jesse	1			422
Lane, Adron	1			
Lane, Samuel	1	1		137
Lane, Tidence	1	1		250
McCubbin, John	1			
McCubbin, Zachariah		1		200
Murray, Morgan				250
Murray, Shaderick	1			150
Murray, Thomas				145
Murray, Thoas Jr.	1			145
Nolan, George	1	4		560
Rigs, Elias	1			
Rigs, Isaiah	1			
Sanders, Frederick				50
Shipley, James	1			245
Shipley, Nathan	1			250
Shipley, Peter	1			150

Note: In the list of justices ordered by the court for the year 1801, Capt. Lane's Company is listed as Nathan Shipley's Company. MHMcC.

....

Captain Longmire's Company for 1801

Names	Poles white	Poles black	Stud horses	Quantity of Land
Acton, James Sr.				116
Acton, James Jr.	1			
Arvin, Samuel	1			100
Barns, Joseph	1			450
Brown, John	1			270
Burass, Elijah	1			
Carroll, William	1			
Clouse, Elijah	1			
Clouse, George Jr.	1			
Clouse, George Sr.				100
Clouse, John	1			
Cole, Israel	1			61
Colyer, Charles				102 3/4
Culbertson, Joseph	1			220
Deakins, James	1			210
Deakins, John	1			50
Deakins, Richard				113
Dillard, Martha		9		200
Doyle, Patrick				44
Edwards, Able	1			101
Edwards, John	1			50
Edwards, Thomas	1			50
Elkins, William	1			
Evans, Farlar	1			
Evans, Thomas				45
Gibson, Thomas				68

Captain Longmire's Company (cont'd)

Names	Poles white	Poles black	Stud horses	Quantity of Land
Harreld, John	1			
Haun, Adam	1			150
Holt, Ephraim	1			50
Holt, Jacob	1			100
Holt, Peter				130
			John Swingle in trust	
Howell, Thomas Jr.	1			
Hutchins, Charles	1			
Jarvis, Alexander				47
Keener, John	1		1 at $2.00	
Layman, Christopher	1			
Lewis, William	1			
Longmire, John	1	1		200
Longmire, John, Executor for Charles Longmire Estate	1			301
Longmire, Joseph	1			175
Love, Robert, Executor of Saml Culbertson's Estate				496
Love, Robert	1	5		631 3/4
McAfee, James				281
			Joseph Culbertson in trust	
McInturff, Gasper				100
McRunnelds, Thomas	1			111 3/4
Nelson, Berryman	1			
Nelson, William				100
Patterson, William	1			
Polly, John	1			
Odle, Abraham	1			110
Odle, Reuben	1			
Randolph, Junior (?)	1			
Reeder, William	1			
Rinehart, John	1			100
Taylor, Nathaniel of Carter				200
Tinker, William	1			
Tittle, John	1			180
Witt, Jesse	1			96

Taken by Robert Love

....

Capt. Morrison's Company - 1801

Names	Poles white	Poles black	studs	Land
Ball, Amos	1			420
Boring, Absolam				91
Boring, Jacob	1			
Boring, William				176
Carr, John		3		232
Cevhover, Necolas	1			
Cittsmiller, Marten	1			
Cocks, William	1			400
Collens, Joseph				100

1801

Capt. Morrison's Company (cont'd)

Names	Poles white	black	studs	Land
Corathers, Jonthen	1			240
Danils, Anne				260
Denton, James	1			
Denhem, Phillip	1			
Denton, Joseph				185
Denton, Samuel				402
Dewold, Gabril	1			
Dewold, Henry				640
Duncan, Charls	1			444
Duncan, Joel	1			
Dunken, Marshel	1			
Dungins, Jeremiah		4		1000
Duzann, William	1			50
Eagan, Barnebes		1		200
Engle, John	1			200
Fains, Samuel a State				440
Ford, Horatio	1			100
Gibbs, Thomas	1			
Hammer, Isaac	1			250
Hammer, Jacob	1			100
Hammer, John Jr.	1			240
Hammer, John Sr.		2		265
Hammer, Jonathan	1			
Hammer, Joseph	1			
Hoose, Jacob Jr.	1			
Humphris, Moses	1			100
Huston, John	1	1		
Jobb, David	1	2		280
Jones, Darling	1			195
Killey, Kinchen				200
King, Hinry	1			370
King, James	1			50
King, Thomas		1		600
King, William	1	2		480
Little, John	1			
Little, Jones				320
Malvin, Joseph				200
Masengill, Henry Sr.		1		
Massingel, Henry				700
McCloud, William	1			
Miller, John	1			340
Miller, Peter				250
Mitchel, Adam				580
Mitchel, John	1			300
Morrison, James	1			50
Morrison, Joseph	1			200
Nelson, George	1			
Nelson, James	1			240
Nelson, William Cr.		2		500
Nelson, William	1			
Rader, Henry	1			
Range, Peter				553

Capt. Morrison's Company (cont'd)

Names	Poles white	Poles black	studs	Land
Reeves, Edward	1			
Smith, Zebulen	1			
Starns, Peter	1			177
Stefeson, Margaret		1		440
Stover, Christian	1			
Swoner, John	1			
Tipton, Joshua	1			
Tipton, Reece	1			
Ward, William				250
White, Ann				300
Woods, William				177
Young, John Jr.	1			
Young, John Cr.		2		252
Young, Robert		1		640

....

Capt. Norwood's Comp. - 1801

Names	Poles white	Poles black	studs	Land	
Baken, Isaac		1		300	
Baken, Jenny	1				
Baken, John				197	
Bean, Edmon	1	1		150	
Beard, Robert	1			140	
Birley, Mickal	1				
Bowman, John	1			270	
Buttron, William	1				
Car, Thomas	1				
Cowen, John	1	1		117	
Cox, James		2		70	
Crabtree, James	1				
Crabtree, John				103	
Crouch, Jesse	1			200	
Crouch, John	1			320	
Denham, David	1			95	
Dungworth, Charles	1			500	
Ellis, James	1		1	572	$3.00
Ellis, Tilman	1				
Ellis, William	1	3		325	
Garner, Brice	1				
Gates, Jacob Jr.	1				
Gates, Jacob Sr.				200	
Gates, John	1			128	
Gates, Richard	1			111	
Ha, Arther	1			140	
Haile, Abednego	1	6		492	
Hall, James	1				
Hall, Nath				150	
Hall, William	1			140	
Hammar, Boltis				119	
Hammar, Richard	1			100	

Capt. Norwood's Comp. (cont'd)

Names	Poles white	black	studs	Land	
Hendry, William	1	2	1	140	$2.00
Henry, Rachel				45	
Hoass, Jacob		1		937	
Hoass, Peter	1			220	
Hodges, John	2			190	
Hodges, Roland	1				
Humphres, Juhue				100	
Hunt, Saml	1				
Hunt, Thomas	1			460	
Jenkins, George	1				
Jenkins, George Sr.	1	1		500	
Low, Andrew	1			160	
Lowe, Andrew	1			160	
Lyon, Ezekel				200	
Lyon, John		1		173	
McCray, Georg	1				
McDonnal, John	1				
McDonnal, John	1				
McDonnel, James	1				
Mains, Isaac				200	
Melone, Williamson	1				
Melven, Joseph	1			335	
Melven, Joseph Elder	1			203	
Melven, Saml.				100	
Mickel, Robart				400	
Milborn, Samuel	1				
Millon, Jacob	1				
Norwood, John	1			300	
Owen, James				136	
Pitcock, John	1			93	
Porter, Charles	1			64	
Pritchet, Charles	1			320	
Pritchet, Thomas	1			220	
Right, James	1				
Starns, William	1				
Wotson, John	1				
York, William	1			131	

....

Capt. Roberson's Company - 1801

Names	Poles white	black	Studs	Land	
Ballanger, Johnnathan	1				
Bayles, George	1				
Bayles, Reubin	2			431	
Boothe, Joseph				250	
Briant, Ambrus	1				
Brown, Benjamin	1			200	
Brown, Jacob	1	3	1	200	$2.50
Brown, John G.	1			276	
Brown, Ruth		3		326	

Capt. Roberson's Company (cont'd)

Names	Poles white	Poles black	Studs	Land
Brown, Solomon	1			150
Brown, Thomas	1			326
Burker, George				130
Burket, Andrew	1			
Carsner, Jacob				330
Chester, William P.	1			150
Colyar, William		3		310
Edwards, Eli	1			
Elkin, David	1			
Embree, Isaac	1			
Embree, Jacob	1			185
Feinch, Peter				200
Fickey (Fukey), John	1			
Fulks, David	1			
Goforth, Absolum	1			
Gibbins, James	1			
Gyre, Christain	1			
Gyer, Henry	1			
Gyre, Jacob	1			
Gyre, Jacob & Henry, Adm. of Jacob Gyre Deceast				1000
Hammond, Christopher				100
Hamton, John	1			
Hamton, Mary				200
Hanley, John	1			200
Hare, Jacob	1			229
Ingle, William				80
Ireland, Thomas	1			
Jinkins, Henry	1			100
Jones, Richard				130
Keicher, Joseph	1			
Kirlin, Joseph	1			
Lamon, David				200
Lineburger, Nicholus	1			50
May, Cassimore	1			56
Moore, Peter	1			
Neal, George	1			186½
Neal, Henry	1			97
Neal, William Jr.	1			
Neal, William Sr.				85
Payn, John	1			
Pearmon, James	1			
Purvis, James	1			
Roberson, Charles	1	1		327
Roberson, George	1			
Rogers, Joseph	1			50
Sevier, James	1	4		950
Sevier, John Jr.	1	6		3740
Shannon, Elijah	1			178
Shannon, John	1			
Shannon, Joseph	1			
Sheffield, George	1			
Shirrel, George				100

1801

Capt. Roberson's Company (cont'd)

Names	Poles white	Poles black	Studs	Land
Sivier, John Governor		10		300
Sliger, Casper	1			63
Slyger, Henry	1			114½
Templin, William	1			
Tucker, Abraham	1			100
Waldrip, James	1			
Wear, John D				100
Winkles, James	1			

....

Capt. Squibbs Company - 1801

Names	Poles white	Poles black	Studs	Land	Lotts
Adams, John	1			100	
Broyles, Abraham	1			100	
Broyles, James	1		1	250	
Broyles, Nicholas		3		130	
Broyles, Samuel	1		(D C	240	
Crookshanks, George				133	
Cunningham, Hugh	1			160	
Cunningham, John	1			160	
Cunningham, Samuel	1	3			
Estate of Adam Dunwiday				350	
Edwards, Ely	1				
Embree, John	1			200½	
Embree, Thomas	2			113	1
Gillespie, George	2	6		1590	
Gilespie, James	1	3		400	
Gilespie, Thomas	1	6		811	
Greham, Chas.	1			540	
Hannah, Andrew	2			320	
Holley, John	1				
Jurdon, Lewis	1			375	
Kelsay, Estate of Samuel				240	
Law, James	1				
Lowry, Adam	1			176	1
McAllister, John	1			945	
McCrackin, John Jr.	1				
McCrackin, John Sr.				150	
McEwen, Margaret				365	
McLin, Alexr.	1			240	
Macy, Clement	1				
Macy, Thomas	1			100	
Mathews, Alexander	1				
Mathews, Alexander	1	3		465	
Messor, Joseph Nelson	1			225	
Milegon, John	1			235	
Nelson, Henry		4		394	
Nelson, John	1	2		200	
Patton, William	1				
Payne, Jessee Sr.	1	2		595	

Capt. Squibbs Company (cont'd)

Names	Poles white	Poles black	Studs	Land	Lotts
Rush, William	1		1		
Scou, Thomas		3	1	300	
Squibb, John	1			314	
Stephenson, Ellis				367	
Sturgeon, Robert	1				
Sturgeon, Simpson					
Telfour, Thomas	1			200	
Willet, Zedock	1			300	
Willhight, Ruben	1			90	
Wilson, Issac	1			350	
Yeager, Solomon	1	2		300	

....

Capt. Henry Taylor's Company - 1801

Names	Poles white	Poles black	Std	Land
Andess, Frederick	1			243
Bayles, Danl.	1			170
Bayles, Danl. Sr.				100
Bayles, John				215
Bell, John				304
Bewley, Anthony	1			200
Blithe, Saml				50
Booth, David	1			
Borin, Absolem	1			
Borin, Absolem Sr.	1			150
Borin, Chaney	1			300
Borin, Ezekiel				70
Borin, Joshua	1			
Bowman, Peter	1			
Boyd, Henry	1			
Brooks, Jane				300
Brumet, Miciah	1			
Burress, Jno.	1			100
Casidy, Jas.	1			
Casidy, Robert	1			200
Cooper, Joseph				69
Crecelius, John	1			100
Delaney, Jas.	1			200
Disney, Thos.	1			
Drans, Benjn.	1			75
Fine, John	1			350
Fitzgarrold, George	1			22
France, John	1			104
Grag, John	1			
Harris, John C.	1			
Hartsel, Abraham	1			
Hartsel, Hannah				60
Harvey, Jae	1			50
Headrick, Charls				140
Homell, Peter	1			

Capt. Henry Taylor's Company (cont'd)

Names	Poles white	Poles black	Std	Land	
Howard, John				100	
Hufman, David	1			236	
Hunneycut, Moses	1				
Hunter, Jacob	1	1		330	$1.50
Hunter, John				391	
Hunter, Joseph	1				
Irwin, Frances	1				
Irwin, John	1			150	
Irwin, Wm.	1				
Kerby, Malachi	1				
Leach, Wm.				100	
Lilburn, Andrew	1		1	100	$1.50
Murrey, Ephraim	1			452	
North, George	1			100	
Ossemus, Henry	1			150	
Parker, John	1				
Parker, Josiah	1				
Parks, Nathan	1	1			
Parks, Philip	1			100	
Pitner, John	1			170	
Price, Rachel				546	
Rader, Adam	1	1		340	
Ragan, Jeremiah	1	1		595	
Rees, Jas.	1	1		141	
Roads, Elisha	1				
Rose, Hosea				320	
Ruble, Henry	1				
Ruble, John	1			320	
Ruble, Peter				623	
Smith, Edward				218	
Smith, John	1			163	
Stermer, George				200	
Stout, Joseph				201	
Stout, Peter	1			148	
Swanegar, John	1				
Taylor, Henry	1			300	
Tipton, John		3	1	332	$2.00
Tipton, Joshua	1				
Tipton, Mary				50	
Toland, Jacob	1				
Walker, Barbary				270	
Watson, Martha				115	
Watson, Mary				100	
Watson, Susannah				100	
Watson, Wm.	1			100	
Wheeler, Wm.	1				
Witt, Burges	1				
Witt, Solomon	1				
Wotson, Nancy				200	
Young, Mary		3		343	
Young, Joseph	1	4		915	
Young, Rebeckah		1		320	

Taken by Jno. Bayless, J.P.

A list of the taxable property in Capt. William Taylor's Co.

Names	Land	Poles Wh	Poles Bl	Studs	Town lots
Adair, James	100	1			
Allison, Robert	650		4		
Anderson, John	199	1	1		
Bails, Isaac Sr.	90				
Bails, Jacob	299				
Bails, Joseph		1			
Bell, George	145	1			
Bowman, Elias	100	1			
Brabston, Thomas	278	1	1		2
Brabston, Ephraim	170	1			
Bullington, Benjamin		1			
Bullington, William	99				
Campbel, Abraham	130	1			
Campbel, John	180	1			
Carson, David	125	1			
Carson, Robert	125	1			
Charlton, Painton	610		1		
Clem, William	100	1			
Cunningham, James	125	1	1		
Curts, John		1			1
Davis, John		1			
Davis, Nathaniel	400	1	1		
Depue, Isaac	228	1			
Duncan, Andrew	229				
Duncan, Joseph	423		1		
Farguson, Alexander	50	1			
Farguson, Henry		1			
Farguson, John	299				
Farguson, John Jr.		1			
Fuston, John		1			
Glass, William Jr.		1			
Glass, William Sr.	384				
Gray, William	300	1			
Guin, Thomas	100				
Guin, William		1			
Hair, Henry	6	1			
Hartman, Levi		1			
Hickman, Elisha		1			
Hunt, Uriah	950	1	1		
Jones, Nathaniel	90	1		1	
Kees, Phillip	100	1			
McAdams, Hugh		1			
McAdams, Robert		1			
McCary, Joseph		1			
McClure, James		1			
McLin, Robert	200				
McLin, William	100	1			
Marsh, Hanery	238	1			
Mathes, William		1			
Miller, John Blair	250				
Nelson, Nathan		1			
Nelson, Thomas		1			

Capt. William Taylor's Co. (cont'd)

Names	Land	Poles wh	Poles bl	Studs	Town lots
Oar, Thomas	70				
Par, Robert		1			
Patton, John		1			
Pursell, George		1			1
Purselly, William	214				
Ralston, John	155	1			
Richard, Lewis	186	1			
Robertson, James	245	1			
Russel, David	330				
Simpson, James		1			
Simpson, John		1			
Simpson, Robert		1			
Shaw, Forneis	200				
Smith, William		1			2
Steale, Andrew		1	1		2
Stewart, David	398	1	1		
Stewart, James		1			
Sutherlin, Thomas		1			
Strain, John	100	1			
Taylor, John		1			
Taylor, Leeroy	254		1		
Taylor, Capt. William		1			
Tucker, Joseph	387	1			2
Tucker, Nicholas	70	1			
Walker, William	184	1			
Webb, John	59	1			
Whits, Lewis	150	1			
Wood, William	155				

....

Scraps - 1801

Scrap No. 1:
The taxable property of Laurance Glaise for the year 1801 consisting of two Negroes, five hundred and seventy acres of land.

- - - - - - -

Scrap No. 2:
List of taxable property for the year 1801 of John Rhea.
One hundred and eighty acres of land on the waters of Big Limestone, one town lott in Jonesborough.

J. S. Gordon, Esqr.

....

Amount of taxes for 1801

Names	S. Tax	C. Tax	Add.C.Tax	Poor tax
Capt. Glasscockes	32.21	32.21	32.21	11.76½
Capt. Squibb	32.23	32.23	32.23	10.40½
Capt. Browns (Should be Capt. Roberson's, taken by Capt. Brown)	31.88	29.63	30.38	8.56½
Capt. Gann	26.83	26.83	26.83	9.71
Capt. Longmire	18.65	16.90	17.65	5.28
Capt. Norwood's	25.21	20.71	22.21	8.95½
Capt. Calvert	25.21½	23.	23.21½	8.46
Capt. Wm. Taylor	25.15½	25.15½	25.15½	9.21½
Capt. H. Taylor	32. 1	27.74	31. 1	10.47½
Capt. Biddle	20.59	20.59	20.59	7.76½
Capt. Aikens	10.15½	7.90½	9.15½	1.90
Town Lotts	18.64	18.64	18.64	
	$297.47	$281.54	$289.27½	$92.49½
Capt. Lane Co.	31.98	29.73	30.48	9.72
Capt. Morrison	34.52¼	34.52¼	34.52¼	12.53
	$363.97¼	$345.79¼	$354.37¼	$114.74½

....

A LIST OF WASHINGTON COUNTY OFFICIALS 1778-1801

Note: The following data taken from 1) Minutes of the Court of Pleas & Quarter Sessions of Washington County, 1778-1801; 2) The Journal of Gov. William Blount, Terr. S of River Ohio, 1790-1796; 3) Commission Book of Gov. John Sevier, 1796-1801.

Chairmen:
1778.........John Carter
1779......... " "
1780......... " "
1780, 11/27..Charles Robertson (1st Court after Kings Mt.)

Sheriffs:
1778.........Valentine Sevier (Brother of John Sevier)
1779......... " " ; Clevias Barksdale, Dep. Sh.
1780.........Clevias Barksdale
1781, 5/19... " " ; Thomas Talbot, Dep. Sh.
1782, 5/27... " "
1784, 8/ ...Thomas Talbot
1787, 2/1....Thomas Mitchell
1787.........Jonathan Pugh (mortally wounded 2/29/1787
Battle of Franklin)
1787.........Jacob Tipton (N.C.)
1788, 5/12...George Mitchell,
res 5/14/88 & Edmund Williams unanimously elected
1789, 5/2....Michael Harrison; Edmund Harrison, Dep. Sh.
1790, 5/2.... " " ; John Carter, Dep. Sh.
Terr. S River Ohio
1790, 11/9...Michael Harrison; George Williams, Peter McNamee
& Wm Alexander, Dep. Sh.
1791, 5/10...Charles Robertson; Rusell Been, Robt Irvine, Dep. Sh.
1792, 5/1....George Gillespie; Allen Gillespie, Dep. Sh.
1793, 5/6.... " " " " " "
1794, 4/16...(2 yrs) " " " " "
1795, 2/ ...George Gillespie Sh & Tax Collector
1796, 1/27... " " " " "
Tennessee
1798, 5/ ...2 yrs..Brice Blair
1799, 2/ ...Brice Blair
1799, 8/1....George Gillespie elected High Sheriff

Clerk of Court of Pleas & Ouarter Sessions:
1778.........John Sevier
1779......... " "
1785, 12/5...Wm Murphy
1787, 2/1....John Tipton; Thomas Gourley, Dep Clk. N C
Court held at home of Wm Davis
1787, 8/1....John Tipton resigns and Thomas Gourley Clerk
1788, 11/1...Thomas Gourley
1789, 5/2....Edmund Williams, Dep Clk.
S W Terr.
1790, 11/9...James Sevier
He served until 1836.

Entry Takers:
1775.........John Carter
1778.........John Carter
1781.........Landon Carter

Trustees:
1778.........John Sevier
1779.........John Sevier
1780, 5/25...John Sevier
1795, 8/7....Landon Carter
1796.........Charles McCray
1798.........John Sevier (Jr.)

Register:
1778.........John McMahon
1789, 5/2....William Stephenson (Stinson)
S W Terr.
1790, 11/9... " "

Ranger & StrayMaster:
1778.........Jacob Womack
1787, 5/9....Wm McNabb, former Ranger
1789, 11/2...Elijah Cooper
1790, 2/2.... " "
1790, 12/20..George Williams in place of Elijah Cooper, resigned
1796, 5/ ...John Adams

Coroner:
1787, 5/8....Alexander Moffett
1789, 5/2....David Brown
1791, 7/26...Joseph Greer
1796, 5/ ...Nathaniel Davis

States Attorney:
1779.........Ephraim Dunlap
1785, 11/7...Joshua Williams, Head County Lawyer
1788, 5/12...Andrew Jackson & John McNairy admitted to practice in this court
S W Terr.
1790, 11/9...James Rees
1794, 9/6....John Sevier, Jr., County Attorney

Surveyor:
1778.........James Stuart
1789, 5/2.... " " ; Joseph Brown, Dep S.
S W Terr.
1794, 5/22... " " ; Nathan Shipley, Dep. S.

Commissioners of Confiscated Estates:

One half of proceeds of confiscated estates went to the state and one half to the family.

1779, 5/27...John Sevier, Jesse Walton & Zachariah Isbell
1782, 5/27...John Sevier, Wm. Cocke, Valentine Sevier

The oldest record found in Washington County, Tennessee; brought to light August 1, 1933 by Mary Hardin McCown (Mrs. L.W.).

BILL OF SALE

LUMPKINS to WM BEEN

Know all men by these presents that I George Lumpkin now of Watauga formerly of Pittsylvania County, Virginia have bargained and sold and by these presents do bargain and sell unto William Been Senior of Watauga aforesaid for an in consideration of the sum of One hundred & seventy three pounds fourteen shillings & one penny Current money of Virginia by the said Been advanced for the use of me the said Lumpkin to satisfy a debt due from him to a certain James Buchanan of Augusta County (if the said debt be of the amount aforesaid) my negroes following towit Jo a fellow of about twenty one years old & Dinah about twenty two To have & to hold unto the said William Been his heirs & assigns forever with warranty to the said Been his heirs and assigns against me the said Lumpkin my heirs & assigns forever

Witness my hand & seal this sixteenth day of October one thousand seven hundred & seventy three

Andrew Greer

John Toddys George Lumpkin (Seal)

If the said Lumpkin shall pay the consideration money within mentioned this bill of sale to be void at anytime (?) whatever.

William Been (Seal)

Acknowledged before us

Andrew Greer
John Toddys

Smith a Cornet
Smith

(On the back side of paper)

Account-- 209.9.10

May Term
Jud.

1776-- James Smith Dr. to-
Wm. Bailey Smith

To Surveyor's Fees--	172.0.0	
To 300 Printed Deeds-5/	75.0.0	
To set of Surveyor's instruments---	18.0.0	
To a blank book---	7.10.0	
	272.10.0	272.10.0

1775-- 16th Octbr.----
Contra.--

By William Dunkham---	17.6.4	
By John Calaham 40/	2.0.0	
By forty one printed deeds 5/-	10.0.0	
By Henry Liles-	2.13.4	
By Col. John Carter	1.8.8	
By Mr. Joshua Houghton	3.14.0	
By Col. John Sevier	2.13.4	
By Capt. James Robertson	1.8.8	
By Patience Cooper	2.13.4	
By Joshua Barton	1.8.8	
By Capt. Thomas Price	13.6.8	
By Andrew Greer	2.13.4	
By Benja. Cobb	1.8.8	
		63.0.2
E E	63.0.2	209.9.10

E E Wm Bailey Smith.

Note by MHMcC:
This record antedates Washington County (1777) and also Washington District (July 5, 1776). Could it have been a Bill presented at a court held by the Watauga Association?
James Smith, who was most likely Clerk of the Watauga Association, purchased of Wm Bailey Smith, Surveyor, his surveying outfit, when the latter went to Kentucky to enter the service with Richard Henderson & his Associates.
This was the oldest record discovered in the basement clean-up by the T E R A, 1935.

Cleavias Barksdill to Charles Roberson

Bill of Sale April 10, 1782

Know all Men by these presents that whereas A Writ of Fiere Facias having date 28th day of February Anno. Dom. 1782 at the suit of Charles Robertson against James Crawford issued from the County Court of pleas and quarter sessions for the County of Washington directed to Clevias Barksdill Sheriff of the County aforesaid commanding the said Sheriff that of the goods and Chattles Lands and Teniments of the said James Crawford he should levy and make the sum of Twenty Thousand pounds in the same Court recovered against him by virtue of which writ a certain entry of five Hundred acres of Land with the Improvements thereon belonging to the said Crawford was duely Executed by the said Sheriff Advertised exposed to sale at publick Auction to the highest bidder agreable to Law The said entry being Numbered in the office Book No. 857. And the lands situate lying and being in Washington County North Carolina on the North side of Nolechuckey River including the plantation whare the said Crawford formerly liv'd And this day Charles Robertson appears at the said Auction and bids Fifty two thousand one hundred pounds Current Money for the said entry of land with the Improvements being the highest bidder. Now Know ye that I the said Cleavias Barksdill for and in Consideration of the Said fifty two thousand one hundred pounds to me in hand paid by the said Charles Robertson the receipt whereof is hereby acknowleged have bargained sold and set over and by these presents do bargain sell and set over unto the said Charles Robertson his Heirs and assigns forever The said entry of five Hundred acres of land with the Improvements as aforesaid so far as the same is liable to be Executed and sold as aforesaid-- To have and to hold the above bargained premeses with the appurtinances to the same belonging to this the said Charles Robertson his heirs and assigns forever according to the effect and opperation of his purchase herein specified and such grant for the same as he at his own expence shall be able to procure and shall obtain from the State. In Testimony Whareof I the Said Cleavais Barksdill Sheriff of the Said County of Washington hearunto set my hand and affixed my seal this 10 day of April Anno. Dom. 1782.

Saml Williams
James Stinson

Cleavees Barksdill Seal

(Sheriff)

Note: This was likely the property of James Crawford, who deserted on September 27 from the Kings Mountain Men, on their march to the Battle on October 7, 1780. The rule was that the proceeds from the sale of confiscated property was given- half to the state and the other half to the family of the deserter. This was also the date - 1782 - when Col. Charles Robertson moved from his Sinking Creek farm to the Nolachucky river area. MHMcC.

Miscellaneous Data Found in Washington County, Tennessee
Court House, Jonesboro, Tennessee, County Court Clerk's Office

Received of Mr. Goines Patterson his quota of salary for the years 1798 and 1799 by me, from Mrs. Marget McEwen,

Feb. 7, 1800 Saml. Doak

(This receipt is written on the back of a page torn from a copybook: "Many men of many minds many birds of many kinds. Many men". Likely Mr. Patterson was a teacher at Washington College.)

....

Jacob Brown

Know all men by these presents That I Jacob Brown do owe and am indebted unto Gabriel Brown of Ninty Six District in province of South Carolina the sum of Two Hundred and Ninety two pound currcy. of sd province for payment of which I Hereby bind myself my Heirs, Executors and Administrators unto the sd Gabriel Brown his Heirs, Executors, admrs and assigns

Witness my hand and sale this Twenty sixth day of August 1775

John McDonald Jacob Brown seal
Jonathan Cain

Back side:

Received of the Within note one hundred and forty pounds Received by me
December 23, 1775 Gabrial Brown

Debt due Ŀ 152 former Currency

Intrust to this date which is ten years 121-11-10½ Like money

....

273-11-10½ Total

In sterling Ŀ 39-1-73/4

....

I Mathew Talbott Do Promas to pay or caus to be paid unto francis Donlany his heirs or asigns the whole and just sum of fore pound ten shilling curent mony of Vergina for Vauler resed of him as Witness my hand This 9th Day of march 1771.

Mathew Talbott

....

UNDATED SCRAPS--

Col Outlaw's List of Land

I give in 690 acres of land on the head of Limestone Creek, porland(?) in the name of Richard Caswell
400 dto on Boons Creek
320 part of the tract Epown (?) lives on if
Frank Elleson has not given it in.

John Waddill, Jr, agent
for Alex Outlaw AL Outlaw

....

The Taxable Property of James Stuart, Esqr.

1 tract of land on Nolichuckey		424
1 Ditto	Do	200
1 Ditto	Do	200
1 Ditto	nown by Condlins Place	160
1 Ditto	on Cherokee	150
1 Ditto	on Indian Creek in Robt (S) Hearts name..	150
1 Ditto	waters of Cherokee	150
1 Ditto	joining the town land	200
1 Ditto	joining Nathaniel Davis	400
1 Ditto	Ditto	150
1 Ditto	belonging to James Chater on little Limestone	100

2 Lot No 28, 29
4 Lots of the Estate of Col Belfor (?), Decesed, No 6-35-47-48

1 Lot David Deaderick & James Stuart 1 Lot No 34

8 Negrows from 10 to 50
1 White Pole
2 Ditto- Thomas Stuart & John Paxton
1

A List of Capt Robert Blair Taxable property to wit:
1 white pole 1 black pole Land 175 acres

....

A List of William Cobb's Taxable property
1240 acres of Land in Washington county on the waters of Watauga river
640 acres of land in Greene County, mouth of lick Creek

One white pole
Twenty three Black polls

Note: On the back...

Major & c	3
Roger & c	2
Jim & c	3
Nea	2
Moses	4
Jo.& Moses	2
	4
	1
	21

UNDATED SCRAPS--

	pl	Land	Scalps
Crouch, Joseph	1	355	25

....

An account of Nathnl Davis taxable property

to one pole and six hundred acres of land

....

A list of Robert Love taxable property in Washington County

to tract of land on the north side of Chuckey rive held by deed	200
1 do held by deed joining to river	166 2/3
1 do joining Martin's Creek	100
1 do on the south sid of Chuckey river	70
the seventy acres held by a title- all the rest by deed	
to 100 do held by deed joining Martins Creek	100
	636 2/3

....

A list of Isaac Prathers taxable property in Washington County

	pole	Land
To 1 pole	1	
To 50 acres of land joining Indian Creek on the south side of Chucke river held by occupent claim		50
To do joining said Creek held by occupent claim		100

....

A List of Certificates recd of Capt Joshuway Hadly at Hillsboro August 1st 1788, the Names of the Persons to hoam granted, the date Eshued, their number, and to what amt in L.S.D.

Persons Names	When Eshued	Number	Amt of the Indent in Pounds Shillings & Pence		
Wm Woolley	1 Sept 84	1984	29	5	0
Aron Beuley	31 Augst 84	1958	20	5	0
Joseph Seviar	12 June 83	3321	6	19	6
Henry Mueke	16 Aug 82	2949	2	0	0
John Smith	12 June 83	3327	6	19	6
Joseph Brown	12 June 83	3312	6	19	6
John Hopton	12 June 83	3233	-	12	0
Joseph McWraths	19 Feb 84	6928	13	14	6
Littleton Brooks	30 June 84	4289	12	14	6
Fedrick Stump	30 June 84	4287	30	0	0
Jacob Albright	14 Nov 83	5232	-	10	0
P. Cobb	12 June 83	3268	8	16	0
			138	15	6

These Indents recd from Capt Hadley
for Lardner Clarke Nashville

On back: "Tickets recd from Capt Hadley for Lardner Clark -

£ 138 - 15 - 6 -

to what

Hadley says he should have."

NOTE: Evidently a list of "Guard Certificates" issued for military service after Yorktown, 1781, and used as a medium of exchange turned in to the store of Lardner Clarke in Nashville, Tennessee. (See Tenn Historical Mag - March, 1917.) It was discovered during the T RE R A Project in 1935. Mrs. L.W. McCown, Supervisor.

"A LIST of NAMES on the PENSION OFFICE at Jonesboro which owe the Clerk of the COUNTY COURT for Seal of Office"

(This loose paper was found in vault in Washington County, Tenn. July, 1935 by T E R A Project. Mrs. L.W. McCown, Supervisor.)

Robt. Henry.....50 (Wash. Pa.)
Wm. Barron......50 (Wash. N.C.)
Nathan Perren...50 (Sull. Mass.)
John Edwards....50 (Wash. Md.)
Cassemore May...50 (Wash. Pa.)
Frances Hughs...50 (Gr. N.C.)
Adam Ingle......50 (Wash. Pa.)
Vachael Leghr...50 (Sull. Va.)
(Light)
George House....50 (Gr. Va.)
Richd Kelly.....50 (Car. Va.)
Adam Har(t)man..50 (Wash. Va.)
John Douglas....50 (Wash & Sull NC)
Amon Hale.......50 (Wash. Md.)
Wm Smith........50 (Wash. Pa.)
Loyd Ford.......50 (Wash. Md.)
Thos. Bell......50 (Wash. Va.)
John Scott......50 (Wash. --)
John Blalock....50 (Car. Va.)
Andrew Taylor...50 (Car. N C)
Charles Paiter..50 (--- --)
Joseph Wilson...50 (Car & Claib NC)
Wm Kendle.......50 (Sev. S C)
John Morrison...50 (Gr. Va.)
Jacob Brown.....50 (Wash. S C)
Samuel Vance....50 (Gr. Va.)
Jacob Brown BS..50 (Wash. N C)
Thos. Bryant....50 (Gr. Va.)
William Copas...50 (Sull. Va.)
John Greer......50 (Car. N C)
Joseph Duncan...50 (Wash. Va.)
Andrew Hannah...50 (Wash. N C)

Babb, Seth..........(--- --)
Taylor, Isaac.......(Car. N C)
McGill, James.......(Gr. Va.)
(Magill)
Wilson, John........(Car. N C)
Lilburn, Andrew.....(Wash. Va.)
Wm Cloyd............(Wash. Pa.)
Greenway, Wm........(Wash. Va.)
James Jack..........(Gr. Va.)
Charles Moreland....(Car. Va.)
Philip Wolever......(Gr. Pa.)
James Campbell......(Car. Va.)
Leroy Taylor........(Wash. N C)
Robert Treadway.....(Sull. N C)
Ben Birdwell........(Sull. N C)
Nathan Gann.........(Wash. N C)
Azariah Doty........(Gr. N C)
George Brown........(Wash. N C)
Henry Long..........(Gr. N C)
Wm Slaughter........(Wash. Va.)
Leonard Bowers......(Car. Va.)
Charles Howell......(Wash. Va.)
John Strain.........(Wash. N C)
Michael Broyles.....(Wash. Va.)
Flower Mullins......(Haw. N C)
Mary Taylor.........(Wash. N C)
Sol. Hendrix........(Car. Md.)
Adam Painter........(Wash. Va.)
Wm. Good............(---- ---)
(Godsey)..........(Sull. Va.)
Thos. King..........(Sull. Pa.)
Ben. Dillard........(Gr. Va.)
Davd. Creemer.......(Gr. Md.)
Gilbert Evans.......(Gr. Pa.)
Peter Kent..........(Gr. Va.)
Jeremiah Campbell...(Car. N C)
John Gass...........(Gr. N C)
John Miller.........(Car. Va.)
John (M) Smithpeter.(Wash. Va.)
John King...........(Sull. Pa.)
Jacob Hawk..........(Sull. Va.)

NOTE: This list is undated- but is before 1836- as Casimore May died in 1836. It was made out after Pension Act of 1832, and is in handwriting of Samuel Greer, Dep Clk for James Sevier 1832-1836, and Clerk 1836-1844. Checked with Armstrong's "2400 Pensioners of Rev & War of 1812". I have added the County of residence and State of service of each. MHMcCown.

www.ingramcontent.com/pod-product-compliance
Lightning Source LLC
Chambersburg PA
CBHW081431270326
41932CB00019B/3159

* 9 7 8 0 7 8 8 4 8 9 7 1 6 *